AFRICAN FOOD SYSTEMS IN CRISIS

Food and Nutrition in History and Anthropology
A series edited by Solomon H. Katz, University of Pennsylvania

Volume 1   **FOOD, ECOLOGY AND CULTURE: Readings in the Anthropology of Dietary Practices**
Edited by John R. K. Robson

Volume 2   **FAMINE: ITS CAUSES, EFFECTS AND MANAGEMENT**
Edited by John R. K. Robson

Volume 3   **INFANT CARE AND FEEDING IN THE SOUTH PACIFIC**
Edited by Leslie B. Marshall

Volume 4   **FOOD ENERGY IN TROPICAL ECOSYSTEMS**
Edited by Dorothy J. Cattle and Karl H. Schwerin

Volume 5   **THE INFANT-FEEDING TRIAD: Infant, Mother, and Household**
Barry M. Popkin, Tamar Lasky, Judith Litvin, Deborah Spicer and Monica E. Yamamoto

Volume 6   **THE EFFECTS OF UNDERNUTRITION ON CHILDREN'S BEHAVIOR**
David E. Barrett and Deborah A. Frank

Volume 7   **AFRICAN FOOD SYSTEMS IN CRISIS
Part One: Microperspectives**
Edited by Rebecca Huss-Ashmore and Solomon H. Katz

**AFRICAN FOOD SYSTEMS IN CRISIS
Part Two: Contending with Change**
Edited by Rebecca Huss-Ashmore and Solomon H. Katz

Volume 8   **TRADITIONAL PLANT FOODS OF CANADIAN INDIGENOUS PEOPLES: Nutrition, Botany and Use**
Harriet Kuhnlein and Nancy J. Turner

Volume 9   **THE POLITICAL ECONOMY OF AFRICAN FAMINE**
Edited by R. E. Downs, Donna O. Kerner and Stephen P. Reyna

Volume 10   **INVESTIGATIONS OF ANCIENT HUMAN TISSUE: Chemical Analyses in Anthropology**
Edited by Mary K. Sandford

This book is part of a series. The publisher will accept continuation orders which may be cancelled at any time and which provide for automatic billing and shipping of each title in the series upon publication. Please write for details.

AFRICAN FOOD SYSTEMS IN CRISIS

Part Two: Contending with Change

Edited by

REBECCA HUSS-ASHMORE

Department of Anthropology
University of Pennsylvania

and

SOLOMON H. KATZ

The W. M. Krogman Center
for Child Growth and Development
University of Pennsylvania

GORDON AND BREACH SCIENCE PUBLISHERS

USA   Switzerland   Australia   Belgium   France   Germany   Great Britain
India   Japan   Malaysia   Netherlands   Russia   Singapore

First published 1990
Second printing 1993

Gordon and Breach Science Publishers

820 Town Center Drive
Langhorne, Pennsylvania 19047
United States of America

Glinkastrasse 13-15
O-1086 Berlin
Germany

Y-Parc
Chemin de la Sallaz
1400 Yverdon, Switzerland

Post Office Box 90
Reading, Berkshire RG1 8JL
Great Britain

Private Bag 8
Camberwell, Victoria 3124
Australia

3-14-9, Okubo
Shinjuku-ku, Tokyo 169
Japan

58, rue Lhomond
75005 Paris
France

Emmaplein 5
1075 AW Amsterdam
Netherlands

Library of Congress Cataloging-in-Publication Data

(Revised for Pt. 2)
African food systems in crisis.
    (Food and nutrition in history and anthropology, 0275—5769)
    Includes bibliographies and index.
    Contents: pt. 1. Microperspectives —   pt. 2. Contending with change.
    1. Food supply—Africa.   2. Produce trade—Africa.
3. Agriculture—Africa.   4. Famines—Africa.   5. Africa—Economic
conditions—1960– .   I. Huss-Ashmore, Rebecca.   II. Katz, Solomon H.,
1939– .   III. Series.
HD9017.A2A39   1989   363.8'096   88–25949
ISBN 2–88124–306–1 (pt. 1)
ISBN 2–88124–307–x hardcover (pt. 2); 2–88124–333–9 paperback (pt. 2)

CONTENTS

Preface vii

*I. Changing African Food Systems—Issues in Anthropology
and Development*
1. Donors and Deserts: The Political Ecology of
Destructive Development in the Sahel
Michael M. Horowitz 3

2. River Basin Development: Dilemmas for Peasants
and Planners
William Derman 29

3. Land Concentration, Existential Development,
and Food in the Sahel
Stephen P. Reyna 43

4. Gender, Land, and Hunger in Eastern Zaire
Brooke Grundfest Schoepf and Claude Schoepf 75

5. Profiles of Men and Women Smallholder Farmers
in Malawi
Anita Spring 107

II. Strategies for Increasing Food Security
6. Curriculum Development in the Study of African
Food Issues at a U.S. Land Grant University
Della E. McMillan 139

7. Towards a Participatory Evaluation Methodology:
The Southern African Pilot Learning Process
Ann Seidman 159

8. Development Alternatives and the African Food Crisis
    David A. Cleveland   181

9. The Role of Cassava in African Famine Prevention
    Fatimah Linda C. Jackson and Robert T. Jackson   207

10. Seasonality of Vegetable Use and Production
    on Swazi Nation Land: Problems and Interventions
    John J. Curry, Rebecca Huss-Ashmore,
        Doyle Grenoble and Douglas Gama   227

11. The Lesson of Rwanda's Agricultural Crisis:
    Increase Productivity, Not Food Aid
    Edward Robins   245

12. Food, Farmers, and Organizations in Africa:
    Anthropological Perspectives, with Implications
    for Development Assistance
    Patrick Fleuret   269

Index   289

PREFACE

This is the second in a series of volumes produced by the Task Force on African Famine of the American Anthropological Association. Like its predecessor (*African Food Systems in Crisis, Part One: Microperspectives*), it addresses both the causes of food system failure in Africa and strategies for dealing with these. However, where the first volume emphasized informal structures for coping with drought and hunger, this volume concentrates on planned change. Specifically, it outlines the role of economic development in both constraining and improving food supply. Thus while Part One documented the traditional local-level response to production shortfalls and consumption shortages, Part Two presents the often contradictory results of outside intervention.

Although development is intended to improve the economic welfare (and biological well-being) of target populations, history shows that it has not always done so. Early projects emphasized industrialization and growth in the GNP, predicting that the benefits of capitalization at the national level would "trickle down" to the rural population. Failure of benefits to trickle down led to a reappraisal of development theory, with an increased emphasis on agriculture as a source of national capital and a series of programs targeting the poor. Such "basic needs" programs improved education, health care and communications for many rural people, while international agricultural research produced the Green Revolution in Asia and Latin America. Despite these advances, it is estimated that 500 million people worldwide are currently undernourished. Nutritional problems are particularly severe in Africa, where food production per capita continues to decline.

Food system failure in Africa is blamed on a variety of environmental, social and economic factors. Uncertain rainfall, poor soils, limited agricultural technology, colonial history, agriculture policy, growing population, traditional social structure and warfare have all been cited as causes of Africa's food crisis. Famines have made this crisis visible and have triggered short-term international response. However, neither short-term famine relief nor longer-term development programs have made a permanent impact on the production-consumption gap.

Why have aid programs in Africa failed to increase food supply? These volumes suggest that part of the answer lies in the insensitivity of such programs to the real concerns of the small-scale rural producer/consumer, the African "peasant." Contrary to conventional wisdom, the African producer is neither technologically backward nor helpless in the face of an unpredictable environment. As the papers in Part One show, rural Africans have a detailed knowledge of their environment and have developed an array of risk-aversive production strategies. Further, African societies have a range of social responses by which the impact of environmental hazard and production shortage may be reduced. These responses include systems of demographic regulation, food sharing, migration and extensive kin networks. Development programs which interfere with these traditional coping strategies are unlikely to be adopted.

In an important paper delivered to the American Anthropological Association in 1985, Art Hansen pointed out the importance of tradition for understanding the impact of food-related interventions.[1] Tradition, in this context, refers to information transmitted through time: institutionalized beliefs, rules and behaviors. Given this definition, it is not only rural Africans who have traditions, but also the agencies providing aid, as well as the scholars who study and codify their interactions. Many of us who deal with African food problems are unaware of the impact of this multiplicity of traditions. We may be aware of (at most) the traditions of African peasants in one or two geographic locations, but tend to ignore our own traditions or deny that we have them. Yet an inattention to the beliefs and rules of all the actors involved may decrease the chances that aid programs will succeed. An awareness of our own traditions, as well as those of others involved in changing African food systems, should improve communication.

Translating and communicating the traditions of other people is one of the classic tasks of anthropologists. Hansen has implied that this

---

[1] "Disaster Relief Traditions: Theirs, Yours, and Ours." Paper presented to the American Anthropological Association Annual Meeting, Washington, DC. December, 1985.

expertise has been underutilized by those promulgating development, at least partly because of anthropological traditions. These include long periods of fieldwork (usually in small, remote communities), sensitivity to and advocacy of local beliefs, an emphasis on qualitative over quantitative data, a methodology relying heavily on participation, a "natural history" approach, and a preference for presentation of results in monograph form. On the one hand, this means that anthropologists often have excellent insights into the workings of other cultures, including their food systems. This microperspective may enable them to identify constraints to production which would otherwise be inaccessible to planners. On the other hand, the length of time necessary to gather data, the reluctance of many anthropologists to give advice or to change the societies in which they work, and the academic orientation and language of resulting publications also mean that few aid-providers ever see the information. Anthropologists and other social scientists concerned with African food crises need to be aware of their own traditions and the role that these play in constraining or enhancing information flow.

The type of aid provided to Africa is also influenced by the traditions of the agencies supplying interventions. Governments and others involved in the intervention process traditionally distinguish between emergency assistance (relief) and long-term assistance (development). Acute crises seem to call for relief, even though acute crises may be only the culminating events of long-term, progressive and systemic problems. The traditional remedy for long-term food problems has been to increase production through improved technology. This has involved an emphasis on mechanization, cash cropping for export, economies of scale, privatization of land, and high yield cultigens. For many African farmers, these strategies have proved costly in terms of initial investment, increased environmental risk, disturbed social relations and labor demands. Further, the traditional Euro-American emphasis on male farming systems has led to a neglect of female farmers, the traditional food producers for much of the African continent.

Perhaps the most insidious of development traditions has been the common donor view that aid recipients are passive (or worse, that they are a problem to be fixed or eliminated). Hansen has emphasized that famine sufferers are not only victims, they are also survivors who contribute to their own survival. African cultures and social organizations represent more or less successful relationships between people and their human and nonhuman environments, worked out over time. Cultural strategies include both unconscious buffering mechanisms to ameliorate environmental impact and conscious coping strategies to diminish suffering or risk. These strategies occasionally fail, but are generally resilient. At the very least, aid programs (whether short-term or long-term) should not disrupt the processes already in place to help people survive and recover. Further, assistance will become more useful if it complements and reinforces these existing patterns.

Hansen's views are echoed by the papers in this volume. Many of the authors, particularly in the first section, examine the logic behind African development projects and demonstrate how that logic has failed in particular cases. In the introductory article, M. Horowitz argues that development interventions may not only be ineffective, but may actually be harmful. Projects intended to improve environment and productivity often have exactly the opposite effect, degrading the habitat and increasing social differentiation. Horowitz indicates that these unexpected outcomes are the result of a distrust of indigenous rural production systems on the part of donors. Such donors are often more concerned with short-term returns on their investments than with sustainable development. The traditional strategies and the perceived needs of the local population are generally ignored in the process.

In the two papers that follow, W. Derman and S. P. Reyna provide examples of development strategies intended to increase food production and income in West Africa. In both these cases, the strategies rely heavily on the development of irrigationable lands, often intended for cash cropping. Derman shows that the development of the Gambia River basin has produced a series of conflicts for the developers, who must respond to the demands of West African national governments, as well as for the local peasants, whose land may be appropriated for dams. Similarly, Reyna shows that changing patterns of donor investment in Burkina Faso have resulted in land concentration. Expropriation of land due to demographic factors, the operation of parastatal organizations, and private ownership has reduced peasant control over food production, with an accompanying increase in poverty.

Land shortage has also been a factor in the growth of hunger in Zaire. B. Schoepf and C. Schoepf argue that cash cropping increases competition for land. Changing gender relations are also linked to cash cropping, as women's labor is increasingly expropriated for the production of men's crops. Thus both land and labor are removed from food production, a process made worse by the increasing search for wage employment and increasing purchase of land by emerging local elites. The importance of gender in African production systems has been known since Ester Boserup's first identification of female farming systems in Africa.[2] However, gender is an issue which continues to be rediscovered in the African context. As A. Spring demonstrates for Malawi, female farming systems are becoming increasingly feminized as male labor is drawn into cash cropping or migratory wage labor. Spring shows that male- and female-headed households do not differ in their basic farming skills and practices. However, access to services and exposure to new technologies have been greater for male farmers in this setting, with negative consequences for women's production, income and quality of life. This gender bias in development and production can only be detrimental to long-term food security.

The second part of this volume concentrates on strategies for improving African food security. With the dismal record of conventional development approaches in Africa, a number of new strategies are being tried. These include new approaches to education, a concern for grass-roots opinion, attention to food consumption as well as production, and various forms of broad-spectrum integrated development. Thus D. E. McMillan recounts the establishment of an innovative curriculum at the University of Florida, integrating social and technical science for students interested in African agriculture and food issues. This program was designed to equip students with the background to make intelligent and sensitive decisions regarding food policy in developing countries. Such programs could have a major influence in making development more relevant to the concerns of rural people, and less destructive to their long-term economic and social interests. A. Seidman points out that education for policy is not enough to improve food shortages and economic conditions in Africa. She argues that the problems engendered by development can only be

---

[2] *Woman's Role in Economic Development.* St. Martin's Press, New York. 1970.

solved with the cooperation and intensive involvement of the developing communities themselves. The Pilot Learning Process that she describes is an innovative approach to education for self-reliance,
designed to enhance the quality and effectiveness of grass-roots
projects.

D. Cleveland also emphasizes the importance of local control for
effective development. He argues that industrial large-scale agriculture has had a mixed record even in developed countries and should
not be taken as the only possible solution for those in the Third
World. He sees the promotion of sustainable agriculture as a necessary part of the drive to increase food production for Africa. This can
only be done if there is recognition that food systems go beyond production economics and technology. Nutritional and social consequences of food systems must also be included in planning.

The next two papers attempt to take the development debate beyond
the issues of food production by including concerns for food consumption and the biological outcomes of food choices. L. C. Jackson
and R. T. Jackson indicate that cassava, often considered a famine
food in Africa, may have an important role to play in famine prevention. They point out that famine is both a social and a biological problem, causing population dislocation and increased mortality and
morbidity. Despite its low protein content, cassava is a highly productive plant which is ecologically sound in most areas of Africa. Traditional processing techniques reduce potentially harmful cyanates to
safe levels, and cyanate ingestion may even be adaptive in malarial
areas. Thus traditional Western bias against tropical root crops should
not blind agricultural development to the potential contributions of
cassava to African food security. Contrary to other papers in these
volumes, the chapter by J. J. Curry and colleagues shows that development projects can be responsive to food consumption concerns.
Drawing on the experience of the Swaziland Cropping Systems
Project, the authors explain how seasonality of vegetable availability
was identified as a dietary concern and was addressed by agronomic
and horticultural sections of the project. Research to improve vegetable varieties targeted a period of shortage in late winter and spring.

The final papers in this section are written by development practitioners. Because both authors are also anthropologists, their views reflect their social science training as well as their development
experience. Using the example of Rwanda, E. Robins argues that

food aid, even on an emergency basis, may be detrimental to long-term food security. While such aid can be an appropriate temporary response, it can disguise more serious and pervasive problems of agricultural production. He argues for a multipronged attack on the food problem, involving improved technology, more stable food markets, and increased opportunities for off-farm income generation. This diversified approach to development is also advocated by P. Fleuret, who points out that the food production problem is not the same as the food problem. Access to food involves more than production, and is generally worse for landless households, those without cash income, and those headed by women, many of whom are poor and poorly educated. Fleuret argues that the definition of the problem influences the solution, so that a broad definition is more likely to generate effective answers. Solutions should also be flexible in keeping with changing and unpredictable economic and ecological conditions. Planners should not strive for optimal solutions, but for flexible and feasible programs that provide a diversity of options for alleviating poverty and hunger.

Taken together, these papers provide an alternative view of the role of development in the African food crisis. This view is essentially anthropological (despite the inclusion of one economist), and draws upon many of the traditions of that discipline. It is primarily a view from the ground up, one that legitimizes the concerns of indigenous African populations. In this view, African traditions and African production systems are seen as resources, rather than problems. Developing those resources, rather than destroying or replacing them, will be a difficult task. This volume and its predecessor add a necessary dimension to the continuing dialogue.

Rebecca Huss-Ashmore

Part I

CHANGING AFRICAN FOOD SYSTEMS— ISSUES IN ANTHROPOLOGY AND DEVELOPMENT

Donors and Deserts:
The Political Ecology of Destructive Development in the Sahel

Michael M Horowitz[1]

Department of Anthropology
State University of New York at Binghamton,
Binghamton, NY 13901

Why do major lenders finance and why do many African governments accept financing for environmentally and socioeconomically destructive interventions? That is, why do development interventions designed to enhance the habitat and improve the income and productivity of small-scale rural households so often have exactly contrary outcomes? In this paper, I suggest that the answer lies, in part, in planners' general disdain for local production systems and in the association many draw between local production systems and resource degradation. Paradoxically, the emphasis on replacing such systems, rather than on enhancing them, has intensified, rather than limited, environmental abuse. I also suggest explanations that emerge from the very nature of the multilateral financial institutions, often more preoccupied with "moving" money than with carrying out sound development. In concentrating on these institutions, I do not mean to exempt national governments from responsibility, but only to provide some focus to an argument that already attempts to cover too broad a terrain.

[1]Michael Horowitz is Professor of Anthropology at State University of New York at Binghamton and Director of the Institute for Development Anthropology. Earlier drafts of this paper were helpfully reviewed by the author's colleagues at the Institute, to whom grateful acknowledgment is hereby recorded. Especial thanks are due Ms. Monica Sella, IDA economist, for her very fine reading of the final version.

I. The Problem

I have recently reviewed a draft "Livestock Strategy Statement" (1987) prepared by a major multilateral development lender. In a brief 110 pages, the draft[2] document attempts to cover a tremendous variety of domestic animals—pigs, poultry, goats, sheep, and cattle; fish in association with pigs and aquatic poultry; and even wild ungulates on game ranches. All the principal livestock areas in the developing world are included, with a focus on five distinct production systems: grain-intensive, pastoral, ranching, mixed crop/livestock, and dairying. While there are many admirable observations in this ambitious undertaking, two points stand out of especial interest to issues of African famine and food supply: first, at no point in the document—even in its statistical tables—is there any mention of camels; second, the donor opposes herd movement through open-range grazing, which, for many scientists, is *the critical adaptive strategy* of pastoral production systems on dry rangelands. I am not sure why camels are ignored, since they figure prominently in mixed crop and livestock systems as well as in arid zone pastoralism; I suspect that the authors simply dismissed them as archaic, anachronisms in a modern economy. I think I do know why the donor is hostile to ruminant herding on dry ranges.

This donor's attitude toward, and perception of, a traditional herding production system is just one instance of a widespread disregard for local production systems among development planners. Despite some Bank-sponsored rhetoric to the contrary (for example, the excellent collection edited by Cernea [1985]), multilateral bank officers, the largest number of whom are economists, often show a deep and fundamental distrust, indeed a contempt, for the rural production systems of Third World peoples. This distrust leads to the a priori assumption that these systems are inherently maladaptive obstacles to development that must be overcome. Those of us with long-term field experience in the rural Third World, on the other hand, see these

---

[2]I stress the term "draft" in discussing this document, since the forthcoming published version may well take into account objections that I, and perhaps other readers, have raised. The draft paper is, however, consistent with a long history of donor thinking about pastoralism.

peoples and their production systems as the basic resources with which development can take root. Financial institutions, such as the World Bank, that are wedded to sectoral as opposed to integrated approaches to development, find dealing with such systems inherently awkward.[3]

World Bank and other donor projects, moreover, too often favor those groups seeking maximum short-term gain rather than those whose objective is long-term sustainable survival.[4] E. Goldsmith (1985), editor of *The Ecologist*, puts it this way: both poverty and resource abuse are caused by policies and actions that seek rapid returns on investments, such as converting rainforest into ranching areas or flooding tropical landscapes by large dams for hydropower and large-scale irrigation. These investments, which render most rural people around the sites worse off than they were previously, find their advocacy at the FAO and their financing at the World Bank and at the regional multilateral banks, says Goldsmith.

One need not subscribe whole-hog to Goldsmith's conspiracy theory—when he says, for example, "the FAO . . . has been, for many years, under the complete domination of the agro-chemical industry"—to agree that the consequences of much of the "development" financed by the multilateral banks has, on balance, contributed both to impoverishing the rural populace and to wounding the habitat. This is not to say that no good has been done by these organizations, that the rural poor have experienced no benefits, or that no environmentally sound interventions have been funded; but a good deal of blame for socioeconomic and environmental destruction rests on the doorsteps of the Bank and other major funding organizations.

---

[3]A clear example of the sectoral as opposed to integrated approach to development is found in river basin planning, where dams are most often the prerogative of the energy division of the donor organization, rendering moot a more desirable multisectoral approach (Scudder 1988:201).

[4]Discussing the encroachment of large-scale farming onto pastoral rangelands in the eastern Sudan funded by Saudi and other Arab donors, John Morton (1988:1) writes: "The normal framework is for private investors, usually urban merchants, to obtain from the parastatal Mechanized Farming Corporation a lease on a 1000 or 1500 acre plot . . . The structure of profitability encourages the adoption of highly deleterious farming practices for a few years, after which a new plot can be leased."

At a meeting in 1986 called to examine the environmental contributions—both positive and negative—of the World Bank,[5] there was a broad sense among the ecologists present that the Bank's net impact has not been beneficial, especially where tropical rain forests were concerned, but there was less consensus on why that was the case.

A representative of the World Resources Institute[6] suggested that part of the fault lay with the limited professional staff and finances that the Bank marshals to appraise environmental impacts of large-scale infrastructural projects, such as hydropower dams. He recommended that the major donors undergird, with additional funding, the Bank's environmental planning and evaluation capacity.

Other members of the panel were either unpersuaded or actively opposed to providing the Bank with additional funds. Catherine Caufield, author of *In the Rainforest* (1985), held that **any** funding of the World Bank exacerbates destruction of tropical woodlands. She and others argued that the Bank is not a potential solution, if only it had sufficient staff, but actually a prime cause of massive environmental degradation, informed by an environmentally destructive perspective on Third World development. The organizers of the conference wrote:

> Tragically, the very development activities funded by the Bank and other foreign aid institutions are causing much of the massive deforestation, erosion and desertification that are devastating large areas of the Third World. Attempts to solve the acute problems of underdevelopment are aggravating existing environmental problems and creating new ones.

Ecologist critics have argued that large-scale capital intensive development projects, "such as dams, roads, plantations and ranches, and mass migration . . . are easier to administer than smaller (and more viable) projects." This is probably true. Management time is considered a very scarce commodity, and larger projects are therefore "less costly" than smaller ones. Thus, it is far more difficult to obtain a hearing for a $500,000 proposal than for a $5,000,000 or even

---

[5]Citizens Conference on Tropical Forests, Indigenous Peoples, and the World Bank, Washington, DC, 28–30 September 1986.

[6]WRI had collaborated with the Bank in producing a study of rain forests, *Tropical Forests: a Call to Action*. Report of an International Task Force Convened by the World Resources Institute, the World Bank, and the UN Development Programme, Washington: WRI, 1985.

a $50,000,000 one. And success within a large donor organization, as Judith Tendler (1975) wrote more than a decade ago, is often associated more with the expeditiousness with which large amounts of money are "moved," than with the quality of the consequent development. To complicate matters, the World Bank until very recently has held the view that much of the responsibility for resource degradation rests with the poor. A. W. Clausen, immediate past president of the World Bank, has said, "poverty puts . . . severe—and often irreversible—strains on the natural environment . . . [A]t survival levels people are sometimes compelled to exploit their environment too intensively [and] poverty has often resulted in long years of mismanagement of our natural resources, evidencing itself in overgrazing, erosion, denuded forests, and surface water pollution."

The Bank's perspective is an instance of "blaming the victim" (Wood and Schmink 1978). It puts the blame for environmental degradation on poverty as if poverty were an independent variable. In other words, the Bank president saw degradation as an outcome of a competition between a population and its land, rather than as a consequence of competition among different groups for access to productive resources.

Ultimately, it boils down to the fact that major development financing organizations tend to see in people and their production systems the problem; we look to people and their production systems for the solution. And not coincidentally, the mutual suspicion and often adversarial relationships that exists between economists and anthropologists derive from these opposed viewpoints.[7]

I would like to demonstrate this point by exploring development activities among pastoral herding peoples on African semiarid rangelands. I will more briefly illuminate it with a view of large dam con-

---

[7]This position is not so much unrecognized by the World Bank as it is ignored in project design and implementation. A recent Bank-published (Falloux and Mukendi 1988:2–3) consideration of development in semiarid regions of West Africa makes the point boldly: "Past developmental efforts in the Sahel have failed to cope with the problem of desertification. Some have clearly exacerbated the problem. These efforts were not successful because governments and donor agencies failed to fully appreciate the role of traditional production systems, did not consult with rural communities, and generally underestimated the strengths of local institutions."

struction and river basin development on the continent. These two "sectors"—livestock herding and river basin development—are selected not because they uniquely illustrate the problem, but simply because my personal experience as a development anthropologist in sudano-sahelian Africa has focused largely on interventions involving animals and rivers. Multilateral bank and, indeed, some bilateral donor-funded projects in rainfed agriculture, in resource management, and even in health could as well be cited in support of the argument made here.

II. Pastoral Production Systems in Africa

The draft livestock strategy statement summarizes its basic position in regard to pastoral production systems: "Pastoral grazing systems under communal land ownership *are* showing increasingly serious irreversible damage due to overgrazing beyond a sustainable carrying capacity" (p. 102). The solution to the problem is "to identify a defined body of land with a defined body of people," and thereby to make them responsible for the state of the land.

This accusation, which has considerable antiquity, was given its modern form by Garrett Hardin (1968) in his famous paper in *Science* on the "tragedy of the commons." The logic is that the disjunction between common ownership of land and individual ownership of livestock generates a situation in which rational action to increase individual benefit by herd enlargement conflicts with behaviors beneficial to the community. The costs of each additional animal placed on the common range are borne by all users, while the benefits of herd increase pertain exclusively to the individual owner. Therefore, pastoral herders are accused of not manifesting "a conservation ethic oriented toward long-term preservation of the ecological resource" (Picardi 1975:164–165).

Since each owner seeks to maximize herd size, the argument continues, the charge rapidly exceeds the carrying capacity of the range, finally resulting in overgrazing, erosion, declining productivity, xerification, and desertification.

During the years since the 1968–1974 sahelian drought largely set the agenda for donor activities in the African livestock "sector," the simple assertion of herder-induced degradation, often bracketed to the assurance that open range grazing replaces "palatable perennials with unpalatable annuals,"[8] has been sufficient to elaborate projects calling for fundamental changes in pastoral practice. The "tragedy of the commons" scenario is persuasive, especially when accompanied with quantitative data on carrying capacities. It is also consistent with the dominant development paradigm of our day, enshrined in International Monetary Fund lending conditionality, that calls for privatization of resources (and investments): identifying "a defined body of land with a defined body of people." However persuasive the anti-nomadic scenario, it is not necessarily true.[9]

It is mainly among development planners, economists (with the prominent exception of ILCA's Stephen Sandford [1983]), and some agronomists and range scientists that anti-nomadism finds its main support. What is remarkable is how little hard evidence there is in support of the claims. In place of data and analysis, one author cites another or simply invokes "common knowledge." Lamprey (1983:656) states categorically that the evidence pointing to overgrazing as the cause of "widespread damage to semiarid and arid zone grasslands . . . [is] overwhelming," but fails to share that over-

---

[8]"Heavy grazing by cattle selectively removes the most palatable perennial native grasses called 'decreasers' and results in patches of bare soil, increases of less productive and nutritious annual grasses called 'increasers' or invasion by foreign species called 'exotics' " (World Resources Institute 1986:74).

[9]What I have termed an "anti-nomad morality" (Horowitz 1979), providing ready rationalizations to control pastoral herding, predates modern development writing by at least 600 years. Ibn Khaldun in the 14th century elaborated the basic attack that continues to inform development planners today. A great advocate of sedentary life, Ibn Khaldun (1967:304) wrote: " . . . civilization always collapsed in places where the Arabs took over and conquered, and . . . such settlements were depopulated and the very earth there turned into something that was no longer earth . . . " In the late 19th century, these accusations were echoed by Palmer (1977:292) writing about the Sinai and the Negev: " . . . wherever [the Bedouin] goes, he brings with him ruin, violence, and neglect. To call him a 'son of the desert' is a misnomer; half the desert owes its existence to him." Antinomadism has found support even among 20th century anthropologists (Herskovits 1926; Murdock 1959; Lomax and Arensberg 1977), although rarely among those with first-hand field work among a pastoral people.

whelming evidence with the reader.[10] FAO (1973:14, emphasis added) escalates the argument to an assault on the very character of pastoralists:" . . . caring for nothing, disdaining manual labor, balking at paying taxes, and being unwilling to sell their animals . . . ; they do not make the economic contribution to their countries that is *rightfully* expected of them." More recently, FAO (1980:56) continued to attribute degradation on rangelands to mismanagement by pastoralists: "It is basically a problem of the misuse of land . . . [M]uch of the problem results from the customs, value systems and attitudes of the people concerning grazing lands and livestock, together with the lack of government mechanisms for effective control."

I suggest, on the contrary, that it is planners' and technicians' understandings of pastoral production systems that are basically in error, and that these errors lead inevitably to flawed programs and projects. The standard portrait of herders on dry lands, however persuasive and however attractive for some scientists, is a socioeconomic and ecological caricature rather than a scientific description. This caricature serves to justify a development posture that has both a disappointing performance record and disastrous environmental consequences (Darling and Farvar 1972; Talbot 1972).

African countries in which pastoralism forms a prominent compo-

---

[10]Lamprey's 1975 claim of a steady southward migration of the desert in northern Kordofan, Sudan, has been cited by a number of writers, most recently by Reeves and Frankenberger (1981). It has also been challenged by researchers from Lund University. Ahlcrona (1988:17) writes that Ulf Helldén's (1978, 1984) analyses of satellite imagery found no such shift. "Neither could Helldén verify any southward sand dune encroachment. To the contrary, he found that the dune complex has been *stable* between 1962 (air photos), 1972 and 1979." Helldén's observations were confirmed by Lennart Olsson (1984, 1985) and by K. Olsson (1985). Writing of the claimed shift in vegetation that is supposedly diagnostic of desertification, the latter author noted "no wood species seemed to have been eradicated from the area, no ecological zones had shifted southwards and the boundaries between different vegetation associations appeared to be the same as they were 80 years ago." I suspect that anti-nomad morality is so powerful among development planners, that many of them will continue to invoke Lamprey's findings and ignore those of his critics. This is not to deny that desertification is indeed a major problem, but rather to insist on the need for a more rigorous documentation of its occurrences and causes. Homewood and Rodgers usefully discuss these issues.

nent of the economy are poor and often landlocked.[11] It is little wonder that governments and donors view the vast herds of cattle and sheep (if not camels and goats) as prime commodities to be offered on regional and world markets. The principal objective of interventions from the government perspective is increased production of meat, some of which is destined for export and the remainder for domestic urban markets, sold sometimes at officially depressed prices to provide cheap food to civil service and private sector urban consumers. Donor organizations add another set of objectives:

- to retard or reverse environmental degradation while improving the forage quality of the range;
- to improve producer income and the quality of pastoral life; and
- to provide a favorable economic rate of return.

It is not easy to increase production while improving rangeland conditions, and to keep consumer prices low while improving producer income—all the while assuring an adequate return on investment. The concurrent satisfaction of all these objectives through development actions never, repeat, never occurs.

Livestock sector interventions normally involve a combination of veterinary measures, new water points, and some kind of range management (usually based on increased offtake and destocking, rotational grazing, and limitation of range access to specifically designated herders). Projects sometimes also include supplemental feeding, feedlots, abattoirs, pastoral associations and cooperatives, credit, functional literacy programs, pest and parasite vector controls, and genetic improvement of stock, and they generally prohibit range fires.[12] "Over the 1965–80 period, it is estimated that donors chan-

---

[11]Subsaharan African pastoralists are most numerous in Sudan, Somalia, Chad, Ethiopia, Kenya, Mali, Mauritania, Niger, Senegal, Burkina Faso, Uganda, and Tanzania respectively.

[12]In East Africa, pastoral peoples have seen their lands alienated not only to agriculturalists, but also to game and tourist parks—wildlife reserves—managed by conservationists. This has had certain ironic if unanticipated outcomes. In Tanzanian Maasailand, "The concentration of people and livestock in the Ngorongoro highlands in the early 1960s, and the continuing penetration and expansion of agriculture into the Conservation Area led the authorities to take an increasingly hard and uncompromising stance. Rules and

neled around $600,000,000 into livestock projects in Africa'' (Eicher 1985:31). Yet apart from veterinary actions, which are often—though not invariably—appreciated by herders, **none of the range management, hydrologic, genetic, and marketing interventions has measurably increased production, enhanced producer income, retarded environmental degradation, or provided a satisfactory economic rate of return on investment.** Livestock development projects in pastoral areas have such poor performance records that many donors, including the World Bank and the US Agency for International Development, are exceedingly reluctant today to do anything at all in the sector.

What went wrong? Why have planners and technicians been unable to design and implement actions that would achieve their objectives?

III. A Critique of the Donor View of Pastoral Production Systems

In answer to this question, let us return to the ''tragedy of the commons.'' There is little convincing evidence that, controlling for environment, private ranges are more productive or better managed than public ones. There is some evidence to the contrary, indicating that ''livestock productivity in pastoral areas has been seriously underestimated, and that on many criteria pastoral systems are actually more productive than commercial ranching enterprises.'' (Horowitz and Little 1987:71).

In southern Ethiopia, for example, Cossins (1985:10) found that the pastoral ''Borana system is very productive; compared with Australian commercial ranches in a very similar climatic environment, the Borana produce nearly four times as much

---

regulations hardened. Grazing in the forest reserve and in the water catchment areas in the highlands was prohibited, and all grass burning banned. This was to have serious consequences for the highland pastures. Where unpalatable grasses previously had been kept at bay by burning, they now expanded over the entire highland plateau, suppressing the palatable grasses and thus radically reducing the dry season pastures. The spread and expansion of tall and coarse grasses in the highlands also led to an increase in the incidence of tick-borne diseases, as ticks thrive in the tall, moist highland grasses'' (Aarhem 1984:194, citing Branagan 1974).

protein and six times as much food energy from each hectare.'' Rather than looking at productivity per animals, which is a measure used in commercial ranching
areas, [Cossins] uses a per land unit measure, which is of greater significance to
pastoral producers. In terms of productivity per unit of cost (labor and other), the
Borana system also has an advantage over commercial ranches. The amount of US
dollar investment required to produce one kg of animal protein is $0.14–0.28 for
the Borana system, $2.01 for commercial ranches in Laikipia, Kenya, and $1.93–
3.89 for Australian ranches. If production of food energy (milk and meat) is used
as an indicator, the difference in benefits from pastoral production is even more
outstanding (ibid.).

Data from Botswana support Cossin's conclusion, revealing that
Botswana pastoral production systems are "95% more productive in
terms of liveweight production equivalents than ranching systems on a
per hectare basis" (De Ridder and Wagenaar 1984:6–7). The data
also speak to the issue of carrying capacity:

Because of uncertainty over stocking rates in traditional systems, a sensitivity
analysis was carried out to estimate the stocking rate at which productivity in
traditional systems would fall to that of ranching, assuming other production parameters were constant. This estimated stocking rate was 9.5 ha/livestock unit,
compared with the observed stocking rate in traditional systems of around 6 ha/
livestock unit (ibid.:7).

Lowering the stocking rate would reduce both productivity per unit
land and the number of persons who can be sustained in the area.
ILCA's Sandford (1983:119–120) writes that "overstocking and environmental deterioration appear to be just as common in areas of
rangeland where, as in parts of the USA and Australia, both land and
livestock are individually owned." Allan Savory (1986) argues that
degradation may be extreme where no animals are grazed at all!

The evidence points to greater productivity from traditional public
ranges; it also points to longstanding management strategies for inhib-
iting the abuse of pastoralism's communal system. The anthropological literature on pastoralism notes restrictions on both access and use
of "communal" ranges, widespread claims on the use and disposition
of "private" livestock, and constraints on the numbers of animals
herded. In other words, pastoralists, no less than anyone else, live in
communities, and these communities have moral bases that do not
allow for unchecked personal aggrandizement at the expense of one's
fellows (e.g., Marie 1985). To be sure, the transition from more egalitarian domestic communities to more differentiated commoditized
ones is clearly associated with a decline in the commitment to general

morality, but **this transition is normally accompanied by the very privatization of public resources** that Hardin and others who embrace the tragedy-of-the-commons argument favor.[13]

The notion of "overgrazing," so central to discussions of desertification on rangelands, assumes that there is some maximum weight of animals that can be sustained on a given range more or less indefinitely. When that gross weight is exceeded, one of two alternative scenarios is supposed to happen. Either a number of animals is removed from the range—through starvation, forced migration, or sale—and the "proper ratio" between charge and carrying capacity restored; or the capacity of the range to sustain that weight is permanently impaired. Anders Hjort (1981:173–174) refers to these two notions, respectively, as the **equilibrium** and **degradation** models. He proposes a third alternative, a **resiliency** model, that sees both stocking rate and carrying capacity in some kind of association such that temporary increases in load cause short-term declines in the carrying capacity, but that capacity is restored over time as the charge on pasture is reduced.

A good deal of discussion in the Sahel and in other arid and semiarid pastoral regions turns on the appropriateness of the particular model held without its being made explicit. Anthropologists of the structural school, prominent in the study of pastoralism until a few years ago, tended to impose equilibrium models on their analyses. American and British range scientists, for the most part, historically identified with the degradation model, and that is the one most commonly invoked in documents regarding livestock sector development (and is implicit in the draft livestock strategy statement mentioned above).

---

[13]An instructive example can be seen in the USAID-financed Lesotho Grazing Lands Management Project. An evaluation carried out in 1985 notes that the project area was removed from common use and given to a newly formed grazing association, the members of which, affluent herd owners, have exclusive rights to pasture. State power is invoked to keep others, including former users, off the range by impounding trespassing stock. An irony of the situation is that while environmental improvement is a project objective, the affluent and powerful members of the association ignore grazing regulations with impunity: "by virtue of their stature, [they] may demand exemption . . . " These upper class herd owners, in other words, enjoying reduced competition on the range from a large number of small herders, are unconstrained by rules designed to maintain productivity and soil fertility.

Increasingly, persons with extensive field research in pastoral areas show considerable dissatisfaction with both, and find the resiliency model according better with the empirical situation. Resiliency is implicit in the alternative range exploitation strategies explored by Sandford (1982:62). These he contrasts as "opportunistic" and "conservative."

An *opportunistic* pastoral strategy is defined as one which varies the number of livestock in accordance with the current availability of forage. Such a strategy enables the extra forage available in good years to be converted directly into economic output (milk, meat) or into productive capital in the form of a bigger breeding herd. The economic output may be immediately consumed or it may be exchanged for easily storable wealth, such as money or jewelry, that can be re-exchanged for consumables when needed. In bad years, livestock numbers are reduced. . . .

A *conservative* strategy is defined as one which maintains a population of grazing animals at a relatively constant level, without overgrazing, through good and bad years alike. A conservative strategy implies that during good years livestock numbers are not allowed to increase to utilize all available forage.

The notion of "carrying capacity" might provide a quantifiable index, rendering it appropriately "scientific," but how is it to be calculated? A salient feature of arid and semiarid rangelands is the enormous and unpredictable variation in the quantity, frequency, and spatial distribution of rainfall and therefore of graze and browse. Holding constant the nutrient profile of the soil, it has been demonstrated that forage production varies with rainfall (Diarra and Bremen 1975, cited in Sandford 1982:65). Since the amount of forage is as unpredictable as the amount of rainfall, and in some years will be reduced to near zero, the selection of a conservative figure for carrying capacity will inevitably mean that **in most years the range could sustain far more animals** than actually utilize it. Sandford (1982) refers to this as **understocking,** and asks which strategy is economically sounder over the long run: one that habitually overstocks or one that habitually understocks? Livestock development rhetoric tends to favor the latter strategy, in direct opposition to the more opportunistic use of rangelands practiced by African herders.[14]

---

[14]Note that on the sahelian and sudanian ranges where annual species dominate—and have dominated for several hundred years at least—unconsumed

Some recent findings by range biologists also question the appropriateness of the degradation model of carrying capacity for designing ecologically sound livestock sector interventions. The ecology team on USAID's Niger Range and Livestock Project discovered that, contrary to conventional range scientist wisdom, moderate grazing in the early rainy season (which, in fact, is the practice of Nigerien pastoralists) provides for greater residual moisture—a soil moisture reserve—than does the lighter grazing pressure more often recommended by pasture management specialists. Increased soil moisture at the end of the rainy season affects the quality of the vegetation by decreasing percent dry matter, extending the "green feed" period, and by increasing perennial regrowth, thus possibly allowing additional animal gains (Swift 1984:758).

The ecologists, directed by Robert Bement, himself a Colorado rancher, discovered that many pastures are actually **underutilised,** and recommended harvesting these grasses for hay and silage to provide high-protein feed supplements in the dry season.

One may thus question whether pastoral herding strategies of "overgrazing" degrade the environment. Let us go a step further: can they improve pasture? There is clear evidence of conditions under which undergrazing is detrimental. Conant (1982) documents the invasion and colonization by nonpalatable thorny acacias of a rangeland in northern Kenya that had been removed from pastoralism for several years, "rested" in the jargon. Others have cited the importance of livestock feeding in reducing the canopy habitat required by *Glossinae* ("tsetse" fly) for their reproduction (Putt and Shaw 1983:517). Savory (1986) insists that a large number of animals grazing intensively for a short period—resembling common pastoral practice—is more beneficial to the range than a smaller number maintained, as in Western-style ranching, for a longer period.

Let us linger for a moment on the issue of canopy, for overgrazing is often indicted where a marked lowering of canopy height is observed. "When I was a boy (or a young range manager, first posted in Kenya [or Senegal or Botswana]), the grass came up to here," the

---

graze cannot be saved from one year to the next, although it might possibly contribute to improved soil structure and fertility. Understocking does not necessarily generate money in the bank.

speaker indicates with upstretched arms. "Now it hardly reaches my knees." Is a high canopy indicative of a more productive pasture? A recent paper in *Science* (Lewin 1985:567) on gregarious grazing, while specific to wild ruminants, is suggestive for livestock:

> Continual grazing clearly presents a very strong selection pressure, and so this direct, short-term reaction is eventually translated to an evolutionary response, with a shift in the genetic and phenotypic characteristics of the surviving plants. There is, therefore, a coevolution between grazers and their "prey" . . . ; for the plants there is an effect on their morphology, and for the animals, an effect on behavior.

Lewin does not speculate on the implications of his findings for domesticated stock, but they would seem to be obvious. Grazing animals, rather than necessarily degrading their environment, may over time **transform** it by favoring the reproduction of those species that better respond to their consumptive requirements. By increasing the biomass per unit volume—instead of the usual measure per unit area—gregariousness increases the efficiency of grazing:

> The high biomass concentration in grazed, short grasses is the result of a more densely packed foliage within the canopy volume, which becomes ecologically significant for grazers. The most important property in their food source is energy intake per bite, not the amount of standing biomass. It is possible for a herbivore to starve in the midst of apparent plenty, if the quality of food culled in each tongue-swing is of a low concentration.

> Stobbs calculated that for a cow-size grazer, a bite size of about 0.3 gram of usable nutrients was necessary for survival, a figure that translates to 0.8 milligrams per milliliter biomass concentration. McNaughton's data from the Serengeti show that vegetation taller than 40 cm would be deficient in support of such an animal. An animal grazing on a 10 cm greensward would be reaping rich rewards of available energy per bite. Moreover, plants cropped at this level are in a more juvenile state, and therefore offer higher protein content and greater digestibility (Lewin 1985:568).

While findings such as these do not in themselves negate the theoretical utility of the "carrying capacity" concept, they should at the least have us regard any specific claims about the number/weight of animals that can be sustained on the range (cf. Lamprey 1983) with a good deal of skepticism.

Nothing that I have said above denies that rangelands are under threat. The threat comes not so much from pastoral herding, however, as from various forms of sedentary landuse—the migration of agriculture across the "agronomic dry boundary" (Ibrahim 1978); the removal of land from food crop production for a concentration on export crops, especially under irrigation, which contributes to the spread of "subsistence" agriculture onto unsuitable lands (Horowitz and Salem-Murdock 1987); [15] and sedentary livestock raising, including ranching—each of which is either encouraged or is a consequence of agricultural policies of the World Bank and other major development funding organizations.

IV. African River Basin Development

Development projects among pastoral livestock producers have often attempted, usually on the basis of distorted understandings of pastoral socioeconomics and ecology, to replace existing production systems rather than to enhance them, to focus on national or rather elite and urban accounts rather than on increasing income for small-scale producers. The results have been failures.

A similar outcome has characterized donor efforts in river basin development in arid and semiarid regions of Africa. Once again, rather than improve local production for the benefit of thousands of small-scale farmers, the donors have financed efforts aimed at radical transformation of these production systems for the benefit of domestic urban consumers and the industrial export market. A current case in point is the Senegal Valley.

In 1986–1988, two major dams in the valley were completed. The Diama Dam, near the mouth of the river, is designed primarily to limit saline pollution of the river from the upstream migration of the Atlantic Ocean during periods of reduced downstream flow. It will also provide a reservoir for irrigation and to supplement potable water

---

[15]In a discussion of migration from rural Mali to the capital city of Bamako, the authors note: "This contact zone between savanna and steppe around the 600 mm isohyet is a highly threatened part of the Sahelian ecosystem, probably more so than the Sahel proper (i.e. the fringe between desert and steppe) (Penning de Vries et al. 1982). Natural soil fertility in both ecological zones is roughly equal, but the somewhat wetter southern Sahel is much more intensively used (cultivation instead of livestock herding) and is therefore more exposed to ecological degradation" (van Westen and Klute 1986:44).

drawn off from the Guier and R'kiz lakes. The Manantali Dam across the major tributary of the Senegal, the Bafing River in southwestern Mali, creates a reservoir of almost 500 square kilometers containing more than 11 billion cubic meters of water (Ciubotariu 1988:6). According to the Senegal Valley Development Authority (OMVS), comprised of representatives from Mali, Senegal, and Mauritania, the Manantali Dam has three principal development objectives:

• irrigation of an additional 375,000 hectares in the Valley, of which 240,000 will be in Senegal, 126,000 in Mauritania, and 9,000 in Mali;
• riverine navigation throughout the year from St. Louis at the mouth of the river to Kayes, giving landlocked Mali direct access to the sea; and
• annual generation of up to 800 GW of electricity.

Additionally, the dams are supposed to improve the drinking water situation for Dakar.

What is not envisaged is the enhancement of the Senegal Valley's **existing** agricultural and pastoral production systems, which would directly increase earnings and living standards for upwards of a million residents.

Agriculture in the Senegal Valley has four traditional components and one new one. During the short summer rains, the people farm cereal grains, mainly millet, on sandy upland fields at some distance from the river. Second, in most years at the end of the rainy season, the river floods, and as the waters recede, some 100,000 hectares of floodplain lands are sown in sorghum, cow peas, maize, and other cultigens. Third, the area sustains substantial herds of ruminant livestock that graze sandy pastures during the rainy season, then move to the cropped millet fields when these pastures give out, and finally, in the later dry season, to the floodlplains where they browse cropped sorghum stalks, shrubs, and nutritious grasses that colonize uncultivated fields. Fourth, these lateral floodplains are essential habitats for the reproduction of fish, which are captured both on the plains and in the river channel. The flood also recharges the surface aquifer, from which many villages obtain water for domestic use, and provides the soil moisture required by *Acacia nilotica,* the dominant floodplain tree species. Thus, beyond rainfed millet farming characteristic of sahelian agriculture, the annual flood in the Senegal Valley sustains a complex agri-silvi-halio-pastoral production system, and enables a relatively dense population to subsist in a semiarid region.

During the past decades a number of irrigated perimeters—lands that are levelled and bunded to facilitate appropriate coverage by waters pumped from the river and distributed along a series of canals—were introduced along the river valley in Mauritania and Senegal. They are managed by parastatal corporations who not only supervise production and provide inputs of seed, water, agricultural chemicals, and machinery, but who also have been responsible for the marketing of crops (mainly sugar and rice). The large perimeters share very high costs of installation, management, and periodic rehabilitation; low yields; and low returns to tenant farmers, who respond with high rates of absenteeism and migration from the valley.[16]

Despite the poor performance of these State-owned perimeters (Guinard 1988), the OMVS, representing member governments, seeks to terminate the annual flood that would provide for low input-cost employment, production, and income for many thousands of peasant households. Yet while few would suggest building a dam in order to regularize a flood artificially, Manantali does have the capability of doing just that, with modest costs to its potential for hydropower generation and irrigation. And as Scudder (1988) has written, a controlled flood in conjunction with electricity, irrigation, and transport, might well prove in the long run to constitute the dam's most beneficial development feature, providing for improved recession cultivation, agroforestry, aquifer recharge, and pastoralism.

What makes Manantali unusual is not that it will interfere with the flood. Almost every dam built in Africa has caused a tremendous decline in downstream flood recession cultivation, and the resultant loss of income to the smallholders who depended on the flood for much of their livelihood. Those who manage dams represent hydropower and irrigation interests. While there are conflicts even among these for control over the reservoir, neither is willing to see their precious water "wasted" on traditional farming. But Manantali was completed without installation of its turbines, and there will be a

---

[16]Production and returns from small village- and privately-owned and managed irrigated perimeters in the Senegal Valley are more attractive than from large State-run schemes, but even among these only about half the total hectarage is farmed at any time.

period minimally of several years before the dam will provide any electricity. For this period, a controlled annual flood could take place without having to compete against the demands of powerful urban and industrial electricity consumers. Therefore, a rare opportunity exists to test the hypothesis that the advantages to traditional production systems from a controlled release will outweigh the costs in some reduction of potential hydropower and possibly some diminution in the availability of water for irrigation.

The official position of the OMVS (1987), supported by the donors, is that the years prior to the installation of hydroelectric infrastructure at Manantali and the establishment of transmission lines from the dam to the anticipated consumption centers will be employed in "weaning" riparian farmers from recession cultivation to irrigation. Since the record of large-scale government-managed irrigation in Africa is not much more attractive than that of pastoral livestock development projects, one can predict, sadly but with a fair degree of confidence, that a major consequence will be a substantial increase in national debt burdens without a commensurate improvement in agricultural production and with very little, if any, improvement in earnings and living standards for rural producers.

Recognition of the potential of the dams to enhance existing production systems, rather than merely to replace them, would fundamentally improve not only the well-being of inhabitants of the region but also of their entire nations. As Thayer Scudder (1988) has written, it is the rising disposable income of low income rural households that is the engine for development. As such households move beyond subsistence, their increasing purchasing power has a greater multiplier effect than large-scale export-oriented irrigated production because their increased demand is for goods and services, such as materials and furnishings for improved housing, that can be locally manufactured and installed. Increased disposable income on farms stimulates increased nonfarm employment in rural and urban enterprise development. But this approach to development requires a willingness on the part of donors and host governments to deal respectfully with small-scale producers and their production systems. Neither the larger donors nor most African governments have heretofore shown much genuine willingness to do so.

In the case of Manantali, a World Bank expert (Andersen 1987) argued that the most efficient use of the dam would be to support a single energy transmission line that would bring power to the city of

Dakar. Alternative uses of the dam—for irrigation, flood recession agriculture, or environmental rehabilitation—must not be permitted to reduce hydropower production below its potential of 800 gigawatts. Not even the enhancement of irrigation through electrification of the pumps is envisaged in Andersen's analysis to assure rapid repayment of the dam construction loans. The Bank is supported in its single-mindedness by two bilateral donors whose nationals, it is assumed, would be contracted to provide the necessary infrastructure for power generation and transmission lines. The Arab donors (Saudi Arabia, Abu Dhabi, Kuwait, and the Islamic Development Bank) and USAID have continued to push for agricultural production, seeing the World Bank's insistence on rapid debt repayment rather than some form of rescheduling as shortsighted.

In its Ministerial Council meeting of April 3–4, 1989, the Senegal River Development Organization decided on the location of power transmission lines: one will go from the dam eastward to Bamako (made necessary because of the silting of the Selingue reservoir whose generators were supposed to assure Bamako's power needs) and the other westward along the Senegal Valley, with the potential greatly to facilitate development in the region. The preceding January, the Senegalese Minister of Plan and Cooperation for the first time vetted the possibility of incorporating a controlled flood in the long-term management of the Manantali Dam, because of its beneficial effects on the environment, fisheries, and flood recession cultivation (Salem-Murdock, Horowitz, and Scudder 1989). Even the World Bank has now acknowledged the significance of recession farming for the middle valley of the Senegal, although almost all their agricultural investments in the region have focused on irrigation (World Bank 1989). Despite this acknowledgment, there is as yet no assurance of a permanently institutionalized controlled release from Manantali that would replicate the natural flood, and an overly optimistic posture is surely premature given the powerful constituencies who favor a total transformation of the existing ecological and production systems.

V. Conclusion

Following years of stonewalling its critics, the World Bank, under the leadership of its new president, Barber Conable, has begun to respond to pressure from environmentalists, and especially from the United States Congress and Treasury Department. Despite its current reduction in force—the elimination this year of several hundred professional positions—the World Bank is reported to be creating a new environment department, with a large staff, to assure the ecological soundness of its portfolio. Persons with environmental responsibilities are also now assigned to the regional departments.

For these changes to be more than cosmetic, the environmental specialists will have to be vested with real authority to approve or reject spending, and that authority will have to be exercised.

Still, no solution to the environmental crises of the Third World will be forthcoming if the projects exclude local populations in their identification, design, implementation, and evaluation. In a review of World Bank and other major donor-funded pastoral projects in Africa, conducted incidentally on behalf of the World Bank, I found that not a single project had any more than a transparent veneer of participation on the part of the supposed beneficiary populations. The commitment of the World Bank and the multilateral regional banks to involve local populations in development activities has been even less exemplary than their recognizably poor environmental record. Their portfolios continue to emphasize top-down development in which the supposed beneficiaries are passive recipients of externally conceived and directed interventions. For example, rural populations have been involuntarily relocated from their homes as consequences of World Bank-supported dam construction—sometimes, as in the Kiambere Dam Project on the Tana River in Kenya, with minuscule financial "compensation," but with no thought given to maintenance of their communities or enhancement of their production systems.[17] As we have seen, the Bank continues to insist on the saliency of the "tragedy of the commons" logic in rangeland projects, despite the dreadful evaluations these projects have received and despite the mounting evidence that communal pastures are more productive and environmentally better managed than private ranches.

---

[17]The World Bank has now adopted a rigorous policy towards involuntary relocation that resists cash payments for relocatees, and emphasizes the need for local participation in the process (Cernea 1988).

Is it possible to design environmentally and socioeconomically sound livestock and river basin development projects, or should one avoid these "sectors" altogether? I believe it is possible, but these interventions must seek in the first instance to increase the disposable income and improve the living standards of local populations. Activities among pastoral herders must avoid affecting mobility and/or threatening the ability of the herd to support large numbers of persons. River basin development should incorporate improvements in existing production systems, such as flood recession farming, fisheries, and agropastoralism, as well as experiment with different forms of irrigation. The sine qua non of actions that are both environmentally and socioeconomically sound is actively to involve the people.

There is a lesson to be learned here. The United States Congress and other major donor parliaments are unlikely to authorize increased funding for foreign economic assistance, especially for the multilateral banks (where they have less control than over bilateral assistance), when important domestic programs confront declining budgets. Yet development that is modest in scale, and that is based on sound socioeconomic and ecological understandings that remain under the control of local populations, is not only the key to the successes of some of the smaller donor and private voluntary organizations, but is also no more costly in the short term, and much less costly over the long term.

World Bank President Conable is to be congratulated for his concern for balancing economic growth with environmental protection. To assure a development both equitable and sustainable, the Bank and the other major funding organizations need to make an equal commitment to the protection and enhancement of rural Third World peoples and their production systems.

References

Aarhem, Kaj 1984 "Two sides of development: Maasai pastoralism and wild-life conservation in Ngorongoro, Tanzania," Ethnos 3/4:186–210.

Andersen, Dennis 1987 "Scope of Tariff and Project Justification Studies." Unpublished report prepared by the World Bank (WAPDR) for the Senegal Valley Development Organization (OMVS).

Ahlcrona, Eva 1988 The Impact of Climate and Man on Land Transformation in Central Sudan: Applications of Remote Sensing. Lund: Lund University Press.

Branagan, D. 1974 "A conflict between tourist interests and pastoralism in the Ngorongoro highlands of Tanzania." In *Tourism in Africa and the Management of Related Resources: Proceedings of a Seminar at the Centre of African Studies,* May 3–4, 1974. University of Edinburgh.

Caufield, Catherine 1985 *In the Rainforest.* New York: Knopf.

Cernea, Michael M., ed. 1985 *Putting People First: Sociological Variables in Rural Development.* New York: Oxford University Press for the World Bank.

————— 1988 *Involuntary Resettlement in Development Projects: Policy Guidelines in World Bank-Financed Projects.* Technical paper No. 80. Washington, DC: The World Bank.

Ciubotariu, Victor 1988 "L'Aménagement Hydraulique du Fleuve Sénégal et les Objectifs de Développement qui s'y Rattachent." Paper presented at the Canadian Association for African Studies meetings, Kingston, Ontario, 11 May 1988.

Conant, Francis P. 1982 "Thorns paired, sharply recurved: cultural controls and rangeland quality in East Africa." In *Desertification and Development: Dryland Ecology in Social Perspective.* B. Spooner and H.S. Mann, eds. New York: Academic Press.

Cossins, N.J. 1985 "The productivity and potential of pastoral systems." ILCA Bulletin 21:10–15.

Darling, F. Frazer, and Mary A. Farvar 1972 "Ecological consequences of sedentarization of nomads." In *The Careless Technology: Ecology and International Development.* M.T. Farvar and J.P. Milton, eds. Garden City, NY: The Natural History Press. pp. 671–682.

deRidder, N., and K.T. Wagenaar 1984 "A comparison between the productivity of traditional livestock systems and ranching in eastern Botswana." ILCA Newsletter 3(3):5–7.

Diarra, L., and Henk Bremen 1975 "Influence of rainfall on the productivity of grasslands." In *Evaluation and Mapping of Tropical Rangelands.* Addis Ababa: ILCA. Pp. 171–174.

Eicher, Carl K. 1985 "Agricultural research for African development: problems and priorities for 1985–2000." Unpublished paper prepared for a World Bank conference on Research Priorities for Subsaharan Africa. Bellagio, Italy, Feb. 25–March 1, 1985.

Falloux, F., and A. Mukendi, eds. 1988 *Desertification Control and Renewable Resource Management in the Sahelian and Sudanian Zones of West Africa.* Technical Paper No. 70. Washington, DC: The World Bank.

FAO 1973 *Propositions Préliminaires pour une Approche Intégrée du Développement à Long Terme de la Zone Sahélienne de l'Afrique de l'Ouest.* Document de Travail de la FAO WS-D7404. Rome: Food and Agriculture Organisation of the United Nations.

————— 1980 *Natural Resources and the Human Environment for Food and Agriculture.* Environment Paper No. 1. Rome: FAO.

Goldsmith, E. 1985 "Open letter to Mr. Clausen, President of the World Bank." The Ecologist 7.

26   Michael Horowitz

Guinard, André 1988 "Les activités agricoles dans la basse et la moyenne vallée du Sénégal: problèmes et propositions de solutions." Report written for the Institute for Development Anthropology.

Hardin, G.J. 1968 "The tragedy of the commons." Science 162:1243–1248.

Helldén, Ulf 1978 *Evaluation of Landsat-2 Imagery for Desertification Studies in Northern Kordofan, Sudan.* Lund: Lund University Press.

——— 1984 *Drought Impact Monitoring: A Remote Sensing Study of Desertification in Kordofan, Sudan.* Lund: Lund University Press.

Herskovits, Melville J. 1926 "The cattle complex in East Africa." American Anthropologist 28:230–72, 361–80, 494–528, 633–64.

Hjort, Anders 1981 "A critique of 'ecological' models of pastoral land use." Ethnos 46(3/4):171–89.

Homewood, Katherine, and W.A. Rodgers 1987 "Pastoralism, conservation and the grazing controversy." In *Conservation in Africa: People, Policies and Practice.* D. Anderson and R. Grove, eds. Cambridge: Cambridge University Press.

Horowitz, Michael M 1979 *The Sociology of Pastoralism and African Livestock Projects.* AID Program Evaluation Discussion Paper No. 6. Washington, DC: Agency for International Development.

Horowitz, Michael M., and Peter D. Little 1987 "African pastoralism and poverty: some implications for drought and famine." In *Drought and Hunger in Africa.* M.H. Glantz, ed. Cambridge: Cambridge University Press.

Horowitz, Michael M., and Muneera Salem-Murdock 1987 "The political economy of desertification in White Nile Province, Sudan." In *Lands at Risk in the Third World: Local-Level Perspectives.* P.D. Little and M.M. Horowitz, eds. Boulder: Westview Press.

Ibn Khaldun 1967 *The Maqaddimah.* Vol. 1, trans. F. Rosenthal. Princeton: Princeton University Press.

Ibrahim, Fouad N. 1978 *The Problems of Desertification in the Republic of the Sudan with Special Reference to Northern Darfur Province.* Khartoum: Khartoum University Press.

Lamprey, H.F. 1975 "Report on the Desert Encroachment Reconnaissance in Northern Sudan, 21 October to 10 November 1975." Paris: UNESCO/UNEP.

——— 1983 "Pastoralism yesterday and today: the over-grazing problems." In *Ecosystems of the World 13: Tropical Savannas.* F. Bourlière, ed. Amsterdam: Elsevier Scientific Publishing Co.

Lewin, R. 1985 "Gregarious graziers eat better." Science 228(4699):567–568.

Lomax, A., and C.M. Arensberg 1977 "A worldwide evolutionary classification of culture by subsistence systems." Current Anthropology 18(4):659–701.

Marie, J. 1985 "Elevage et problèmes fonciers dans le delta intérieur du Niger au Mali." Cahiers de la Recherche-Développement 7:38–42.

Morton, J. 1988 The Decline of Lahawin Pastoralism (Kassala Province, Eastern Sudan). Pastoral Development Network, Paper 25c. London: Overseas Development Institute.

Murdock, George P. 1959 *Africa, Its Peoples and Their Culture History.* New York: McGraw-Hill Book Co., Inc.

Olsson, K. 1985 *Remote Sensing for Fuelwood Resources and Land Degradation Studies in Kordofan, the Sudan.* Lund: Lund University Press.

Olsson, Lennart 1984 *DIAPAC (Digital Image Analysis Package) Users' Manual.* Department of Physical Geography, University of Lund.

—— 1985 *An Integrated Study of Desertification.* Meddelanden Från Lunds Universitets Geografiska Institution, Avhandlingar XCVIII. Department of Physical Geography, University of Lund.

OMVS 1987 "Compte-rendu de la réunion spéciale OMVS/bailleurs de fonds sur le projet de production et de transport de l'énergie de la centrale hydroélectrique de Manantali." Dakar: Senegal River Development Organization (OMVS).

Palmer, E.H. 1977 *The Desert of the Exodus.* Vols. I and II. New York: Arno Press.

Picardi, A.C. 1975 "A systems analysis of pastoralism in the West African Sahel." In *Framework for Evaluating Long-term Strategies for the Development of the Sahel-Sudan Region.* Annex 5. Center for Policy Alternatives. Cambridge, MA: Massachusetts Institute of Technology.

Penning de Vries, F.W.T., et al 1982 *La Productivité des Pâturages Sahéliens.* Wageningen: Centre for Agricultural Publishing and Documentaries.

Putt, S.N.H., and A.P.M. Shaw 1983 "The Socioeconomic Effects of the Control of Tsetse Transmitted Trypanosomiasis in Nigeria." In *Proceedings of the Third International Symposium on Veterinary Epidemiology and Economics.* Edwardsville, KS: Veterinary Medicine Publishing Co. Pp. 515–523.

Reeves, Edward B., and Timothy Frankenberger 1981 *Socioeconomic Constraints to the Production, Distribution and Consumption of Sorghum, Millet and Cash Crops in North Kordofan, Sudan: A Farming Systems Approach.* Report No. 1. Lexington: University of Kentucky.

Salem-Murdock, Muneera, Michael M. Horowitz, and Thayer Scudder 1989 *Senegal River Basin Monitoring Activity: Progress Report IV.* Binghamton, NY: Institute for Development Anthropology.

Sandford, S. 1982 "Pastoral strategies and desertification: opportunism and conservatism in dry lands." In *Desertification and Development: Dryland Ecology in Social Perspective.* B. Spooner and H.S. Mann, eds. London & New York: Academic Press.

—— 1983 *Management of Pastoral Development in the Third World.* Chichester, England: John Wiley & Sons.

Savory, Allan 1986 The Savory Letter, the Newsletter for Holistic Resource Managers 14:1–4.

Scudder, Thayer 1988 *The African Experience with River Basin Development: Achievements to Date, the Role of Institutions, and Strategies for the Future.* Binghamton, NY: Institute for Development Anthropology.

Swift, Jeremy, ed. 1984 *Pastoral Development in Central Niger: Report of the Niger Range and Livestock Project.* Niamey: USAID.

Talbot, L.M. 1972 "Ecological consequences of rangeland development in Masailand, East Africa." In *The Careless Technology: Ecology and Development.* M.T. Farvar and J.P. Milton, eds. Garden City, NY: The Natural History Press. Pp. 694–711.

Tendler, Judith 1975 *Inside Foreign Aid.* Baltimore: The Johns Hopkins University Press.

van Westen, A.C.M. and M.C. Klute 1986 "From Bamako with love: a case study of migrants and their remittances." Tijdschrift voor Econ. en Soc. Geografie 77(1):42–49.

Wood, Charles H., and Marianne Schmink 1978 *Blaming the Victim: Small Farmer Production in an Amazon Colonization Project.* Studies in Third World Societies, Publication No. 7, "Changing Agricultural Systems in Latin America."

World Bank 1989 *The World Bank and Senegal, 1960–87.* Washington: Operations Evaluation Department, The World Bank.

World Resources Institute 1986 *World Resources 1986.* New York: Basic Books, Inc.

River Basin Development: Dilemmas For Peasants and Planners

William Derman

Department of Anthropology
Michigan State University
East Lansing, MI   48824-1118

West Africa faces multiple crises, among them: increasing hunger, environmental degradation, indebtedness, diminution of export revenues, and rates of urbanization that stretch all available resources, among others. These crises are interconnected, although this paper focuses only on river basin development as one proposed option to generate solutions to some, but not all, of these problems.

With the decline in total rainfall since 1968 and the often poor timing of the rains, water availability is a critical constraint. In the Gambia River Basin, as in many parts of West Africa, the more effective utilization of the few river systems is seen as a key means of increasing and intensifing agricultural production and avoiding reliance on the importation of fossil fuels. River basin development, which includes irrigated agriculture, has been part of donor-proposed solutions (for example, the long-term Sahel development program and the Organization of African Unity's strategy known as the Lagos Plan of Action) for coping with Africa's food crisis.

In terms of development strategies, the late 1980's are a time of transition from emphasis on smallholders, direct assistance to the poor, and popular participation, to increased production (both for domestic use and export), with less attention paid to how it may be done. Rural populations have come to be viewed as a resource for production, rather than as people who produce in order to live, whose culture and way of life have intrinsic value. It has become difficult for planners and developmentalists to consider fully how rural people live, rather than just how much they produce.[1]

This paper examines how planners in West African nations are caught between the donors and their own rural populations. I argue that these planners are not unwitting actors in a play written in Washington, Paris, or Riyadh but are themselves playwrights, although they lack sufficient internal resources to produce their work. Moreover, their relations with the actors and actresses (the rural West African populations) are sullen at best, and tempestuous at worst, as they try to engage them in roles which violate the canons of the profession. (Perhaps if peasants were regarded as professionals they might gain greater respect.) The concern here is to understand the central dilemmas for the planners, on the one hand, and the rural populations, on the other. The basic issue of whether the overall Gambia River Basin development strategy is likely to succeed is discussed, but only insofar as it forms the essential background to the structure and content of what appear to be, at least for the present, intractable problems. In my view, the contradictory interests and perspectives simultaneously at work require enormous political mobilization to resolve, but at the present time rural populations and peasantries are disenchanted by, and suspicious of, many of the current programs and policies of their central government. Their past experiences with their respective national governments and their agencies tend to be viewed in negative terms; these past experiences include pricing policies, extension services, input supply and corruption. The dilemmas for planners revolve around how to attain the necessary outside resources and funding to construct a series of dams and how to increase both the presence and power of the state in the rural areas. The dilemmas for the peasantries are to keep the state at bay while using both donor and national state programs and resources to increase income and security of rural life.[2]

---

[1]This is paraphrased from Arturo Warman's elegant study of the peasants of Morelos, *We Come to Object: The Peasants of Morelos and The National State* (Baltimore: Johns Hopkins University Press 1980). While there are many important differences between Mexico and West Africa, there are also important parallels concerning state efforts to control and direct peasant energies and organizations.

[2]I use the terms "rural populations" and "peasantries" to emphasize rural differentiation and to avoid the connotations of the term "farmer". Farmers

Rivers and their drainage networks are natural energy systems for economic planning and development. The formation and implementation of river basin development has to overcome ecological, regional, and national differences. The nub of one set of difficulties concerns who does the planning. The planning process proceeds from the overall objectives (typically irrigation, production of hydropower, navigation) to the more specific questions of where the dams should be located, what their characteristics should be, whether turbines should or can be installed, where the electricity will go, and what kinds of crops should be grown with what technological packages on the proposed irrigated perimeters. The state or its agency seeks and maneuvers for control over the outcome of river basin development. It does this against both multinational donors, who want to maximize influence for their donations and loans, and peasants, who want to maintain the rural economy, as tattered as it is.

To illustrate the interactions between national planners, donor agencies, and rural populations I will examine the Gambia River Basin Development Organization.[3] This organization reflects contemporary belief in the efficacy of top-down planning despite qualms from the rural sectors and some donors.[4] Although many individuals in donor development organizations and West African governments would prefer alternative planning models, this view has not yet penetrated the higher levels of decision-making in The Gambia, Guinea, and Senegal.

The Gambia River Development Organization (OMVG)

The Gambia River Development Organization is currently made up of four nations: The Gambia, Guinea-Conakry, Senegal, and Guinea-

---

and farms can imply a productive and social organization like that of European and American farm enterprises which is not the case in most of the Gambia River Basin

[3]The Gambia River Basin Development Organization is usually known by its French acronym OMVG, L'Organisation pour la mise en valeur du fleuve Gambie.

[4]For a powerful series of arguments against top-down planning see Rural Development: *Putting The Last First* by Robert Chambers, Longman, Harlow 1983.

Bissau. As an interstate organization, clear limits are set with respect to its power and authority. The latter resides, for example, in determining water-use policy but not the type of irrigation authority to be organized. The major policy decisions are made by the four presidents and a council of ministers. These two groups make the major decisions, informed by the head of OMVG (the high commissioner, currently Malik John) and a relatively large technical staff, which includes expatriate experts. The four presidents, council of ministers, and the high commission have adopted a three-dam strategy as the keystone for basin development. The governments of the four nations have assumed they express the wishes of their respective populations and thus did not need to consult the rural population or solicit its input. This, of course, is not unusual in current postcolonial peasant-state relations or in most large development projects. One might add that since the rural populations are not well informed about planned developments and the results of studies, many rumors and much misinformation circulate in the countryside.

The development strategy for the Gambia River Basin is still being planned but has not been implemented. No dams have been built, although a design study has been done of one, a feasibility study has been made of a second, and the studies on the third have begun. The three projects are an antisalt barrage at Balingho in The Gambia and high dams at Kekreti (in Niokolo-Koba National Park) in Senegal, and at Kouya, near the confluence of the Litti and The Gambia River in the Guinean Fouta-Djallon highlands. No irrigation perimeters are being constructed, but there is a design for the prototype of such schemes after the dam has been completed. In addition, there is a relatively large (by West African standards) irrigation project at Jahaly Pacharr in The Gambia, which many Gambian officials would like to see serve as the model for future irrigation projects. Because the present low water levels in the river lead to the advance of the salt tongue, it is currently not feasible to increase significantly the amount of land under dry season irrigation.[5] As an aside, current plans to increase dry-season perimeters in eastern Senegal may jeopardize Ja-

---

[5]The Gambia River, due to its relatively level topography and the reach tidal influences, can be saline quite far upriver. The degree of salinity depend primarily on the river flow. During August and September, the salt tongue is

haly Pacharr and other dry season perimeters in The Gambia under conditions of poor rainfall and low river flow.

The essence of OMVG's strategy for the moment rests on the three dams, which are to provide adequate water in the dry and rainy season for the irrigation of more than 85,000 hectares (53,500 in The Gambia, 16,500 in Senegal, and 15,000 in Guinea-Conakry, although this latter total has not been subject to the same detailed studies as those carried out in Senegal and The Gambia). Most of the land is slated for double-cropped irrigated rice, but other crops will be grown on soils less suitable for rice. The two high dams are to produce hydroelectricity to be used for potential mines and urban areas. The antisalt barrage is also to serve as a bridge to facilitate transport within Senegal and between The Gambia River's north and south banks (the nearest bridge being Goulombo, 450 kilometers upriver), and boat locks will be constructed at Balingho to improve and increase river transport. The subsidiary aspects of OMVG's program, including forestry, livestock, and rainfed agriculture, take a distant second place to securing funding for the dams, which are the centerpiece of the current strategy.

The logic for the dam/irrigation strategy rests on a model developed by Clark Ross for OMVG and the UN Development Programme, which examined the outcome for projected continued population growth. This model, which projects increasing food dependency without basic changes in the basin's agricultural systems, helped form the base for developing programs to increase agricultural production. Since the model was developed (and subsequently updated) there has been no diminution of population increase in Guinea, The Gambia, and Senegal. It might be noted, however, that the rate of population increase in the rural areas of at least The Gambia is much less than in the urban areas. Nonetheless, most agree that the consistently high importation of basic foods by Senegalese, Guineans, and Gambians both within and without the Gambia River Basin is a major problem reflecting an overarching agrarian crisis. Deteriorating patterns of rainfall, dramatic population increases, and high rates of urbanization have led to the conclusion that intensification of agriculture must proceed as rapidly as possible.

---

pushed quite far west but returns almost as far as Jahaly Pacharr by the end of the dry season.

West African governments currently place highest priority on food security and self-sufficiency, combined with self-sustaining agricultural growth. This represents a shift in focus from the pre-drought 1960s in West Africa. While not questioning the importance of these goals, it is unclear the extent to which they have been developed to fit with changing donor analyses and requirements. Thus, while relatively isolated agricultural areas may not have been given the highest priority by national governments, they may be important to some donors, who then create new opportunities for assistance that national governments may not want to undertake. River basin development fits more with national priorities, however, than do other rural development projects.[6] I have suggested elsewhere (Derman 1977 and 1984)[7] that the donors have undertaken projects in areas considered peripheral to national governments. Partly this is due to donor concerns for rural peoples who were not benefitting from externally provided assistance, and partly to West African governments leveraging donors to provide resources that they were unwilling or unable to provide. This approach has led to some tensions between national governments and donors over control and management of these projects. In addition, many of them are abandoned by national governments if funding is not continued.

The requisites for outside funding for river basin development often render the rationale for such projects different than those envisaged by planners. This is a complex, multi-layered issue. Often, political goals are hidden behind donor requirements or other masks, making project analysis difficult. Quite clearly, the major issue for West African governments is not the nutritional well-being of peasants, but the provision of cheap food for urban populations (including the

---

[6]The Gambia River Basin is of differential importance to the four nations. It is peripheral to Guinea-Bissau, marginal to Guinea-Conakry, important to Senegal (but not compared to the Senegal River Basin), and absolutely critical to The Gambia. The latter's survival depends upon the river and its utilization, which is not the case for the other nations.

[7]Derman, William 1977 "Agrarian structures, class formation and development in the Sahel". Unpublished paper.

Derman, William 1984 "USAID in the Sahel: Development and Poverty" in *The Politics of Agriculture in Tropical Africa* edited by Jonathan Barker. Sage. Beverly Hills, CA.

large number of state employees) and the politically volatile popular classes, combined with sustaining national revenues. Although difficult to assess at present, there is a strong desire among government employees to invest in rice production and own land, an urge historically lacking but now spurred by the likelihood of donor backing and anticipated price supports for rice crops.[8] This is not to say many members of West African governments are not concerned about the well-being of rural populations, but that political concerns dictate other priorities.

What, then, are the dynamics underlying the Gambia River Development Organization? Embedded within OMVG is a vision—even as one disagrees with the specifics—of a West Africa less subject to the vagaries of climate, enjoying a more productive agriculture, and having a greatly enlarged hydroelectric grid. This vision has its roots in industrialization and the power of advanced technology to overcome constraints to economic progress (development). It is also a vision of controlling and mastering water to overcome what is conceived as the decisive limitation to intensifying agriculture. The Minister of Water Resources for The Gambia visited the Tennessee Valley Authority in the United States and upon his return observed that environmental and socioeconomic studies must have been done there to avoid the negative consequences of such vast construction. He went on to comment sharply that those who would deny West Africa dams are denying Africans the same technology they themselves used in order to industrialize and achieve economic progress. Whether the minister is factually correct is not the issue. What is important is the political point he made, and the responsive chord he struck among many Gambian planners.

What kinds of dilemmas are faced by national political leaders and planners in the effort to secure funding for the dams and implement an irrigation strategy? A major set concerns the difficulties of multi-

---

[8]The problem with government employees using their political positions to obtain land lies less at the"productive level" than in its consequences for rural peasantries, already under severe pressure. Indeed, one might project that one could have increased production while increasing poverty in the countryside. The urban private claims on land are becoming apparent in the lower Senegalese River Valley. It is a highly sensitive subject, and therefore its extent and overall importance are difficult to assess.

national cooperation, both in forging an alliance of interests among four nations and with potential donors who have their own interests in their development assistance programs. Neither task is easy, and both currently border on failure. What holds the four nations together is that each wants, first and foremost, its own dam,[9] which is perceived as the key goal (and symbol) of the development program for the basin. This has become more complicated than anticipated because the ecology, topography, and soils along the river imply different strategies for each part. These strategies are, in the final analysis, determined by each nation. These then have to be integrated. At best, planning will take into account and protect the interests of each nation.

At one level, OMVG and member states are saying that, in an imperfect world, give us the best of what is available and let us try. At another level, they are not in a position to generate the capital internally or provide the material and knowledge necessary to plan and implement the proposed strategy. This renders them dependent on donors, which leads to conflict. In the case of OMVG, it is questionable whether the organization would have been created and sustained without donor assistance, yet when one of the donor contractors, the University of Michigan, reached conclusions inconsistent with the pace and scale of OMVG plans, considerable controversy arose. (I will return to this in the conclusion.) Given the larger economic crisis in which the four nations involved find themselves, they are dependent on donors to implement their development strategies.

The initial political climate in which OMVG was formed is very different from the current one. OMVG benefited from the multilateral and donor cooperative emphasis of the late 1970s. For example, the UN Development Programme and the Sahel Development Program stressed an integration and coordination of donor efforts, partly due to the reluctance of any single donor to commit to a strategy before it was fully developed. Then the political and economic climate began to shift, and (for different reasons) Senegal, Guinea (Conakry), and The

---

[9]With the exception of Guinea-Bissau, which is marginal to the basin. But if OMVG becomes more regionally and river oriented beyond the Gambia Basin, it shares many rivers with Guinea-Conakry and contains the potential to increase rice production, which would assist all member states of OMVG.

Gambia had to renegotiate their foreign debts and comply with IMF and World Bank requirements. The donor perception of the Gambia River Basin possibilities changed greatly between the late 1970s and 1986, with the result that OMVG has had to find alternative donors and play one against another. This strategy is inevitably quite limited due to the weak leverage of these nations. Furthermore, the donors seek not only to influence OMVG but also one another, which has produced conflict among OMVG, UNDP, the French, the British, and USAID. USAID has been ambivalent about river basin development, although it has been a major donor of OMVG. In addition, it funded the controversial studies by the University of Michigan. The coordination of donor activities has thus been difficult for OMVG. Ironically, it has relied on expatriates provided by donor organizations to OMVG. The consequence has been an extraordinarily time-consuming effort to meet donor wishes and needs, even if contradictory. (I will return to this in the conclusion.) The outcome for rural populations in this process is clear, if painful. In the search for financing, it is difficult to focus on the rural populations's long-term needs, and the degree to which they are included in the thinking of planners, other than rhetorically, is problematic.

Development Dilemmas: The Peasant Side

On the other side of the arena are the producers, the rural populations, in whom there has been little interest to date. Space limitations preclude details about the rural history of The Gambia, Guinea, and Senegal and the various efforts by the state to increase rural production. In general, The Gambia and Senegal have tried to control peanut production, the major agricultural export of both nations. Guinean agricultural history within the basin is quite different, since the state relies on mineral exports for its revenues; agriculture, particularly in the isolated zones of the basin, has played a peripheral role, nationally but not necessarily for local units of government. Partly in response to excessive reliance on groundnut production, combined with low prices, increased food imports, and a decline in rural productivity, Senegal and The Gambia seek to diversify their agricultural production. One must add the desire by bureaucrats to buy land and hire labor, a tendency which remains embryonic basinwide but increasingly a factor in specific local areas. Throughout much of the basin, peasants retain control over land and the range of associated productive decisions. The proposed shift toward double-cropped irrigated rice entails changing the relationships of peasants to land and labor.

I found no evidence that members of state agencies view peasants as other than objects to be taught, educated, guided and coerced into following state plans. Peasants are not viewed as resources from whom one could learn. The ideology of development as expressed by bureaucrats does not include peasants and their concerns, except as they touch upon the functioning of a given agency. It is fair to say that peasants are seen as enemies of progress and often are treated as such, even though they are crucial to the material well-being of their respective nations or regions.

I emphasize this point not because it is new or even surprising, but because of the persistence of the hierarchical relationship between state and peasants. The current development framework within OMVG (and that of the donors) reflects the wider problem of the state's inability to reorganize or "capture" the peasantry. What would this mean specifically for the Gambia River Basin? It is difficult to project plans and tendencies into what would actually happen, for it is important to recall that none of the dams are currently under construction. Nonetheless, there is a history of irrigation in both Senegal and The Gambia, along with the ambitious development plans in the Senegal River Basin. In areas along the river in The Gambia and in small zones of Senegal, rice is cultivated through tidal irrigation and flood recession and in low zones which flood. These have been areas for agricultural expansion since the nineteenth century, first with the spread of groundnuts and then with the exhaustion of upland fields. These zones are predominantly cultivated by women, who do not "own" the land but have use rights. It is precisely this land which will be affected by the antisalt barrage, preventing tides, and the high dam in Senegal, preventing floods. Much of this area will be developed for irrigation, changing land tenure and land-use patterns. Up to now, efforts to develop double-cropped perimeters have not been successful (with the exception of Jahaly-Pacharr).

The development plans emphasize the utilization of national land law to wrest control from those who now have rights in perpetuity in order to lease the land back to those who will follow an irrigation authority's or larger scale farmer's production schedule. This will alter the peasants' relationship with the land and with one another. Even if production is increased, and rice can be exported to the cities, there will be an intensification of labor and inputs for rice producers. This will put the current ecology at risk.[10] In sum, peasants will be asked either to assume virtually all the risks associated with double-cropped, irrigated rice production and large-scale environmental changes, or to participate in schemes which remove most of the risks, such as Jahaly Pacharr. In these schemes, the donors do not expect to recapture this initial capital investment. They therefore willingly, at least for the present, provide the infrastructure, seeds, fertilizer, technical expertise, and fuel that enable participants to grow rice successfully. The replication of Jahaly-Pacharr[11] under current world and Gambian economic conditions is highly improbable.

Conclusion

No proper conclusion can be drawn, since I have been discussing dilemmas associated with river basin planning, not implementation. The plans remain plans only, and conclusions must be speculative.

---

[10]In particular see *Aquatic Ecology and Gambia River Basin Development* by Russell Moll and John Dorr. University of Michigan Gambia River Basin Studies, Ann Arbor. 1985. For a longer discussion of dam impacts see *Rural Development in The Gambia River Basin* by William Derman, et al. same series.

[11]The project has achieved high yields of rice for its first two full years (eight tons per hectare per season, or sixteen per year), but it is capital intensive. The irrigation part of the project requires full water control. There is an improved swamp rice component which utilizes the tidal action of the river. The consequences of the project on those who participate are currently being studied. Two primary concerns have been raised about its long-term success. First, the high level of capital input can never be recovered, and therefore similar projects cannot be begun in the current economic situation. Second, the high level of management activity required to get plot holders to their fields on time and to carry out all the necessary tasks cannot be sustained. In addition, I understand there has been a problem in the timely delivery of fuel to keep the pumps going. The Gambia suffers from chronic shortages of hard currency with which to purchase fuel, combined with an aging and inadequate fleet of fuel trucks.

The fact that peasants are voiceless is, unfortunately, not exceptional. Nevertheless, greater attention must be given to targeting beneficiaries, even if benefits may never flow. I am not sanguine about prospects for a change in strategy. Bureaucratically, OMVG and member states are committed to dams, which they view as largely positive; they think any negative features can be mitigated. The raising of new concerns about the viability of The Gambia River Basin development strategy has not pleased either member states or OMVG. From their perspective, to question their rationale breaks with several years of study, beginning with the UN Development Programme's multidonor mission, which formulated the preinvestment program.

In additon, organizations such as OMVG rapidly create their own environment and importance while seeking to expand their resources and influence. OMVG has not at all been a passive actor in the face of what it perceives as inconsistent donors. Neither donor agencies nor national bureaucracies value rural history or the political and historical conditions of West African rural populations. Left to themselves, OMVG and member states would construct the dams as quickly as possible, but they are constrained by shifts in capital availability, by the deterioration of their own economies, and by their incapacity to undertake any further loans. They cannot make decisions independently of donors. In a more global context, they claim that they act in the name of the rural populations. Without early, consistent involvement, without strategies for listening to and learning from those who actually cultivate, without respect for the knowledge of those who, for better or worse, provide both food and cash crops, cooperation between bureaucrats and peasants is improbable.

It becomes clear that to suggest solutions means shifting the relationship between donors and hosts and between nations and their rural majorities. Under present circumstances, the likelihood of either is small. Evidence from the social sciences concerning the staying power of rural elites and their links to an increasingly powerful national bureaucracy leads one to be cautious concerning the benefits of local participation. Not because it is wrong, but because it is hard to see why and how this will benefit those who hold power.

The dilemmas are, for the moment, irresolvable. National planners are unwilling or unable to reorient programs and projects to meet local interests and concerns. Peasantries are themselves powerless to alter state strategies except in relatively passive ways. Some donors holding the critical resources have shifted their priorities creating greater tensions and divisions among the planners. Planners then have to attempt to ally with those donors who are most likely to provide resources. In the national and international arena, the peasantries have no voice. If past experience is a guide to the future, voiceless-ness leads to passiveness, which will prevent the use of the human energies necessary to intensify agriculture while sustaining a deterio-rating environment.

Acknowledgements

I would like to thank Dr. Gordon Appleby for reading this paper. He corrected the smaller mistakes and we argued about some of the larger issues of interpretation. As always, he made perceptive and helpful comments even if the final paper is different than he would have wished. In addition, Scott Whiteford, Terry Hoops and Ruth Scott read an earlier draft and provided constructive criticisms.

References

Derman, William 1977 "Agrarian structures, class formation, and development in the Sahel." Unpublished paper.

———— 1984 "USAID in the Sahel: Development and Poverty." In *The Politics of Agriculture in Tropical Africa*, ed. by Jonathan Barker. Beverly Hills, CA:Sage. pp. 77–97.

Land Concentration, Existential Development, and Food in the Sahel*

Stephen P. Reyna

Department of Sociology and Anthropology
University of New Hampshire
Horton Social Science Center
Durham, NH 03824
(603) 862-1800

I. Introduction

First impressions are often lasting. Musa's place was the jumping off spot for my first fieldwork in Chad. Here, after a morning's drive, we would rest in the shade of a giant kapok tree waiting for a pirogue to ferry us across the Chari to our village. Musa's place was a *joli jardin*—an exuberance of colors and scents of mangoes and papayas, oranges and lemons. We would stare across the river while waiting for a pirogue. Over there, beyond the trees, was the "real" Africa—an immense, dusty plain. The overwhelming impression of "over there" was of the plain's vastness, of the tiny villages scattered in it, and of the great distances separating village from village. Any notion that land concentration might be a problem in this emptiness seemed absurd. Development practitioners and scholars reinforced this impression. Land concentration had occurred in Latin America, South Asia and Southeast Asia. But in Africa, and especially in the West African savanna, with its abundant land and low human population densities, scholars concluded that "communal land ownership . . ." had "produced a relatively egalitarian distribution of farm holdings"

*A version of this paper was presented at the session, "A Comparative Look at Arid Land Demography and Ecology in China, India and the Sahel," at the AAAS annual meetings in Los Angeles, May 26–31, 1985. Please note that the terms savanna and Sahel are used interchangeably in this essay for the region between the forest and desert in West Africa.

(Johnson and Kilby 1975:18).[1] First impressions are often deceiving. This essay addresses two questions: Does the West African savanna have land concentration problems, and if so, what are its implications?

Before answering these questions, I want to clarify the approach and the organization of this essay. Land concentration is the amassing of large amounts of land in the hands of few individuals or institutions. It involves processes that result in a particular structure: one involving bimodal land distributions in which a large number have very little and a very few have a great deal of land.[2] Two processes create land concentration: those which lead to the *acquisition* of land by some and those which lead to its *loss* by others. Appropriation will denote processes of land acquisition. Expropriation will refer to those of land loss. These processes may be intentional or unintentional. Intentional appropriation or expropriation occurs when the institutions involved in a process of land acquisition or loss have formal authority over the attainment of these goals, and when agents in these processes consciously utilize these institutions and the law to achieve land acquisition or loss. State invocation of eminent domain to acquire land for a highway is an example of intentional appropriation. Unintended appropriation and expropriation occur when land is lost or acquired, and when neither the institutions nor the actors involved in the process consciously sought such results. For example, when drought

---

[1] The World Bank document, *Land Reform*, which suggested that sub-Saharan Africa possesses the most egalitarian land tenure systems in the world (1974:12–16) has been influential in perpetuating the view that land concentration problems are absent in the sub-continent.

[2] Conceptual debate is generally absent in the land concentration literature. For example, K. Griffin's *Land Concentration and Rural Poverty* (1976) never defines land concentration. The term land concentration was chosen in this essay over that of land accumulation for two reasons. First, the term accumulation is given very specific meanings by Marx vis-a-vis the production process (cf. *Capital*, Vol. I, 1960:619 and ff; and 784 and ff), and to have the term refer both to production and land distribution seems needlessly confusing. Second, the verb accumulate, according to common dictionary usage, connotes a "steady amassing." This would mean that all bimodal land distributions had to evolve at continuous, arithmetic or geometric rates. This may, indeed, be the case in some instances, but there are others where land appears to be concentrated in a "jerky" fashion. In these cases, there is no "steady amassing."

turned the American Southwest into a dustbowl, it sent a stream of migrants to California, even though no institution or individuals had intended this consequence. Finally, there are processes which lead to the emergence of land concentration and those which reproduce it once it has been established. This essay presents evidence indicating that there are both intentional and unintentional appropriation and expropriation processes that could contribute to the emergence of land concentration in savanna West Africa.

Macro and micro approaches to the study of land concentration are possible. The former, favored by economists and certain sociologists, tends to use the nation as the unit of analysis and to establish associations among a few, highly aggregated indicators such as Lorenz curves or the GNP. The reliability and validity of such indicators is suspect in Third World nations. But a more fundamental problem with such approaches is that they have trouble detecting the beginning of trends, when, for example, the data defining the Lorenz curve have not changed radically. Nor do they observe the actual participants in the process—the individuals involved in land concentration. Such methodologies do not let the observer see the trees for the forest. Micro approaches, favored by anthropologists, typically look at the individuals in 50 or so households in a village for a year or two. Here the quality of the data is uncontestably better, and bears upon the actors in the land concentration process, but it is limited to a small number of people in a tiny area over a brief period. Land concentration occurs among a large number of people, often more than a single nation's territory, over a long period of time. Micro approaches do not let the observer see the forest for the trees.

I have examined, in preparing for this essay, a number of microstudies of anthropologists, geographers, demographers, historians, agronomists, economists of all stripes, project personnel, host country officials, donor country officials as well as my own observations in the course of research or development missions throughout the savanna.[3] Each of these studies has been about a particular place examined over a short time. However, because a fairly large number of studies was consulted that dealt with different places at dif-

---

[3] My observations that bear upon the emergence of land concentration were made in the course of ethnographic research in Chad (1969–70; 1973–74),

ferent times, it has been possible to examine a fairly large area—
that surrounding Burkina Faso—over a fairly long time—since the
beginning of the 20th century. I have taken pains to examine events
from "above" as well as "below"—that is, I have noted the actions
of highly placed donor and host country officials and then sought
to see how these affected ordinary rural folk. The approach has
been a bit like that of a pointilist. Each micro-study has been a
"point"—a place in time and space that is part of the larger canvas.
In a sense, then, one sees both the trees—the daubs of microstudies—and the forest—the emerging land concentration which
they reveal.

The essay is in two parts. The first part analyzes land concentration
in Burkina Faso.[4] It then explores whether the Burkinabe findings are
applicable throughout the region. My analysis of Burkina Faso begins
with an exploration of investment preferences; then I document three
land concentration processes (parastatal land appropriation, "demographic" land expropriation, and private land appropriation) that are
at least partially dependent upon donor investments; and, finally, I
show that a consequence of these processes is the creation of "existential" opportunity structures. In the second section of this essay, I
broaden the focus to other areas of West Africa in a comparative analysis to indicate that land concentration processes similar to those in
Burkina Faso are occurring throughout the West African savanna, and
that for most people, "existential" development is a situation from
which there is no exit.

II. Land Concentration in Burkina Faso

Donor Investments

Public donor investments are important to Burkina Faso's development because the national economy generates almost no capital and

---

Northern Cameroun (1973–74) and Mauritania (1975) as well as during
development missions to Chad (1975, 1977, 1978), Niger (1979, 1982), Mali
(1972, 1980), Burkina Faso (1979, 1980), Senegal (1978), Mauritania (1976,
1979), and the Gambia (1979).

[4] In 1982 Upper Volta was renamed Burkina Faso. At this time, a Voltaic
became a Burkinabe.

because there are few investment opportunities to attract private, foreign capital (McFarland 1976:xx). The nation exhibits two distinct ecological zones: riverain lands near the Volta Rivers and their tributaries, and interior lands uninfluenced by the rivers. In general, the former lands are more fertile than the latter. Since the early 1970s, donor investments have predominantly been in the riverain lands. The *Autorité des Aménagements des Vallées des Volta* (AVV), for example, is an agro-parastatal near the Volta Rivers that is financed by French, German, Dutch, and European Economic Community (EEC) donors. AVV's budget was reported by one AVV staff member to have been approximately $15 million in 1980. For the entire country, the proposed budget for 1980 was approximately $191 million (USAID 1980:25). About a fifth of the national budget and foreign assistance are allocated to rural development (USAID 1980:25). This means that approximately $76 million was invested in rural developments, of which fully a fifth went to AVV. During 1978, AVV had 3,750 hectares in production (Sorgho and Richet 1979:4). Assuming that by 1979 production had increased to approximately 4,000 hectares, then about 20% of Burkina Faso's total rural investment was concentrated on .01% of its total area. Other donor investments in Burkina Faso equally favor parastatal river valley agro-enterprises (Ouedraogo 1979:555). The following section describes how such donor investments affect the appropriation of land by parastatals.

Parastatal Land Appropriation

In 1972, the French bilateral economic development agency (FAC) recommended the creation of a parastatal agency with development responsibility in valleys along the Volta Rivers being cleared of onchocerciasis (Maton *et al.,* 1971).[5] Burkina Faso accepted FAC's rec-

---

[5] Parastatals are state corporations (like the TVA in the United States). They play a significant role in Third World development (Gillis 1980), and since the 1960's have been the institutions most frequently relied upon to "modernize" sub-Saharan agriculture. The literature analyzing West African agro-parastatals is scant. Of use, however, are Constantin and Coulon (1979), Diabate (1977), and Hermann (1981). There has been no extended discussion of parastatals within anthropology, which limits the discipline's ability to participate in lively debates concerning the utility of state corporations.

ommendations. In September, 1974, a Presidential Decree created the AVV and transferred ownership of roughly 30,000 km^2 of the Volta River Valley lands to the state. A 1976 Decree authorized one category of individuals—the AVV and other government officials—to control land utilization and created a second category, the tenants, to till under conditions controlled by AVV.[6] Almost overnight, roughly 12% of the entire country was concentrated in the hands of a single parastatal! The reasons for the rapid concentration of land in the hands of a single parastatal are explored below.

Historical factors influencing foundation of the AVV

AVV's establishment can be argued to hinge upon a convergence of EEC and Burkinabe interests that had been developing since colonial times. Early in the 20th century, French colonial administrators judged Burkina Faso to be economically *"non viable"* (Songre et al. 1974). The result of this judgment was that colonial investments were diverted to more attractive, largely coastal areas; Burkina Faso was used as early as the 1920s to supply laborers for those investments (Londres 1929). At roughly the same time, Burkinabes were obliged to grow cotton to pay taxes and to supply the French textile industry with inexpensive fiber. Cotton was cultivated using the existing technology and organization of production (Ossendowski 1928:276). Farmgate prices were set at low levels dictated by cotton-purchasing monopsonies—organizations granted exclusive rights to purchase cotton. Those investments that were made in Burkina Faso were predominantly in road and rail links needed to transport labor and cotton. French merchant capital offered consumer goods under near monopoly conditions.

Such policies moved Burkina Faso into the French portion of the world capitalist economy and obliged existing farming systems to produce additional outputs demanded by metropolitan capital, while they also diverted labor to more lucrative, coastal investments. Hence, commoditization was intensified under colonial terms-of-trade in which Burkinabe sold labor and commodities cheaply while buying French goods and services dear (Gregory 1974).

---

[6] A copy and analysis of the 1976 Presidential Decree can be found in Reyna (1980).

Development strategy followed colonial patterns in the first decade following independence. Investments in rural areas were few and what agricultural development did occur was implemented by French enterprises—*Compagnie Française pour le Développement des Fibres Textiles* (CFDT), *Société d'Aide Technique et Coopération* (SATEC), and *Compagnie Internationale de Développement Rural* (CIDR). Emphasis continued on the cultivation of cash crops using the existing production organization, with technological improvements " . . . in reality very little" (Marchal 1977:85). Although CFDT was able to increase cotton production, other successes were minimal. Productivity of food generally stagnated or declined (Savonnet 1976:507–512). Most alarmingly, soil deterioration was observed to be increasing in the most densely populated region of the nation—the Mossi Plateau.

This meant, as agriculture was the main source of government revenue, that government revenues were small. It also meant, as Mossi Plateau ecological problems multiplied, that Mossi demands on the bureaucracy to resolve these problems intensified (personal communication, E. Skinner). The 1972–1973 drought greatly intensified government preoccupation with both fiscal and ecological matters. In the early 1970s, then, it was in the bureaucracy's interest to develop the agricultural sector. But how?

In 1973, the World Health Organization began a program to control the blackfly, which breeds along the banks of the Volta Rivers and which is the vector for river blindness (onchocerciasis). This program altered the economic attractiveness of riverain areas because: "With control of the vector, the valleys . . . (could) be resettled, thereby generating new output on 'new lands' . . . " (Berg 1978).

France and other EEC nations were not indifferent as to how these "new lands" should be developed. During the first decade of independence, CFDT had demonstrated that it could grow cotton. Not only would EEC textile concerns benefit from the cotton, but multinational industry could potentially sell their products and allied services to Burkina Faso's cotton sector. Estimates based on projections of AVV investment and operational costs indicate that EEC firms could conservatively do 125 million 1978 dollars worth of business by installing the AVV, and could thereafter conservatively realize 3.5 million 1978 dollars annually by selling farm equipment and supplies to the AVV (Reyna 1983). Further, the bigger the agro-parastatal, the larger the markets for and cotton supplied to EEC agro-industries.

Thus, the creation of a vast agro-parastatal met EEC interests by generating new markets and an increased cotton supply.

So the FAC mission was prepared to tell Burkina Faso's bureaucracy how to develop the agricultural sector. Its 1972 report in effect said: Do it with state corporations. To enhance this recommendation's attractiveness to Burkinabe bureaucrats, the report also played upon their chief preoccupations and announced that: "Government revenues (from a parastatal) would be approximately 3.7 billion F CFA (roughly $18,500,000) over 25 years . . . " (Maton et al. 1971:22) and that 150,000 individuals could be resettled from the Mossi Plateau into the parastatal's domain, reducing the Plateau's problems of overpopulation (Maton et al. 1971:22).

Thus the AVV appeared to address Burkina Faso's fiscal and ecological problems while at the same time helping out western European industry. This conjuncture of EEC and Burkinabe interests certainly influenced the rapidity by which 12% of the nation's land was intentionally appropriated by a single state corporation.

Coerced cash-crop class relations

By 1978, AVV was in full operation with the average tenant farm family cultivating six hectares—40% of which was cotton (Murphy and Sprey 1980). The land control differentials and organization of appropriation which characterized AVV's production relations at this time are analyzed elsewhere (Reyna 1983). With respect to control, it was shown that AVV tenants were obliged to contribute financially to uncertain agricultural decisions in which they did not participate, and which offered no protection should these decisions go awry. AVV managers, on the other hand, were shown to enjoy greater de jure control over land use than private land owners (Reyna 1983:217). It was estimated for 1978 that 63% of the income received for the sale of AVV cotton was appropriated by the Burkinabe state. Under these conditions, a majority of the tenants were in debt and exhibited an "insécurité fondamentale" (Kattenberg 1979:40).

Wallerstein (1976) suggests that consequent upon capitalist core expansion, "coerced cash-crop" classes emerge in the periphery . . . where the peasants are required by some legal process enforced by the state to labor at least part of the time on a large domain producing some product for sale on the world market" (1976:6). A defining feature of such class systems is that state actions directly set the rate of surplus labor appropriation, meaning that appropriation is through primitive accumulation. Wallerstein was largely referring to *encomiendas* in Hispanic America and the "Second Serfdom" in eastern Europe. The AVV tenant class works a vast domain—riverain land. They produce a commodity for the world market—cotton. They are legally coerced in ways controlled by state actions to cultivate this commodity. What distinguishes AVV from 16th century "coerced cash-crop" systems is that in the former, the state owns the means of production. Thus, because of the participation of the state in production relations, it is appropriate to say that parastatal land appropriation resulted in "coerced cash-crop" class relations on Burkinabe lands.

The following section explores the absence of donor investment in the interior.

"Demographic" Expropriation

Little capital is available in the interior because of riverain donor investments. Fertilizer and other inputs are allocated first to agroparastatals. Interior incomes are exceptionally low, which means that farmers cannot afford those few inputs that are available. Agricultural technicians are disproportionately assigned to agro-parastatals, which reduces the quality of agricultural services available in the interior. If an increasing supply of agricultural inputs and services is necessary for productivity increases, stagnation in interior agriculture results from the favoring of parastatals. Below it is shown how stagnation, in the presence of population growth, may harm both the environment and farming systems, driving people from their land.

Burkina Faso's last national census indicates a high 2.06% natural growth rate (Upper Volta 1979). Such rates apparently extend back into the colonial epoch (Marchal 1977:75; Kohler 1972), and may result from the maintenance by colonial policy of fertility at high levels. In fact, French administrators forced Burkinabe farmers to cultivate cash as well as food crops, while providing no labor-saving tools, and they augmented nonagricultural work with *corvée* labor, while reducing labor force size by organizing migration. With more work to do and fewer workers to do it, Suret-Canale concluded that colonial policy intensified agrarian labor requirements (1976). Some scholars have argued that the demand for child labor in agriculture and fertility are positively associated in agrarian societies (Cleveland, 1986; Faulkingham 1977; Handwerker 1977; Reyna 1977; Deere 1978; Javillonar *et al.* 1979:Chapter 2; Weil 1986). Population and emigration increased during the colonial period in Burkina Faso, while mortality and immigration remained roughly constant, suggesting that population increases may have been due to fertility. During this time span, labor demands intensified. Such evidence is consistent with the view that increased labor demand resultant from colonial policy may have contributed to Burkina Faso's population growth.

Population growth fueled density increases on the Mossi Plateau (Marchal 1977:75). This, in turn, has been argued to have restricted access to farmland in Burkina Faso (Boutillier 1964; Kohler 1971; Swanson 1979). Kohler describes a sequence of tenure changes he observed among Mossi at Dakola. As density increased, land ownership passed from lineage to individuals, with control over land passing from lineage to household heads (1971:151). Household elders should not deny access to household members, but can and do exclude non-household, lineage members. Access is thus narrowed because individuals are deprived of guaranteed access to former lineage lands.

Density increases mean decreasing per capita amounts of arable land. Land scarcity, in the absence of new technology, often leads to soil deterioration and productivity declines. This appears to be the case in certain areas on the Mossi Plateau. Marchal describes the situation for an area near Yatenga. Here, between 1925 and 1973, population increased from 250,000 to 500,000 and: "This dense population . . . is faced with a shortage of arable land, a decline in the practice of leaving land to lie fallow, rapid soil deterioration, and a drop in production" (1977:75).

Thus, Mossi Plateau evidence suggests that population increases elevate density, making land scarcer. Then, land scarcity restricts land access and decreases soil fertility, which means that households increasingly possess smaller amounts of arable land. Domestic groups finding themselves in this situation must do things to insure their subsistence. Because alternative employment sources are lacking on their own farms, one of the things they must be prepared to do is to seek off-farm employment—elsewhere! This means they must migrate, i.e. be separated from their own land.

There is a relatively large literature concerning Burkina Faso's migration reviewed in Gregory (1974) and Piché, Gregory, and Coulibaby (1980) that establishes three points. First, the volume of intra- and international migration is great, including perhaps 12% of the total male population (Courel and Pool 1973:1013; Upper Volta 1979). Second, migration is highest among productive age-groups in the most densely populated regions, especially on the Mossi Plateau (Piché, Gregory and Coulibaby 1980). Third, the literature indicates that migrants are motivated to leave, either to augment incomes (Coursel and Pool 1973:1002; Piché, Gregory and Coulibaby 1980:36–38), or to avoid the consequences of population pressure (Kohler 1972). These explanations, in the absence of services and inputs to modernize farming, suggest the following argument. The need to supplement income results, at least partially, from declining productivity consequent in part upon increasing population density; therefore, population movements, in part, may be said to be a "response to declining availability of arable land" (USAID 1980:7).

The preceding evidence suggests that the following process may be separating individuals from the Mossi Plateau lands: high agrarian labor demands help maintain high fertility, which contributes to population size and density increases; these both reduce the amounts of arable land and restrict access to that which remains; and finally, reduction in available arable land constrains on-farm incomes, motivating individuals to migrate to alternative employment opportunities. This process resembles a "demographic" expropriation, for demographic, rather than legal or political, events separate people from their lands.

"Demographic" is not the only form of expropriation in Burkina Faso. Land is enclosed by agro-parastatals, as we saw earlier. It is taken by private individuals acting on their own private behalf, as we shall see in the following section. There are still other expropriation processes occurring, one of which is discussed in the section on Comparative Perspectives.

However, it is plausible that should Burkina Faso's population densities continue to rise, "demographic" expropriation will increase in importance. A final point: though expropriation is occurring in Burkina Faso, the reader should not lose sight of the fact that it is *just* beginning. The vast majority of Burkinabe still have access to some land, and as such, are a semi-proletariat.

Private Land Appropriation

The available social science literature rarely reports private land concentration occurring in Burkina Faso. Rather, what is frequently found are land distributions similar to that described by Saul for the village of Bentenga in southern, central Burkina Faso. Here there were about 200 households cultivating about 2.82 hectares (1983:78) and four larger farms of between 14 and 40 hectares (1983:88–89). Thus, what is puzzling is why private individuals have not more aggressively moved to acquire larger amounts of land. Studies are reviewed below in different interior areas which suggest under what conditions private individuals are motivated to accumulate land.

Eastern ORD

The Eastern ORD is an area of low demand for agricultural commodities according to data collected by the Michigan State University farm-level agricultural survey (personal communication: G. Lassiter). Few individuals purchase large quantities of staples, and though the government wishes to purchase cotton, it does so at farmgate prices unattractive to producers. Nevertheless, Swanson observes that "Traders and functionaries in large communities . . . use their influence and wealth to secure for themselves valuable property (e.g., land)" (insert added for clarity) (1979:6). This land is then worked by wage laborers, usually paid in kind, mainly to produce foodstuffs demanded in local markets. Individuals accumulating land in this manner are officials, traders, "traditional" rulers, or veterans who have greater access to influence and financial capital.

However, only a very small percentage of the farms employ wage labor and these farms are generally rather small. Preliminary results from a three-year, farm-level, agricultural survey by Michigan State University of Eastern ORD households suggests that 10% of the labor supplied to farms is some form of wage labor (personal communication: G. Lassiter). Sharecropping is not reported. In Fada N'Gourma, for example, which is the largest town in the Eastern ORD, an informant estimated there to be 20–30 farms of from 20–30 hectares employing wage labor. If we very generously assume that there are 20 farms of the same size as those in Fada N'Gourma in each of the 25 largest towns in the Eastern ORD, then there are 500 such farms occupying a total of 125 km^2, meaning .25% of the Eastern ORD's

50,000 km^2. Thus private land appears to be being appropriated in the Eastern ORD at a leisurely pace. It is important to note that the larger private farms are located near major towns, where they meet the increased demand for agricultural foodstuffs.

Mossi Plateau

The Mossi Plateau is also a region of relatively low demand for agricultural commodities, but one of far greater population density than in the Eastern region. Evidence suggests that here, as in the Eastern ORD, land is acquired by private individuals at a slow rate.

Equally, officials and other members of the elite are reported to accumulate land near large communities, where the demand for foodstuffs is greater. For example, there is a small dam at Mogtedo, 80 paved kilometers from the capital, Ouagadougou, where, according to Dumont, " . . . more than half the dam's irrigated fields were the property of urban dwellers . . . " (1978:308) and were worked by wage labor. At Boulbi, immediately south of Ouagadougou, a dam was constructed and irrigated rice cultivation begun. Fields were originally allocated to local farmers, but, according to Dumont, " . . . their plots were given to someone else who was in reality the figurehead for a *'fonctionnaire'* " (1978:308). Similarly, in the area around the capital, Skinner reports:

> A small but influential group of *fonctionnaires* in Ouagadougou has become 'gentlemen farmers' or 'civil servant farmers'. . . . As members of the group in Ouagadougou, these men have had little difficulty obtaining land—even valuable rice land—from peri-urban and rural chiefs. They either bring rural relatives to settle on these farms as cultivators or hire youths in Ouagadougou to go work these (1974:51).

The Southwest

Dumont reports on the situation from around Banfora and Bobo Dioulasso in southwest Burkina Faso. This area has lower population densities than the Plateau, but, due to proximity to Ivory Coast markets, has a stronger demand for agricultural commodities. He states:

> One sees appearing more and more orchards, often of mangoes . . . planted above all by those with money; urbanites, bureaucrats, soldiers. These new non-peasant farms are thus the work of a new category of absentee landlords . . . who

have land "attributed" to them by customary authorities. These developing enterprises create a new category of workers, proletarians, detached from their means of production: agricultural wage laborers, often paid 100 F CFA plus a meal (1978:309).

Finnegan observed the existence in southeastern Burkina Faso at Tenkodogo of "several" mango orchards of perhaps 80 trees per orchard. He further reports that orchard owners experienced difficulties in finding a market (1976:317). This is in contrast to the "vast" mango plantations seen in Dumont's area. Thus, the difference between the size of the mango orchards seems associated with demand, with the larger orchards accumulating near areas of greater demand.

The Forest

There is a final area where Burkinabe labor migrates to help form class relations. This is in the forests, first of Ghana and today, largely in the Ivory Coast. Perhaps a sixth of the nation's inhabitants reside in these coastal countries. A 1960 survey found that most were agricultural workers (Courel and Pool 1973:1003). Campbell documented a growth of an Ivorian "planter class" that expanded from an estimated 300 families in 1950 to 20,000 wealthy families who " . . . controlled about one fourth of cultivated land, (and) employed two-thirds of salaried labor . . . " in 1965 (1978:72–73). This labor was supplied by foreign migrants (Campbell 1978:102) drawn almost exclusively from Burkina Faso (Foltz 1967:47). Changing demand for agricultural commodities in the form of "rising coffee and cocoa prices" hastened the emergence of this class because "after 1946 [it] encouraged an increase both in the total output and in the land area cultivated of these two crops" (Campbell 1978:72), which was largely farmed by the wealthy families.

In sum, the rate of private land appropriation appears at least in part sensitive to agricultural commodity demand. In areas of highest agricultural commodity demand (e.g., near large towns, the southwest, and the forest), large farms based on wage labor rapidly emerged, while in those of lower demand (e.g., the Mossi Plateau, the Eastern ORD, and Tenkodogo), such farms occur more slowly. Burkina Faso lacks a substantial comparative advantage in any agricultural commodity required by core industries. This means that metropolitan demand for its products is generally weak. The only real demand for agricultural products is in local, urban centers. But Burkina Faso is overwhelmingly a rural nation, so that urban demand is limited, which at least partially explains the desultory private land appropriation.

A rising bureaucratic gentry

My informants were reticent about discussing the ways private individuals acquire land. Responses tended toward generalities: "We buy it like you," or "We register it." However, it gradually became clear that expectations of generalized and negative reciprocity on the part of those ceding land were important in private land accumulation. Most private lands are acquired by influential people—merchants and more frequently *fonctionnaires*. It is often acquired either by asking for its donation or convincing its owner to sell it, often at a nominal price. It may then be registered with local authorities and a title of ownership is issued. Much land, however, never appears to be registered. Rather, it is appropriated through purely customary means. Saul, for example, reports that the four largest farmers in Bentenga acquired their land through traditional borrowing, gift-giving or the re-activation of lineage rights (1983:89).

Traditional land authorities and registration officials appeared willing to facilitate the elite's interests in land because these individuals have the ability to help or hurt. Thus, land owners and registration authorities acquiesce to influential persons' land appetites in the hope of achieving future rewards (i.e., of generalized reciprocity) or of avoiding future punishments (i.e., of negative reciprocity). One informant suggested, "If they want land, they get it. If you help them, then perhaps they will help you."

More information needs to be acquired before merchants and *fonctionnaires* can be classified as capitalists. However, like capitalists, they privately control the means of production. They often hire wage labor, and they sell their products on a market so that they extract surplus value. What seems more problematic are the degree to which the labor they hire is a true proletariat, because most workers have some access to land, and the degree to which farming results in a steady accumulation of surplus value, about which there is simply no information. Nevertheless, far less problematic is the suggestion that there is a rising, largely bureaucratic gentry intentionally appropriating land in Burkina Faso. A consequence of the three land concentration processes just described is presented in the succeeding section.

"Existential" Development

In Camus' *The Stranger* there is an aged character, Salamano, who owns a dog he hates. One day the dog disappears, and precipitates:

> "The bastard! The filthy cur!" When I asked him where his dog was, he scowled at me and snapped out, "Gone!" . . . A minute or two later I heard Salamano's footsteps and a knock on my door. When I opened it, he halted for a moment in the doorway. "Excuse me. . . . I hope I'm not disturbing you." I asked him in but he shook his head. He was staring at his toe caps, and the gnarled old hands were trembling . . . "They won't really take him from me, will they, . . . ? Surely they wouldn't do a thing like that. If they do—I don't know what will become of me" (1954:48–50).

Salamano and his cur illustrate an existential plight. Such situations are those in which *all* possible alternatives involve some sort of negative utility. Salamano's is a classic existential situation. His cur is his life—but with him, he is miserable, while without him he is also miserable.

Change precipitating sets of alternatives in populations in which all the opportunities possess negative utilities is "existential" development. An "existential" development process is an ordering of events which generates such utility sets. It will be shown below that for the majority of Burkinabe, the processes of appropriation and expropriation described earlier constitute an "existential" development.

The size of the elite in Burkina Faso is tiny. The vast bulk of the population, over 90%, are farmers on small, domestic farms who face the following opportunity structure: they may remain on their own farms, become tenants on parastatal lands, workers on private lands (either in the forest or in Burkina Faso), or move to urban areas. The consumption levels they will enjoy in these four "opportunities" are as follows:

1. There is evidence of " . . . profound disorganization of productive structures . . . " if they stay on their domestic farms (Ancey 1977:6). This suggests, contrary to Meillassoux (1970), that underdevelopment in Burkina Faso does not *preserve* the communal production relations. It destroys them, which hardly suggests opulence. The net average income is a good indicator of consumption levels that these farmers will enjoy. This income was estimated to

be $52 per year per capita (Murphy and Sprey 1980). Such an income, among the lowest in the world, implies extreme poverty.

2. If farmers choose to become tenants on agro-parastatals, their situation may not improve over that of the first option, if the case of the AVV is representative. No projection of AVV tenant incomes, be it the original FAC design mission (Maton *et al.* 1972) or the calculations from AVV's own figures in Bei Agrer (1978) or Sorgho and Richet (1979), suggest that farmers will enjoy income levels that are high enough to lift them from poverty. The most frequently projected net family income level converted to approximately $190 per capita per year at the exchange rates prevailing between the dollar and the central African franc in 1980 (Murphy and Sprey 1980).

The actual situation may be worse than that projected for them by the planners. AVV tenants had two income sources: one from their cereal production and the other from their cotton sale. Murphy, using 1978 production data, showed that there was ''no cereal surplus'' (1980:4). Reyna suggested that by 1985, due to rising production costs, net income on one hectare of cotton would be negative (1980:8).

3. If farmers chose to become wage laborers on private lands, they might earn in Burkina Faso on the order of $2 to $3 per day as calculated by Saul for the Bentenga region in the late 1970's (1983:85). Songre *et al.* calculated their wages in the forest to be about 60¢ to 80¢ in the early 1970's (1974).

4. Finally, those Burkinabe who seize the final opportunity and move to urban areas tend to end up in the most menial jobs in the informal sector as day laborers, guards, prostitutes, petty thieves, etc. whose income levels are low and who are subjected to the increased health hazards that occur in densely crowded urban environments lacking sanitary facilities (Reyna 1980).

There may, and should, be debate over the exact levels of real, disposable income accruing to individuals in the above opportunity structure. It is improbable, however, that incomes in any of the four opportunities will lift a person above poverty. Thus, most Burkinabe face the following opportunities: they can be poor on their own farms, they can be poor as tenants on parastatal lands, they can be poor as laborers on capitalist farms, or they can be poor as urban proletarians. Development has been ''existential'' for Burkinabe: for them, like Salamano, life is full of bad choices.

Parastatal appropriation, "demographic" expropriation, and private appropriation all contribute to this opportunity structure. "Demographic" appropriation deepens the deterioration of income levels on domestic farms, which, at the same time, motivates migration to other opportunities. Parastatal appropriation helps create the opportunity of being a tenant on a state farm. Similarly, private appropriation helps create that of being a worker on private farms. Thus, these processes of land concentration all contribute to Burkina Faso's existential development.

III. Sahelian Perspectives

The West African savanna includes three major river basins—those of the Senegal, Niger, and Chari/Logone Rivers, and a number of lesser ones—including those of the Gambia and Volta Rivers. The pattern of land concentration throughout this region in the 1960s and 1970s generally resembled that in Burkina Faso. This appears to be, at least in part, because donor investments favored agro-parastatals in river valleys.

Following the Sahelian drought (1968–1973) efforts were made to increase the volume and quality of donor investments. Two organizations were created to facilitate this task. One included representatives of the savanna nations (*Comité Permanent Interétats de Lutte contre la Sécheresse dans le Sahel*—hereafter CILSS). The other consisted of the representatives of the donor nations (*Club des Amis du Sahel*—hereafter Club). The two groups were to plan and coordinate the savanna's development. In principle, the groups were supposed to reflect the desires of both the African nations and the donors. In practice, for a number of reasons, not the least of which was that the vast bulk of the planning was done by expatriates employed by donor agencies, the "action plans" developed for the savanna reflected donor interests. These plans proposed little investment in dryland agriculture, and enormous sums for riverain irrigation systems.[7] One estimate had the cost of irrigation infrastructure, excluding the cost of

---

[7] The case of the United Nations Development Program's (1977) Mission to the Lake Chad Basin Commission is typical of the way in which planning for the development of African river basins has been conducted since indepen-

dams, at four billion dollars (CILSS 1977:270). Time has proven these estimates to be far too low. The cost of developing one irrigated hectare, excluding the cost of dams, has risen from between $1000 to $5000 in the 1970s (Argoullon 1972:4) to about $20,000 in the early 1980s (Horowitz 1983:9:1). Mali has a million five hundred thousand irrigable hectares. This means the costs of constructing irrigated perimeters in Mali alone would run about thirty billion dollars. One consultant at a 1978 colloquium contemplating U.S. policy toward West African savanna development observed that:

> . . . when one calls for bids, there is only one French company which definitely has almost a monopoly . . . on all construction including granaries, roads, dams, dikes, and so forth (Joyce 1978:14–15).

The consultant's observations suggest a reason for donor interest in savanna irrigation: such investments transfer donor tax revenues to donor agro-industries, thus subsidizing a crucial donor industrial sector.

Donor preference for riveraine investments led savanna nations to create a large number of agro-parastatals in the 1960s and 1970s that accumulated considerable amounts of land.[8] In the Senegal River Basin, these included *Société Nationale de Développement Rural* (SONADER) in Mauritania and *Société d'Aménagement et d'Exploitation des Terres du Delta* (SAED) in Senegal. In the Malian section of the Niger River Basin, there was the *Office du Niger,* the oldest savanna parastatal, as well as a slew of others, called *Opérations,* initiated in the 1960s. The *Office National des Aménagements Hydro-Agricoles* (ONAHA) became the agency responsible for all as-

---

dence. This mission, in which I was a participant, was charged with formulating a Lake Chad Basin development strategy. It consisted of 35 development "technicians"—*none* of whom were from Lake Chad Basin nations. The "technicians'" professional activities were regulated by four management "experts". These were employees of French and American multinationals. A hefty proportion of the French firm's revenues come from the design and management of agro-parastatal enterprises in the Third World. Predictably, the two most expensive of the mission's recommendations were for the creation of two agro-parastatals.

[8] In 1977, the French firm, *Société Centrale pour Equipement du Territoire Internationale,* published the *Manuel de gestion des périmètres irrigués* (SCET 1977). This work was a "how to" manual detailing "how to" create and manage West African agro-parastatals.

pects of irrigation in the Nigérien section of the Niger River Basin in 1979 (Horowitz 1983:9:8). Finally, in Nigeria's section of this basin, at least 10 agro-parastatals, called River Basin Development Authorities (RBDAs), had been established by 1980 (Watts 1983:493). There were four major parastatals in the Chari and Logone River Basin by 1977. These included *Secteur Éxperimental de Modernisation Agricole de Bongor* (SEMAB), *Société de Développement du Sategui-Deressia, Secteur Expérimental de Modernisation Agricole de Laï-Kélo* (SEMALK), and *Société de Développement du Lac* (SODULAC) (Club 1977).

Evidence concerning the amounts of land appropriated is scanty. Nevertheless, the following information will give some idea of magnitudes. In the Senegal River Basin both SAED and SONADER had by 1978 rights to control the vast majority of lands along the river. At this time, these two parastatals had created irrigated perimeters on 21,000 hectares (*Organisation pour la Mise en Valeur du Fleuve Sénégal* (OMVS) 1978:1). Further, when one consults a 1977 OMVS map, it is clear that SAED and SONADER had already developed plans for irrigated perimeters along the entire river stretch within their two respective nations.

Mali, Niger, and Nigeria are the major nations in the Niger River Basin. Since 1932 and the formation of the *Office du Niger,* Mali has relied heavily upon parastatals for both irrigated and dryland agriculture. By the early 1970s the *Office du Niger* had 50,000 hectares in production and rights to appropriate up to 900,000 more hectares. Other parastatals were also appropriating land along the river. This was especially true of *Opération Riz,* which was acquiring valuable land in the interior delta of the Niger (SCET 1977:Annex). Niger has less potentially irrigable land than either Nigeria or Mali, but when one consults the map prepared for the Horowitz volume, which shows the location of existing and planned irrigated perimeters, one notes that it presents 37 existing or planned agro-parastatal perimeters located in *all* the places where there is irrigable alluvium along the Niger River in Niger (1983:9:1). In Nigeria, the RBDAs had put 15,000 hectares into irrigated perimeters by 1982, had plans to increase this to 100,000 hectares by 1985, and had identified a further 1.5 million hectares as potentially irrigable (Watts 1983:495).

The development of agro-parastatals along the Logone and Chari Rivers has been hampered by the Chadian civil war. Nevertheless, the manager of one small irrigation project on the Chari confided to me in 1977 that he had had considerable difficulty finding a location for his perimeter because irrigable land along the Chari was either being farmed by private individuals or parastatals or had been spoken for by these actors. Along the Chari River by 1976 there were a number of World Bank "small scale" irrigation projects (SATEC 1976). An IBRD map shows them occupying both banks of the river from Koundoul to Bousso (World Bank 1976). These projects did not at that time involve agro-parastatals. However, I was assured by one official that these perimeters were a *"phase pilote"* after which, when the technicians had gotten the knack of irrigation along the Chari, agro-parastatals would be introduced. Irrigation was more advanced along the Logone in the 1970s than along the Chari, due to the greater amounts of alluvium. Here, between Doba and Bongor, were located SEMBAB, SEMRY, and Sategui-Deressia. Equally, by this time, SODULAC had rights over all the fertile, polder lands in the Chadian portion of Lake Chad (Bouquet 1974).

The evidence with regard to private land appropriation is even more elusive than that for parastatal appropriation. However, existing evidence points in the direction of slow, but sure, private land appropriation. Two developments dominate the situation in the Senegal River Basin. First, in Senegal a Muslim religious brotherhood, the Mourides, has acquired "thousands of square miles" (O'Brien 1971:630). The Mourides have organized non-capitalist, but highly exploitative, monocrop production of peanuts. In Senegal, as in Burkina Faso, private individuals such as merchants and officials acquire lands near urban markets. One study reported this occurring around Rosso where foodstuffs were produced for sale in the Mauritanian capital of Nouakchott (Vu Tan Thai 1978:VI:8).

The situation in the Niger River Basin appears to be as follows. Meillassoux has spoken for Mali of the rise of a "bureaucratic" class, but he has neglected to document whether this class goes out as private individuals and accumulates land (1970). My own discussions with officials in Mali suggest that they did indeed seek to acquire *"quelques petits jardins."* Niger appears to resemble Mali. Latour Dejean describes the acquisition of land by an elite of officials and merchants in the Mawri region (1975). Horowitz reports a case where an official even managed to acquire a large amount of land in a government irrigation scheme (1983:9:18).

Private land acquisition apparently was emerging more quickly in Nigeria's portion of the Niger River Basin than in either Mali or Niger. This was due, at least in part, to the far greater amounts of agricultural finance capital available because of Nigeria's oil revenues and World Bank funding (Watts 1983:501–502). This capital disproportionately flows to "bureaucratic elites, influential merchant-traders, and traditional autocracies" (Watts 1983:502), and, as a result, "large-scale, capitalized agrarian producers are emerging" (Watts 1983:505; D'Silva and Raza 1980).

The situation in the Chari-Logone River Basin appears to resemble that in Niger and Mali. I was aware in 1972 of a number of officials who had acquired lands along the Chari River and who were supplying foodstuffs to the Chadian capital, N'Djamena. A 1974 UNDP report noted that merchants had acquired land along the main roads in Chad and were estimated to be producing about 5–6% of the total annual marketed supply in the country (UNDP 1975:150). Thus, throughout the West African savanna, bureaucrats and merchants appear to be seizing "targets of opportunity"—lands close to urban markets. This appropriation may be occurring more rapidly in Nigeria where there is the greatest urban demand and supply of agricultural finance capital.

Analysis of intentional and unintentional expropriation is in its infancy in the Sahel.[9] Agro-parastatals have sprung up throughout the savanna, implying that officials consciously had to devise strategies to expropriate land, which in turn implies that intentional expropriation has been a savanna commonplace. However, there is no extensive literature bearing upon such expropriation.[10]

---

[9] Wells and Norman (1984) have provided a bibliography of Sahelian irrigated agriculture. This work references studies which discuss the amounts of land appropriated by parastatals and then, how these parastatals have performed.

[10] Van der Klei (1978) warned, at least for Senegal, that the "Law of National Domain" might lead to considerable expropriation. However, no literature has emerged dealing with this topic. The work that does exist generally emphasizes the effects of expropriation upon existing land tenure systems. For example, SCET (1977) includes an examination of changes in land tenure that occurred subsequent to creation of agro-parastatals in Senegal, Mali, and Cameroun. Funel and Laucoin explore some of the effects of parastatal irri-

There appear to be two types of unintended Sahelian expropriation. The first is "demographic," and the second we shall term "market" expropriation. "Market" expropriation occurs when farmers' participation in the market does not result in enough income to meet their consumption requirements. This occurs when the sale prices of the crops produced on a small-holder's land are not sufficient to meet his food, clothing, tax, educational, medical, and agricultural input expenses. "Demographic" expropriation results from a reduction in the *amount* of a small-holder's arable land due to soil degradation and the constricting of land tenure consequent upon rising population densities. "Market" expropriation may occur without any reduction in land holdings. Rather, it accompanies changes in market structure. When the sale prices of agricultural commodities produced on an area of land decrease or stagnate, and the costs of production inputs and/or consumer necessities increase to a point that income is not able to meet costs, then the individuals on that land may leave it. When this occurs, their land may be said to have been appropriated by "market" forces.[11]

Investigators might seek "demographic" expropriation in areas of rapid population increase and high population density. Studies in the peanut producing areas of Senegal and in the densely populated flood plain along the Logone River suggest that both these areas may be subject to "demographic" expropriation.[12] "Market" expropriation

---

gation projects upon land tenure in the lacustrine zone of Mali, the Gorgol in Mauritania, and Ibohamane in Niger (1981:30–41).

[11] Market structure appears to play a role in unintentional land expropriation in contemporary North America. Here the prevailing agricultural input and farmgate prices combine to make small farms shaky and large ones viable. A result of this situation for the small farmer is that, even though he or she did not intend it, he or she frequently loses his or her land. Expropriation, thus, is an "unintended" consequence of market structure.

[12] There are a number of studies dealing with the Senegalese peanut basin. These make clear that soil degradation, population increase, and migration are present in the basin (Franke and Chasin 1980; Lericollais 1970; Lacombe 1979; Roch and Rocheteau 1971). Less clear is whether population increase results in soil degradation and whether this in turn provokes migration—both of which are necessary if "demographic" expropriation is to occur. An alternative view might have it that a particular variety of production relations—

would seem most likely in areas of stagnant or declining farmgate prices and inflating prices for consumer goods. For example, the population density was low ($10/km^2$) in the two Barma villages along the Chari in Chad where I conducted fieldwork in 1969–70. Land was abundant in the sense that if one needed a few fields, they were there for the taking. But, paradoxically, there was still not enough land for certain people. Barma at this time cultivated no industrial crops, so their cash incomes were limited to the sale of foodstuffs whose prices had remained low and constant for about a decade. However, cash requirements for such consumption items as cloth, taxes, sugar, tea, and, most importantly for young men, bridewealth had increased steadily. Consider this situation from the vantage of young men.

A household's annual earnings from the sale of foodstuffs were not sufficient to meet bridewealth costs. Bridewealth at this time averaged slightly over 12,000 F CFA, which was equivalent in amount to the purchase of a house for most Westerners. Young, unmarried men lacked the resources (chiefly labor) to place large areas of land in production to grow additional foodstuffs to acquire increased income for use as bridewealth. Hence, their consumption needs (for bridewealth) exceeded their production incomes (from farming). This meant that fully 54% of all unmarried males between the ages of 15 and 29 in the two villages studied spent all or a portion of their year as migrants working for wages. They did so, most said, to acquire the money they needed to marry.[13] Thus, the prevailing market forces made it impossible for such men to reside permanently on their land, which meant that they had been subject to "market" expropriation.

---

those associated with the Mourides—uses the land in ways which leads to its deterioration (cf. Copans 1980). The case of the Logone River flood plain seems less problematic. Here, de Garine writes, "increases in density rapidly brought such a reduction of the cultivable area of traditional plots that younger sons were forced to migrate" (1978:45).

[13] It might be noted that the 1969–70 Barma "bridewealth costs exceeded three years of the gross money value of most farmers' total cereal harvests. This implies that if a farmer stopped eating for three years and sold his entire sorghum crop he still would not have acquired enough money to meet the average bridewealth prevailing at the time" (Reyna 1984:63). C. Raynaut has described what appears to be "market" expropriation among certain Hausa in Niger (1973; 1977).

The preceding paragraphs suggest that different forms of intended and unintended expropriation occurred throughout the Sahel following independence. Available information does not permit estimates of the numbers of small-holders who are at risk of expropriation. However, only 8% of the savanna is arable (Matlock and Cockrum 1974:101). The most fertile of this land is in the river basins, and there appears to have been considerable intentional expropriation of these lands by parastatals between 1960 and 1980. Should agro-parastatal expropriation of the highest quality lands continue, then small-holders would be crowded onto poorer quality soils where—if population and consumer prices continue to escalate in the absence of producers' price increases—they would be prime candidates for "demographic" and "market" expropriation.

Do parastatal and private appropriation in conjunction with different forms of expropriation mean that most savanna small-holders experience "existential" development? Here, I believe, the evidence is clearer. Sahelian nations are classified as among the poorest in the world (World Bank 1981). The poorest Sahelians are small-holders who are also the majority of the population—over 90% of most Sahelian nations' total population. It is clear that small-holders have not advanced from poverty by working on private farms—for such persons are usually the poorer of the poorest. This means that the only existing opportunity for an exit from poverty is the agro-parastatal. However, A. Waldstein, following a survey of different, largely agro-parastatal schemes in the savanna, concluded: " . . . few . . . offer their adherents a net annual income substantially greater than otherwise current among rural cultivators . . . " (1978:39). This means that for the vast majority of small-holders there are presently no opportunities which offer an escape from extreme poverty.[14] This leads us back to the question: does the savanna have a land concentration problem?

---

[14] Most Sahelian parastatals have been functioning for less than a decade, so it might be possible to dismiss their inability to provide increased real incomes as the result of start-up "bugs." However, Mali's *Office du Niger* has been in operation for over half a century, suggesting that it has had time to work out the "bugs." It offers its tenants incomes which allow "only very slightly higher consumption levels" than those prevailing for "traditional" domestic farmers (Netting *et al.* 1980:404).

IV. Return to Musa's Place

Land concentration appears to have been occurring during the 1960s and 1970s in the Sahel. Thanks to donor investments, agro-parastatals appropriated fertile, alluvial land at a rapid rate. Concurrently, a rising bureaucratic and merchant gentry appropriated other valuable lands near to areas of urban demand at a more leisurely pace, while small-holders on their domestic lands were subject to different forms of intentional and unintentional expropriation. This land concentration meant that a new opportunity structure was appearing, one dominated by officials, who—as parastatal administrators or private gentry—were acquiring control over land, while ordinary small-holders watched theirs diminish due to various forms of expropriation.

This opportunity structure has implications for food supply and security. These may be grasped by examining the resources and motivation of the different actors in the sand. The 90% or so of the population resident on its own domestic farms, which is already desperately poor, may find itself subject to increased "demographic" and "market" expropriation, reduced labor supply, and declining farm incomes. Such a population would hardly be in a position to increase food supply and security. Equally, tenants on private and state farms, as well as urban proletariat, would lack the incomes or other resources to ameliorate food problems.

But what of those favored actors in the new opportunity structure who make land-use decisions? These are the parastatal managers and private farm proprietors. They have an over-riding concern to make the greatest profit possible. This has overwhelmingly meant in the past that they cultivated crops with the highest farmgate prices. These tend to be (non-edible) industrial crops or (non-affordable) luxury food-stuffs. In such an opportunity structure, those with the motivation to increase food supply and security lack the resources, while those with the resources lack the motivation.

The existentialists of the 1940s and 1950s, reflecting on the world they saw around them, believed that the opportunity structures available to people provided them with, as the title of one of Sartre's plays expressed it, *No Exit*. Everywhere there was "no exit" from the bad choices provided by the prevailing bad opportunities. If the land concentration trends of the 1960s and 1970s continue, then the average person in rural areas of the West African savanna may be very poor on his or her domestic lands, or on an agro-parastatal's lands, or on a bureaucrat's or merchant's lands. While there may be choices, there will be no exit from poverty. First impressions are indeed often deceiving. Once, when I returned to Musa's place, I asked who this guy Musa was anyway. Musa turned out to be a *"gros patron"*—a most important merchant. He had "eaten", i.e. simply taken, the land for his *"joli jardin"*, and his papayas and mangoes were going as luxuries to tempt the palettes of *nassara* (whitefolk) in the capital.

References

Ancey, G. 1977 Variation Mossi sur le thème: Reproduction de milieux ruraux mis en contraste avec le système capitaliste extérieur. Travaux et Documents de l'ORSTOM. 64.

Argoullon, J. 1972 Potential Areas for the Development of Large-Scale Irrigation in the Upper Valley of the Niger. Paper presented at the International Seminar on Prospects for Irrigation in West Africa. Ibadan, Nigeria: IATA.

Bei Agrer 1978 Programme Global d'Etudes et d'investissements de l'Autorité des Aménagements des Vallées de la Volta (1978–82). Vol. I–VI. Bureau Courtoy, S. A. Blvd. E. Jaquemain, 83-Blell, 1000 Bruxelles.

Berg, E. 1978 Onchocerciasis Control Program: Economic Review Mission. Draft. Ann Arbor: University of Michigan, Department of Economics.

Bouquet, Christian 1974 L'homme et les plaines alluviales en milieux tropicales. Iles et rives du sud-Kanem (Tchad). Etude de géographie régionale. Bordeaux: Travaux et documents de géographie tropicale #13. Centre des Etudes de Géographie Tropicale, Université de Bordeaux.

Boutillier, J.L. 1964 Les Structures Foncières en Haute Volta. Etudes Voltaiques. Mémoire No. 5. Ouagadougou: CVRS.

Campbell, B. 1978 The Ivory Coast. *In* West African States. J. Dunn (ed.). Cambridge: Cambridge University Press. pp. 66–116

Camus, A. 1954 (1942) The Stranger. New York: Vintage.

Chauveau, J.P. 1980 Agricultural Production and Social Formation: The Baule Region of Toumodi-Kokumbo in Historical Perspective. *In* Peasants in Africa. M.A. Klein (ed.) Beverly Hills: Sage. pp. 143–177.

CILSS 1977 Résumé du rapport de synthèse: Equipe cultures irrigiguées. #7768. 3 mai 1977. Bamako: CILSS.

Cleveland, David A. 1976 Fertility Regulation: Kusasi Intensive Cultivators of West Africa (Ghana). *In* Culture and Reproduction: An Anthropological Critique of Demographic Transition Theory. W. Penn Handwerker (ed.). Boulder, CO: Westview.

Club 1977 Eléments pour une programmation des équipements hydro-agricoles 1978–2000. Républic du Tchad. Mars 1977. Paris: Club des Amis du Sahel.

Constantin, F. and C. Coulon 1979 "Enterprises publique et changement politique au Mali." *In* Les Enterprises publiques en Afrique Noire. Voll. Dimitri-Georges Lavroff (ed.). Paris: Editions A, Pedone.

Copans, Jean 1980 Les Marabout de l'arachide: La confrérie mouride et les paysans du Sénégal. Paris: Le Sycomore.

Courel, A. and I. Pool 1973 Haute-Volta. *In* Croissance Demographique et Evolution Socio-Economique en Afrique de l'Ouest. J.C. Caldwell *et al.* (eds.). New York: Population Council.

Deere, C. 1978 Intra-Familial Labor Deployment and the Formation of Peasant Household Income: A Case Study of the Peruvian Sierra. Manuscript. Amherst, MA: University of Massachusetts, Department of Anthropology.

de Garine, Igor 1978 "Population, Production, and Culture in the Plains Societies of Northern Cameroon and Chad: The Anthropologist in Development Projects." Current Anthropology 11(19):42–67.

Diabaté, Mustapha 1977 Les grands problems théoriques et pratiques des sociétés et enterprises d'Etats en afrique (Cote d'Ivoire, Mali, Sénégal). Abidjan: Institut d'ethnosociologie, Université d'Abidjan.

D'Silva, B. and M.R. Raza 1980 "Integrated Rural Development in Nigeria." Food and Policy 5:282–297.

Dumont, R. 1978 Paysans Ecrasés, Terres Massacrées. Paris: Laffont.

Faulkingham, R. 1977 Fertility in Tudu: An Analysis of Constraints on Fertility in a Village in Niger. *In* The Persistence of High Fertility. J.C. Caldwell (ed.). Canberra: ANU Press. pp. 148–58.

Finnegan, G. 1976 Population Movement, Labor Migration, and Social Structure in a Mossi Village. Unpublished Ph.D. dissertation. Ann Arbor, MI: University Microfilms International.

Foltz, W.J. 1967 From French West Africa to the Mali Federation. New Haven: Yale University Press.

Franke R. and B. Chasin 1980 The Seeds of Famine. Totowa, NJ: Rowman and Allanheld.

Funel, J.-M. and G. Laucoin 1981 Développement en zones arides: Politiques d'aménagement hydro-agricoles. Paris: Agence de Coopération Culturelle et technique.

Gillis, M. 1977 Efficiency in State Enterprises: Selected Cases in Mining from Asia and Latin America. Discussion Paper #17. Cambridge, MA: Harvard Institute for International Development.

Griffin, M. 1976 Land Concentration and Rural Poverty. New York: Holmes and Meice.

Gregory, J.W. 1974 Development and In-Migration in Upper Volta. *In* Modern Migrations in Western Africa. S. Amin (ed.). London: Oxford University Press. pp. 305–320.

Handwerker, W.P. 1977 "Family, Fertility and Economics." Current Anthropology 18(2).

Hermann, Eric R. 1981 Analysis of Selected Agricultural Parastatals in the Ivory Coast. Medford, MA: Fletcher School of Law and Diplomacy, Tufts University.

Horowitz, M. 1983 Niger Social and Institutional Profile. Binghamton, NY: IDA.

Javillonar, G. 1979 Rural Development, Women's Roles and Fertility in Developing Countries: Review of the Literature. Chapel Hill, NC: Research Triangle Institute.

Joyce, C.L. 1978 Proceedings; Colloquium ''Towards a Rational U.S. Policy on River Basin Development in the Sahel.'' Washington, DC: Africa Bureau, AID.

Johnston, B.F. and P. Kilby 1975 Agricultural and Structural Transformations: Economic Strategies in Late-Developing Countries. Oxford University Press.

Katternberg, D. 1979 Quelques Aspects de la Culture Mossi. Ouagadougou: AVV. Ministère du développement rural.

Kohler, J.M. 1971 Activites Agricoles et Changements Sociaux dans l'Ouest Mossi. Paris: Mémoires ORSTOM.

———— 1972 Les Migrations des Mossi de l'Ouest. Paris: ORSTOM.

Lacombe, B. 1979 ''Mobilité et migration.'' Cahiers ORSTOM. Série sciences humaines. (VI)4:11–42.

Latour Dejean, E. 1975 La transformation du régime foncier: Appropriation des terres et formation de la classe dirigeante en pays Mawri (Niger). In L'Agriculture africaine et le capitalisme. Samir Amin (ed.). Paris: ANTHROPOLOS-IDEP. pp. 185–232.

Lericollais, A. 1970 ''La détérioration d'un terroir—Sob en pays Serrer.'' Etudes Rurales. 37.38.39:113–128.

Londres, A. 1929 Terre d'Ebène. Paris: Presses Universitaires de France.

Marchal, J.Y. 1977 ''The Evolution of Agrarian Systems in Yatenga.'' African Environment, Vol. II, III and IV:73–87.

Marx, K. 1960 (1867) Capital. Vol. 1. New York: The Modern Library.

Matlock W. and E. Cockrum 1974 A Framework for Evaluating Long-Term Strategies for the Development of the Sahel-Sudan Region. Vol. 2. Cambridge, MA: Center for Policy Studies, Massachusetts Institute of Technology.

Maton, et al. (FAC) 1971 Etudes de Pré-Factibilité: Projet d'Aménagement et de Mise en Valeur des Vallées des Volta. Ouagadougou: Ministère du Plan, de l'Industrie et des Mines.

McFarland, D. 1976 Historical Dictionary of Upper Volta. Metuchen, NJ: Scarecrow Press.

Meillassoux, C. 1970 ''A Class Analysis of the Bureaucratic Process in Mali.'' Journal of Development Studies 6:97–110.

Murphy, J. and L. Sprey 1980 The Volta Valley Authority: Socio-Economic Evaluation of a Resettlement Project in Upper Volta. West Lafayette, IN: Department of Agricultural Economics, Purdue University.

Netting, Robert McC., David A. Cleveland and F. Stier 1980 ''The Conditions of Agricultural Intensification in the West African Savanna.'' In Sahelian Social Development. S.P. Reyna (ed.). Abidjan: REDSO/WA: AID. pp. 187–507.

O'Brien, D.C. 1971 The Mourides of Senegal. London: Oxford University Press.

OMVS 1978 Note succincte sur la situation du développement de la culture irriguée et le renforcement du système de planification dans le bassin du fleuve sénégal. Dakar: OMVS.

ORSTOM 1979 Stratégies d'Aménagement et de Mise en Valeur des Zones Libérées de l'Onchocercose en Haute Volta. ORSTOM Memoire No. 89:275–280. Paris: ORSTOM.

Ossendowski, F. 1928 Slaves of the Sun. New York: Dutton.

Ouedraogo, D. 1979 Genèse et Structure d'Un Espace Enclave: La Haute Volta. ORSTOM Mémoire No. 89:553–559. Paris: ORSTOM.

Piche, V., J. Gregory and S. Coulibaby 1980 "Vers une explication des courants migratoires voltaiques." Labor, Capital, and Society XIII(1).

Remy, C. 1972 Donsin, Les Structures Agraires d'un Village Mossi de la Région de Nobere. Ouagadougou: ORSTOM.

Raynaut, C. 1973 La circulation marchande des céréales et mécanismes d'inégalité economique. Cahiers de centre d'études et de recherches ethnologiques. #2. Bordeaux: Université de Bordeaux.

——— 1977 Circulation monétaire et évolution des structures socio-économiques chez les Haoussas de Niger. Naimey, Niger: in IRSH Library.

Rey, P.P. 1973 Les Alliances de Classe. Paris: Maspéro.

Reyna, S.P. 1977 Economics and Fertility: Waiting for the Demographic Transition in the Dry Zone of Francophone West Africa. In The Persistence of High Fertility. J.C. Caldwell (ed.). Canberra: ANU Press. pp. 393–427.

——— 1980 Impact of Autorité des Aménagements des Vallées des Volta. Abidjan: REDSO/WA. USAID.

——— 1983 "Dual Class Formation and Agrarian Underdevelopment: An Analysis of the Articulation of Production Relations in Upper Volta." Canadian Journal of African Studies 2(17):221–234.

——— 1984 "Barma Bridewealth: Socialization and the Reproduction of Labour in a Domestic African Economy." Africa 4(54):59–72.

Roch, J. and G. Rocheteau 1971 "Economie et population: Le cas du Sénégal." Cahiers ORSTOM. Série sciences humaines. (VIII)1:63–71.

SATEC 1976 Projet d'extension des périmètres villageois irrigués le long du fleuve Chari (Tchad). Paris: SATEC.

Saul, M. 1983 "Work Parties, Wages and Accumulation in a Voltaic Village." American Ethnologist 1(10):77–96.

Savonnet, G. 1976 ORSTOM. 13(1).

SCET 1977 Manuel de gestion des périmètres irrigués. Paris: Ministère de la Coopération.

Skinner, E.P. 1974 African Urban Life: The Transformation of Ouagadougou. Princeton, NJ: Princeton University Press.

Smith, James 1977 Economy and Demography in a Mossi Village. Unpublished doctoral dissertation. Ann Arbor, MI: University Microfilms International.

Songre, A. *et al.* 1974 Réalités et Effet de l'Emigration Massive des Voltaiques dans le Contexte de l'Afrique Occidentale. *In* Modern Migration in Western Africa. London: Oxford University Press.

Sorgho, J. and O. Richet 1979 Les Coûts Récurrents d'Une Installation en Culture Sèche, de 15,000 Families sur des Terres Neuves Aménagées par l'Autorité des Aménagements des Vallées des Volta. Ouagadougou: CILSS.

Suret-Canale, J. 1976 FRENCH COLONIALISM IN TROPICAL AFRICA, *1900–1945*. London: Heinemann.

Swanson, R. 1979 Gourmantche Agriculture. Part I. Land Tenure and Field Cultivation. Fada N'Gourma: EORD.

UNDP 1975 Production et commercialisation des céréales au Tchad. Volume I. N'Djamena, Tchad: UNDP.

Upper Volta 1979 Recencement Nationale 1975. Résultats Provisoires. Ouagadougou: Bureau Statistique.

USAID 1980 Country Development Strategy Statement: Upper Volta. Ouagadougou: USAID.

Van der Klei 1978 Anciens et nouveaux droits fonciers chez les Diola au Sénégal et leurs conséquences pour la répartition des terres. Lama Kara, Togo: Paper presented at the Séminaire International sur la réforme agro-foncier dans les pays du Conseil de l'Entente en Afrique de l'Ouest.

Vu Van Thai 1978 Etude socio-economique de bassin du fleuve Sénégal. Rapport interimaire. (Fin de phase d'observation qualitative). Dakar: Direction de la Planification et de la Coordination: OMVS.

Waldstein, A. 1978 Government Sponsored Agricultural Intensification Schemes in the Sahel: Development for Whom? Abidjan: REDSO/WA. USAID.

Wallerstein, I. 1976 The Modern World System. New York: Academic Press.

Watts, M. 1983 Silent Violence. Berkeley, CA: University of California Press.

Weil, P. 1986 Agricultural Intensification and Fertility in the Gambia (West Africa). *In* Culture and Reproduction: An Anthropological Critique of Demographic Transition Theory. W. Penn Handwerker (ed.). pp. 294–320. Boulder, CO: Westview.

Wells, J.C. and W.R. Norman 1984 Sahelian Irrigated Agriculture: A Review of French Literature Sources. Ithaca, NY: Department of Agricultural Engineering, Cornell University.

World Bank 1974 Land Reform: Sector Policy Paper. Washington, DC: IBRD.

———— 1976 Appraisal of a Rural Projects Fund Chad. Report #1194-CD. Regional Projects Department, West Africa. Dakar: Regional Office.

———— 1981 Accelerated Development in Sub-Saharan Africa: An Agenda for Action. Washington, DC: IBRD.

Gender, Land, and Hunger in Eastern Zaire[1]

Brooke Grundfest Schoepf and Claude Schoepf

13 Spencer Baird Road,
Woods Hole, MA 02543

Introduction

As in most African societies, Zairian women are active in production of food crops, both for home use and for sale. In fact, women are the principal food producers despite the ecological and sociocultural diversity which characterizes this second-largest sub-Saharan nation. Thus increased food production must rest upon knowledge of gender roles and constraints. Yet few studies of Zairian women's status in relation to agricultural activities, income and family nutrition exist. This paper calls attention to linkages between effects of the national political economy, including dependency and internal class formation, and efforts of peasant women to produce food crops in one area of Zaire.[2] It suggests that women's status in family and community is key to their ability to contribute to and benefit from increased production efforts.

---

[1]Revised version of a paper presented at the 84th annual meeting of the American Anthropological Association, Washington, D.C. December 8, 1985.

[2]The methodological approach linking macrolevel political economy with microlevel socioeconomic conditions and social relations was pioneered by a team of anthropologists studying *The People of Puerto Rico* (Steward et al 1956). Their research was funded, as was much of our Zaire work, by the Rockefeller Foundation (Susan Almy, personal communication Nov. 1988). We wish to express our gratitude for the generous support we have received while absolving the Foundation from any responsibility for the contents.

The Area: Eastern Kivu, Zaire

The paper draws upon field data from a study by Claude Schoepf in four localities of Kabare Zone, South Kivu, in 1982 and upon interviews with development workers, community groups and officials by Brooke Schoepf in both South and North Kivu in 1985.[3] The interviews indicate that the general situation in the study communities is similar to that existing in the many areas of land shortage in eastern Kivu.[4] Eastern Kivu Region is part of the Eastern Highlands area of Zaire which extends over more than 1,000 miles, from north of Lake Mobutu and the Ituri River, southward toward Lubumbashi and the Kundelungu massif in southeastern Shaba Region. Major mountain ranges include the snow-capped Rwenzoris, the Virunga chain with active volcanos, and the evergreen forested Mitumbas. The area varies in altitude from somewhat below 1,000 meters to peaks above 5,000 meters and in width (east–west) from 50 to 350 miles (Kabala Matuka 1976; Ames et al. 1981). The landscape, climate, soils and natural vegetation are extremely varied, as are the farming systems and cultures.

This western extension of the Rift Valley Great Lakes region contains deep, highly fertile volcanic soils. However, some of the most serious hunger problems in Zaire are found here. As in most of Zaire, women share in the general condition of the peasantry, which is one of stagnation, neglect and crisis. Exploring the processes of peasant

---

[3]Fieldwork in Kivu includes Claude Schoepf's baseline survey analysis and observations made in 1982 as a member of the USAID-funded INERA Support Project at the Mulungu Research station and Brooke G. Schoepf's interviews with development workers and officials during February-April 1985 while a member of the US Peace Corps' African Food System Initiative (AFSI) Zaire Assessment Team. The acknowledgement of these institutions does not render them in any way responsible for errors of fact or interpretation. The views expressed in this paper are solely those of the authors.

[4]At the time this chapter was drafted (1985), Kivu Region in eastern Zaire was divided administratively into three sub-regions. These are the heavily forested Maniema to the west, and the two eastern sub-regions of South and North Kivu. The latter shares many geographical and cultural characteristics with the eastern Ituri region of Upper Zaire. In 1988 Kivu Region was divided into three small administrative regions each with its own Governor and Legislative Council.

decline in the Eastern Highlands corridor casts light upon the relationship of food production and nutrition to the status of women, internal class formation and international interests.

Major causes of hunger in the region are generally held to be overpopulation, erosion and maternal ignorance. We focus instead on the land question. The focus on land shortage in its historical and contemporary phases serves to put other causes in perspective. Land policies which increase inequality are a major aspect of the food crisis in the Third World (Lele 1975), and they are of growing importance in African poverty. In areas where unemployment or below-subsistence wages are the only alternatives available to those without formal education, capital and political patrons, the consequences of land shortage may be tragic, particularly for women and children in poor households, who are the most severely affected (Boserup 1970; Rogers 1979).

Historical Perspective

During the colonial period huge tracts of land were appropriated by the Crown and concession companies throughout the Eastern Highlands and the Comité National du Kivu (CNKi) was formed to encourage European settlement.[5] Both men and women were subjected to forced labor corvées to provide food for workers in European enterprises, to build roads, carry burdens and so on (Sosne 1979). Several types of wage labor contracts were introduced for African men

---

[5]In 1902, large tracts in the northeastern highlands corridor totaling 4,000,000 hectares were awarded by King Leopold II to the Compagnie des Chemins de Fer du Congo Supérieur aux Grands Lacs (CFL) on the theory that the company would build a railroad link to the Nile. The concession included mineral rights (including the gold fields of Kilo-Moto) and rich lands of volcanic origin. In 1928 the government and CFL formed the Comité National du Kivu (CNKi) with a concession of 12,000,000 hectares eventually reduced to 300,000 around Bukavu. The CNKi then sold off parcels to settlers (Joye and Lewin 1961; Merlier 1962). The pattern of appropriation of peasant lands for incorporation in state domains and their subsequent privatization is an old one which continues in the present. More detailed treatment of the early period appears in Schoepf and Schoepf (1988).

(Bashizi 1978). Plantation labor did not offer a viable alternative to peasant farming, as wages remained well below the "vital minimum" necessary to maintain male workers (Moeller 1930).

As the farming systems of Bushi[6] changed under pressure from capitalist plantations, food crop cultivation was increasingly delegated to women. Traditional food reserves were not maintained and reciprocal exchanges beyond the family compound dwindled. Manioc replaced sorghum and beans, the traditional staple foods;[7] diets were impoverished and the food security of many undermined.

Cash crops including tea, coffee, pyrethrum and quinquina spread and processing plants were established by European settlers and subsidiaries of transnational firms. By 1952 the administrator responsible for Ngweshe Chiefdom, located near the research site, warned that the area was "saturated" with industrial crops (Bosmans 1981). Most family plots in Bushi were too small for minimal subsistence needs (Hecq and Lefébvre 1959).[8] As in other districts around the city of Bukavu, it was difficult for peasants to find land on which to grow food. Many (an estimated 30,000 in 1959) regularly worked on plantations where wages continued to be extremely low.

Following independence in 1960, political violence and military banditry wreaked untold misery and hardship, including widespread malnutrition and some starvation. The food crisis was not only an urban phenomenon. Hunger was also widespread in the countryside;

---

[6]The area inhabited by the Shi people is called Bushi, the language Mashi and the people Bashi. During the colonial period the four main Shi kingdoms were incorporated into Kabare Territory. Following independence they were split into Kabare and Walungu Zones. See Sosne (1979) for an analysis of colonial peasantization and plantation labor to 1972 and Callaghy (1984) for problems of local administration and state control in the first decade of the Mobutu regime.

[7]This despite the relatively low yields of manioc in the medium altitude zone when compared with those of lowland forest and savanna.

[8]Calculating dietary needs on the basis of yield data which were higher than those currently obtained, Hecq and Lefébvre estimated that a family of four which included two children, would need the produce of 1.2 hectares plus salt and palm oil purchases. Since households in Kabare Territory then averaged holdings of less than 1 hectare, cultivators relied upon root crops which filled their stomachs but did not supply adequate nutrients.

as the plantation wage-labor system was disrupted, the landless poor had no means to buy food, and poor peasants also were affected.

In 1965 voluntary organizations staffed by missionaries and local elites joined forces with international relief agencies to form the Comité Anti-Bwaki (CAB)—*bwaki* is the local term for the syndrome known internationally as kwashiorkor. The term is now used in kivu to denote protein-energy malnutrition (PEM). The CAB's concerted efforts combined with partially restored economic activity resulted in limited improvement.[9] Nevertheless, a hard core of severely malnourished children remained: a study reported 20 percent of children under three to be suffering from marasmus (CEMBUAC in CAB 1975:30).

In 1974 the Zairian economy entered a period of crisis and prices of consumer goods rose vertiginously. The Anti-Bwaki Committee reported that: "all centers complain the situation is worsening" in both rural and urban areas (CAB) 1975). The downward trend in living conditions for the majority of Zairians continued as inflation reached a cumulative 6,580 percent by 1984.[10] In 1981 a physician in charge of maternal-child health services noted that despite highly successful health and nutrition programs:

> over the past two years pregnant women appear less well-nourished, the babies are smaller with lower birth weights . . . The evolution of clinical malnourishment shows a steady increase. In Walungu and Kabare Zones [Bushi] virtually the entire population is insufficiently nourished and the majority exhibits stunting" (Vuylsteke 1981: 49).

Tuberculosis, which for several decades has been more prevalent in the Eastern Highlands than in the rest of Zaire, is currently reported to be epidemic. Physicians consider this to be an indicator of declining nutritional status (interviews 1982, 1985).

Kabare and Walungu are the zones of highest population density and land appropriation in Kivu Region. Kabare *Collectivité*, with 98

---

[9]For example, studies conducted in Walungu Zone of South Kivu which along with Kabare Zone had registered the most widespread hunger problems, reported that between 1969 and 1975 malnutrition had been reduced from 41.5 to 35.5 percent among children under fifteen years. In children under one year the rate had declined from 27.2 to 21 percent (Crombe cited in CAB 1975:30-31).

[10]Data supplied by Zaire Department of Agriculture and Rural Development, Bureau of Studies to USAID/Kinshasa.

percent of the population described as rural, had 232 persons per square kilometer in 1981 (Kabare Zone: 1981); most were peasants. Some 65 percent of the best land now is reported occupied by plantations growing export crops, principally quinine, coffee and tea (interviews 1985).[11] As estates occupy accessible areas the more remote regions have become extremely congested. The next section examines the current organization of peasant farming in the interior of Kabare.

Peasant Farming in Kabare

Analysis of a household survey conducted in four mountainous *localitiés* of Kabare *Collectivité* near the Mulungu agricultural research station of Zaire's Institut Nationl de Recherche Agronomique in 1981–82 reveals the outlines of peasant farming systems there (C. Schoepf 1982a). Mulungu station lies 2 degrees South of the equator at altitudes ranging between 1,600 and 2,000 meters. Annual rainfall averages 1,666 millimeters distributed in two distinct seasons, with a short dry spell in January and three-month dry season between July and September. Much of the soil is of volcanic origin; the brown and red basalts are heavy, deep, moderately acid (ph between 4.5 and neutral) and highly fertile. Soils on the higher forested slopes tend to be thin, sandy or yellow clay and lacking in humus. Kahuzi-Biega National Park, home to troops of free-ranging gorillas, borders on the station.

One hundred and sixty households were selected by means of a two-stage random sampling process.[12] Households contain an average

---

[11]Valid Figures are unobtainable. The Kabare Zone Agricultural Officer (*Agronome*) reported in 1979 that 14,500 hectares—20 percent of the Zone's agricultural land—were planted to export crops, mainly on large settler estates and plantations. There were no figures to be had on land recently acquired by Zairian officials and traders (Schulz et al 1982: 36). The plantations are concentrated in Kabare *Colletivité* where they take up a far larger proportion of the land. The other *Collectivité*, Nindja, lying on the western side of the mountains had only 18 persons per square kilometer and no large plantations in 1982.

[12]The baseline survey was designed by consultants in 1979, data collection supervised by the project's rural sociologist in 1980–81. Additional inter-

Table I. Land distribution—Mulungu survey.

	Hectares per household					
	0–.3	.3–.5	.5–1.0	1.0–1.5	1.5–2.0	2.0–2.5
% of Hholds	33	14	20	21	5	2
Cumulative %s	33	47	67	88	93	95

N = 78   x̄ = .83ha   median = .55ha   (Total % error due to rounding)

of 5.2 persons, including 3 children. Seventeen percent of the men report more than one wife. The average family holding for the 78 households whose fields were measured is 0.83 hectare. Not unexpectedly, averages mask considerable differentiation within the landholding peasantry.[13] One-third of all families work plots totalling less than 0.3 hectare; nearly half (47 percent) work less than 0.5 hectare and two-thirds subsist on one hectare or less (see Table 1). Even with intensive cultivation, the holdings of nearly 90 percent are insufficient to support a family. Sixteen percent of the male population engages regularly in wage labor—more than half in agricultural employment. Another 36 percent report seeking paid work, while 20 percent of households occasionally employ hired labor.[14] Regular off-farm employment is reported for less than 1 percent of the female population, although many women work seasonally picking tea on the estates; 9 percent of households are female-headed.

Plots are extremely small: the average household has 3.6 separate fields (median = 3). Thirteen percent of fields are rented. Only one third of the households have swamp land which can be planted to beans (a traditional staple) during the dry season—or year round with

views, re-measurements and analysis were undertaken by Claude Schoepf in 1982.

[13]No landless households were part of the survey. These may exist but were not included on the lists supplied by chiefs. Similarly, female-headed households may be under-reported.

[14]Schulz and colleagues found 32 percent of peasant households in 6 survey villages working on 0.4 hectares or less, while 48.5 percent had between 0.4 and 1 hectare. Some 19.5 percent have 1 to 2.5 hectares and only 1 percent of land holders were bourgeois absentees with large holdings. These last two groups were employers of wage labor (Schulz et al 1982: 36–44).

adequate drainage. Reduction in total size of family holdings appears to have been accompanied by reduction in the number of plots per household and thereby, of ecological diversity. Still, families attempt to obtain dispersed plots of diverse soil types in order to maximize their food security in the face of environmental risks.

More than half the families surveyed reported seasonal hunger beginning toward the end of the dry season when grain stocks are exhausted and lasting until December when new crops ripen. Nearly one-fifth (19 percent) reported family members still hungry after meals. Seven percent reported symptoms of *bwaki* malnutrition in the family. In households where men consume large amounts of banana beer, sex differences in nutrition are likely to be especially pronounced, with men getting far more calories and other nutrients in proportion to work energy expended.

Beans are grown by virtually all families (96 percent), while beer bananas (74 percent) and manioc (74 percent) are grown by most. Yields of the latter crop are low due to the altitude. Most households (74 percent) also grow maize and 43 percent grow sorghum interplanted with beans. Small gardens of sweet potato, yams and taro are planted near the houses by 44 percent. The average household plants 34 percent of its land in beans, mainly interplanted with other crops; 30 percent is devoted to bananas and 30 percent to manioc in various stages of growth. Fallowing has virtually disappeared from the farming system and crop yields are said to be declining despite the use of vegetal debris and other wastes.

In other respects the system appears to have changed little since the study made more than 25 years earlier by Hecq and Lefébvre (1958). In contrast to those who blame peasants for the area's ecological problems (cf. Jurion and Henry 1967), these authors proposed that the indigenous crop rotation system was a rational adaptive response to the constraints and possibilities of the local ecological and sociopolitical systems (Hecq and Lefébvre 1961). "A peasant's dependence on land ties him to his village, keeps him firmly subjected to his chiefs, and obliges him to pay illegal tribute" (Sosne 1979: 200).

Cultivator households are not simple resource pooling units; work and resources are allocated on the basis of differential social power structured on the basis of wealth, sex and age. The Shi normative stereotype allocates agricultural labor to women, who are considered to be stronger and more resilient than men. Once land has been cleared, women do the major share of the labor on all but the beer banana plots. Since most land is under continuous cultivation, men have even less to do on food crop plots than formerly. Continuous cropping encourages vigorous weed growth; women's work has increased in this respect. Women's work loads are heavy throughout the year due to the rainfall distribution which allows two or three crops to be grown each year and to their daily domestic chores, including carrying water up the steep slopes. While there are seasons in which women work longer hours, there is no slack season. Working days of twelve hours are common; time for child care and food preparation is held to a minimum—with deleterious consequences for the nutrition and health of young children.[15]

Banana beer is made, drunk and sold by men, whose labor day as peasants typically ends at noon. In the poorest households where all land is devoted to food production, men may help their wives in land preparation, sowing and weeding when they are at home. As hired laborers, too, men may perform virtually all agricultural tasks. Nevertheless, men with sufficient land of their own tend to work only on cash crops and bananas. To avoid "women's work" is a matter of masculine pride. These gender roles are not necessarily "traditional" or pre-colonial. In the Eastern Highlands where wealthy men were able to establish clientelist relations involving both livestock and land, many poor men worked alongside their wives in the superior's fields.

Not all the food grown is consumed at home. Nearly one-quarter of the beans, about one-third of sorghum and manioc, one-half of maize and two-thirds of banana beer are sold. Predictably, households with

---

[15]Manioc is laborious to process and does not store well. During peak work seasons which coincide with the rains, women tend to spend less time in food processing and cooking. Meal is less finely stamped and less digestible. To save time on wood gathering, cooking may be done only once per day or even every two days, resulting in high bacteria counts. Both conditions lead to high risk of diarrheal diseases, particularly in young children. A study made in The Gambia of bacterial growth in cooked food left standing discovered that in the hot rainy season levels of *E.coli* rise to dangerous levels after one hour (Barrell and Rowland 1979). Furthermore, "poor food handling is caused by unduly arduous work pressure on village mothers" (Rowland et al 1981: 174) which makes food contamination inevitable.

the most land also sell the most produce and are the ones employing non-family labor. However, poor households with insufficient land and crop yields to provide adequate family nutrition also may sell some produce. When shortfalls occur (as in the unusual drought of 1985) they may be able to obtain beans by working for more fortunate neighbors.

All households need cash. As in many areas of Africa, husbands and wives typically keep their cash resources separate. Among the middle peasants, men's incomes result primarily from beer and women's from food sales. Sometimes women sell beans and buy cassava, which is cheaper but of poorer nutritional value, to obtain cash (Newbury and Schoepf 1989). About half of the households raise a few animals which can bring them occasional cash or act as a temporary storehouse of wealth. Goats, sheep and especially cattle are concentrated in the households working larger amounts of land. In one third of the households, children raise guinea pigs which they consume themselves. Adult men, particularly, scorn this source of animal protein.

The landless and peasants with insufficient land must seek wage employment, primarily on farms or in the agro-industrial sector. Despite the low wage rates, Sosne found in 1972 that "plantation jobs remain in high demand as they offer the only source of regular income" (Sosne ibid.). Incomes of most were so low that families could not afford adequate nutrition; those with higher income did purchase foods and improved their diets (CAB 1971).

The National Legume Project's mission was to develop soybean production by improving seed varieties adapted to tropical high altitude envirnoments. In this it achieved some success. The new varieties are now grown by missions which distribute prepared soy flour as part of their nutrition programs. They also purchase peasant-grown soybeans and sorghum. Several large farms use soybeans and sorghum to feed livestock—primarily chickens sold in urban markets to the bourgeoisie. If veterinary programs spread and cattle herds are upgraded (see below) more high-quality feeds will be needed.

With respect to peasant nutrition, however, the impact of new soybeans is limited. A small percentage of women in the sample households—six percent—grow soybeans, mainly for sale to nutrition clinics. The crop is not particularly esteemed as a food, although some use it like peanut flour to thicken the sauce, since neither peanuts nor oil palm grow at this altitude. Most women said they had all they could do to find sufficient land for beans. Their expressed needs were for higher bean yields, cheap, improved hand tools, better storage and especially more land. These needs have become more acute over the intervening years since already low manioc yields have dwindled as a result of the rising incidence of insect pests and diseases.[16]

Peasants and Plantations

Plantations producing export crops are described by many officials and expatriate advisors as the "modern", "dynamic" sector. Peasants, who produce mainly food, are viewed as "traditional" "subsistence" cultivators. Conceived as separate the two sectors actually compete for resources. The dual economy notion serves to obscure their interrelationship *within* the capitalist economy. Ngirabakunzi (1984) writes of Rutshuru Zone in North Kivu:

> In the new mode of production imposed by colonization, the peasantry finds itself both subordinated to capital and marginalized. It lies upstream as a labor supply reservoir, downstream as a consumer of industrial goods, by its side as an economic partner and under its heel as a dominated and declining political and economic force.

Pharmakina, the Zairian subsidiary of a German transnational consortium, operates with Zaire government participation. Reported to be the area's largest land holder, it has extensive concessions totalling some 7,000 hectares in Kabare. Its main processing factory lies on the road to Bukavu, the regional capital. The company's labor policies are reputed to be extremely repressive (Mateso 1977). Nevertheless, as the largest employer it attracts workers from throughout the area. In the 1970s internationally-funded projects began promoting the *"relance"* of export crops by providing subsidized credit and inputs (e.g. the FED's *Relance Théicole*).[17] Although recovery has been

---

[16]As of March 1985 the USAID-funded National Manioc Program had not yet tested disease and pest-resistent varieties for the medium altitude areas.

[17]Members of the state bourgeoisie obtained plantations held by settlers as a result of a 1973 "Zairianization" decree which also created some state farms. Subsequently, under the terms of *rétrocession* decreed in 1975, some Zairians

slowed by high petroleum prices, transport costs and fluctuating terms of trade, the plantations can be made profitable, partly because (as in the colonial period) the government holds minimum wages to below-subsistence levels. Many are labor intensive and use few modern inputs.

While wages in Zaire are among the lowest in the world, wages paid in Kivu are the lowest in Zaire. A plantation worker working a six-hour day got only 2 to 3 Zaires per month, equivalent to $4–6 in 1972 (Sosne 1979: 203). Since that time the rate has been further reduced. In April, 1985 the minimum wage for agricultural work was 6 Zaires per day. Devaluation made this equivalent to US $0.12 daily or $3 per month—below the cost of food subsistence. In Kabare and other areas situated near plantations, women who are landless or whose husbands give them too little land for growing food may work for wages. Young women also may seek plantation work before they marry. Women are concentrated in the lowest paid jobs. Women and children provide most of the casual labor employed in hoeing, tea picking and stripping quinine bark.[18] Better paying jobs in the processing plants are reserved to men. Labor force segmentation creates and maintains wage differentials. One manager explains: "Men will not work in the fields. For these jobs we are forced to hire women" (interview April 1985). He reports that the regular workers are better nourished than are most full-time peasants. A major attraction of plantation work is that it may provide access to land on which to grow some food—and perhaps to health services, as well.

Many plantations require women to leave their babies at home so as not to interfere with the work. Nursed early in the morning and not again until 7, 8 or even 10 hours later, young infants who are given only manioc gruel or water in the interval, literally starve. "In Kivu today, *bwaki* is not just a disease of the weanling child; nurslings are

entered into partnerships with former owners or new investors. The coffee boom of 1977-1980 acted as a spur. While complete figures are unavailable, ranches and plantations now occupy a substantial portion of the best lands throughout the Eastern Highlands corridor. Properties held by the Mobutu family's CELZA company are among the largest and include tea estates in Kabare and Walungu Zones.

[18]At piece rates of 0.60 Zaire per box, some exceptionally fast workers are able to earn more than the minimum wage.

also affected'' (CAB 1984:3). Without digestible, nutritious supplemental foods, babies who suckle infrequently from the breasts of
overworked, underfed mothers, succumb.

Both poor peasant cultivators and landless wage laborers are themselves at risk from both debilitation and acute hunger. Malnutrition
and overwork combine with pregnancy and lactation demands to over-
whelm women, especially. By 1984 the situation had worsened to the
point that "today 5 percent of bwaki cases are adults," mainly nurs-
ing women (CAB 1984: 3; interviews 1985). The Committee pointed
to the need to organize primary health care services and protect the
land from further erosion. Neither the land question nor wage rates
are mentioned in any of the reports consulted.

Cash Crops, Hunger and the Subordination of Women

Over the 20 years of the Anti-Bwaki Committee's existence, its education campaigns have raised people's consciousness of the relative
nutritional values of foods. Where CAB associates have installed
mills for grinding sorghum and maize, these crops have experienced a
limited renaissance. Most mothers in the 1981–82 Mulungu survey
correctly identified nutritious weaning foods and 40 percent had experience in preparing soybean flour (C. Schoepf 1982b). They are
aware that grains and legumes provide healthy diets. Nutrition remains inadequate not because mothers lack information, but because
they lack resources, just as in the period prior to the introduction of
nutrition education (CEMBUAC cited in CAB 1971: 21).

Where the internationally funded projects or local entrepreneurs operate processing plants, peasant men have responded by cultivating
quinine, tea, coffee, and papaya (papaine) depending on the region.
Hired labor is in abundant supply from among the landless and near-
landless of Bushi as well as from Rwanda. Export crops, principally
coffee grown under the shade of banana groves, have come to cover
the lower slopes and plateaux of the eastern mountains in areas accessible by road. The area devoted to food production has declined:

Since they do not have money to buy new lands, the men plant quinine in fields
formerly planted to food crops. . . . . Food crops are pushed away from the roads to
small plots on the steep slopes; overexploited, they give dwindling yields
(Bosmans1981: 51–53).

Peasant export crop production has exacerbated land conflicts and resulted in increasing differentiation, both between households and within households, between women and men. Unhappy about having too little land, women protest that "soon they won't have anything left but quinine roots to suck on." In Bashi culture, "*à très forte dominance masculine,*" men conduct both village and family affairs (Bosmans 1981:51-53). In these households women are pressed into work on men's cash crops, while food, grown on marginal land, is the exclusive business of women. Although women make decisions about their own labor on food crops and control the products, decisions about land allocation within the family are typically made by men who are the holders or inheritors of land obtained by various forms of contractual arrangements. Cash earned by men is seldom contributed to family food purchases.

Conflict between spouses is reported to occur over the use of cash resources. Women readily acknowledge that sometimes they sell produce from their fields without their husbands' knowledge. They need cash to purchase items not produced at home:[19] salt, soap, oil, fish, sugar, tea . . . and cloth.[20] Today cloth is a major consumption item. Everyone—except village toddlers and perhaps some Mbuti deep in the Ituri forest[21]—now goes covered. In both rural and urban areas

---

[19]Some of these consumer items are essential to health; others have become socially necessary. Salt is a dietary essential which is no longer produced from burning marsh grasses or from local salt springs and must be purchased. Iodized or sea salts, essential in preventing goiter, a condition particularly common on Idjwi Island in Lake Kivu, are most expensive. Soap is a major factor in reducing the incidence of diarrheal disease and skin infections. It is thus an essential item in preventing nutrient loss and the loss of labor time due to sickness. Oil and fish also supply nutrients essential to health maintenance. Clothing is socially necessary and offers protection against the damp chill and respiratory infections frequent in the mountain environment. Hides are no longer worn.

[20]The tyranny of cloth in the Ivory Coast is the subject of a brilliant article by Mona Etienne (1980). In Zaire the production process is different, but the tyranny no less harsh.

[21]Some Mbuti bands are enmeshed in commodity relationships with petty traders who supply salt, rice, cloth, clothing and ID cards in exchange for game meat which they resell in urban areas (Hart 1978). Other Mbuti serve in a special unit of the Zairian Armed Forces (FAZ) where they acquired a fearsome reputation in western Shaba (fieldnotes 1978).

cloth is a marker of social status. Men "should" buy gifts of cloth for their wives. Often poor men cannot, for they have other imperatives: the state's taxes and fines, bribes to officials, tools, school expenses, their own used clothes, seeds, medical care, their friends and relations, all require cash. Many women must buy their own cloth and uniforms for school children. They often contribute to school fees as well. Each family attempts to send at least one son to secondary school in hope that he will obtain a salaried post and be able to provide parents' old age security. Declining opportunities and real wages mean that these hopes are increasingly frustrated but, without an alternate strategy the behavior persists. Men argue that women sell too much food, and keep too little for family consumption and seeds.[22] They claim that women have money hidden away (interviews 1985). Women acknowledge that although this is sometimes the case, they have little choice.

Remote as their dispersed hilltop settlements appear, people in eastern Kivu are no longer actors in a purely domestic economy. The past hundred years have shattered rural self-sufficiency and peasants must have cash to maintain their consumption levels. Thus they are as unable to withdraw from the market as they are to secede from the Zairian state.[23] As with other types of victim-blaming or scapegoating

---

[22]The 1985 Peace Corps planning team heard this theme expressed during a meeting with men in a village in Bandundu region, as well. It is a particular instance of a more general tendency to blame women for whatever goes wrong (cf. Schoepf et al. 1988). As a battle between the sexes, this type of scapegoating tends to deflect attention from exploitation by traders and officials. Market women are a favorite target of the latter (cf Lemarchand 1979: 255) and of extortion by the military.

Among the matrilineal Buma, in a neighboring area of Bandundu region, the evolution of manioc cash cropping by women is related to their emancipation from male control via manipulation of gifts of cloth (Hochegger 1973: 27). During the colonial period, when men worked for wages but few cash outlets for women's produce existed, "wives had to implore humbly to obtain a new pagne." As markets expanded with post-independence urban growth, women increased their manioc growing and processing activities. Those who succeeded—mainly older women who could command the labor of adolescent daughters and sons—were able to buy their own cloth, even high quality Dutch wax prints.

[23]To write about "articulation" between pre-capitalist or non-capitalist and capitalist modes of production in the present tense (cf van Binsbergen and

mechanisms, sexism here deflects attention from exploitation by plantations, traders and officials, as well as from the serious land shortage among the poor.

Government officials attribute responsibility for malnutrition to population pressure, to erosion and to peasant men whose banana groves and cash crops take up land that would otherwise be used to grow food (interviews 1985). Beer drinking is also implicated in alcoholism, another serious health problem reported in the area and in physical abuse of women and children. None of these social problems should be blamed upon the victims, however, since they are the result of socially structured patterns of access to strategic resources.

As indicated above, population densities have indeed increased since the 1920s, partly as a result of land alienation. In zones that were less densely populated, the colonial administration provoked permanent migration from Rwanda to provide European settlers with cheap farm labor (Bucyalimwe 1984). Reduced birth intervals and other policies originating in the colonial period also contributed to population increase (Bezy, Peemans, and Wautelet 1981; Schoepf and Schoepf 1981). The latter included ideological, medical and legal assaults upon abortion and infanticide and lowered age at marriage consequent upon male wage labor. Moreover, the intensification of family labor on small plots and the use of older children as plantation workers has led to high population growth rates in other parts of the world (Mamdani 1973; White 1973; McCormack et al. 1986). Although data are lacking, research should be undertaken to identify the interrelated economic and social dynamics underlying population pressure in the Eastern Highlands.

Beer is also a strategic resource. The Mulungu baseline survey found that the average household devoted 30 percent of its land to bananas. Much of the beer was sold, but the poorest 26 percent of households had no banana groves. Where bananas are planted on steep slopes they tend to limit, rather than to exacerbate erosion. Beer is important in social relationships between males, including client-

---

Geschire 1985; Verhagen 1984) is to reduce the transformations of African societies and cultures by colonial capitalism over the past hundred years to a collection of trait-lists (Schoepf 1975a,b; Schoepf and Schoepf 1981; Schoepf in preparation b).

ship relations and payments to officials. Without beer to give men are not considered full adults. Unless the entire structure of land holding is altered, bananas will remain essential to the household economy. Such transformation of land use as is currently taking place does not open new opportunities for peasant food production either by women or men. Attributing malnutrition to bananas and population pressure without looking at the overall pattern of resource control constitutes one more form of victim-blaming.

The apparently simple gender role dichotomy requires qualification. Not all Bashi women are peasants. Not all Bashi women are subordinate to all men today nor were they in the past. In the stratified pre-colonial system, women of the Baluzi ruling clan were ranked above male commoners. Wealthy women could command a client labor force of both men and women. Poor men performed agricultural work of all kinds. The current *Mwamikazi*, a widow of the late *Mwami* of Kabare, is reputed to be extremely clever and powerful. Recognized by the government as Chief of Kabare *Collectivité* (cf Kabare Zone 1981), at the time of fieldwork in 1982 she was politicking to influence the succession to the "traditional" position in favor of her teen-age son, who was not the first-in-line. [24] The peasant house-holds whose farming practices were surveyed, however, are poor commoners. Among them, wives, daughters and sisters are subordinate to husbands, fathers and brothers, all of whom are subordinate to the wealthy and powerful in both the Shi and wider systems of social relations.

As the contributions of women to household income from outside sources increase substantially, changes in gender relations may occur. For example, Nande women from the North Kivu zones of Beni and Lubero have become active in trade both within Zaire and across neighboring frontiers. A few have become quite wealthy (MacGaffey 1986). Others have brought new resources to households headed by poor peasants and wage workers. These women are reported thereby to have increased their claims to personal autonomy and decision-making authority with respect to children.

---

[24]The succession conflict continued and in 1987 was the subject of a parliamentary investigation which reviewed the ethnography without taking sides. The affair remained unsettled until the death of the contender in 1988, when his claim was considered to have become extinct.

Research is needed to determine whether the above perception of gender role changes is correct and if so, whether they are translated into improved nutritional status. Middle class male development workers spoke disparagingly of such women, in terms which reminded us of Packard's (1980) historical account: in the past women who attempted to circumvent male control were scapegoated when misfortunes befell the Nande kingdoms.

This brief section indicates that gender relations deriving from precolonial social organization have taken on new dimensions as the area was subordinated to colonial capitalism. Nevertheless, increasing misery such as that documented here should not be interpreted as entirely precluding women's ability to organize in defense of their interests. Newbury (1984a) reports a tax revolt by Tembo women of neighboring Kalehe Zone in 1982. Supported by their church group,[25] peasant women confronted officials who imposed new taxes. Although they were partially successful in getting some market levies abolished, the women could not address the real causes of their poverty: a declining farming system and dependency on income from crops sold to monopsonist buyers on unfavorable terms.

Land Hunger and Class Formation

In an earlier section we cited studies indicating the role of capitalist agriculture in the impoverishment of the peasantry in this area during

---

[25]The local Catholic organization has provided support for women's survival struggles here, as elsewhere in Zaire in recent years. These include women's rural cooperative participation in Katanga village, southeastern Shaba, and Gandajika, Eastern Kasai, (cf B. G. Schoepf 1980, 1985a,b,c, 1986) and urban women's consciousness-raising groups in Kinshasa (Walu Engundu 1985 personal communication). Several Protestant church leaders interviewed in 1985 appear to be less involved in the social struggle and less clear on the subject of women's special burdens. For example, an Evangelical catechism, *Christ Loved the Church,* which continues to circulate among Swahili-reading Protestants, contains a section on the "work of women". It uses Biblical citations to maintain that women must be submissive to men, that women may neither teach nor ask questions in the church, and still less aspire to leadership (see MacDonald 1967: 56–60). The pattern is an old one, noted for the Catholic Church, as well, by Comhaire-Sylvain in 1950 (cited in Bose rup 1970: 60).

the colonial period. Today further land appropriation is taking place. High government officials, big businessmen, "traditional elites" and local traders or "*opérateurs économiques,*" as well as large firms and Zairo-Expatriate partnerships, all are in quest of peasant-occupied lands, including those held in *kalinzi* tenure. Although many peasants consider them to be tantamount to purchase (CAB 1971: 10) and exhibit proudly the slips of paper evidencing their registry, *kalinzi* lands are actually insecure (C.Schoepf 1982a).

Changes in land law decreed by the Mobutu regime alter the terms by which peasants and others throughout the country hold and gain access to the use of land (Inonga 1976; Lumpungu 1977). The claims of clan and village communities to hold ancestral lands in perpetuity are abolished. While the complementary legislation governing community land holding has yet to be written, the state *de facto* has abrogated community rights—even to permanently occupied lands. In theory, this "national integration" measure (W. MacGaffey 1982) means that all Zairians now can have equal access to land throughout the national territory (Lumpungu 1981). In actual fact, it means that those with power, wealth and influence are able to manipulate the system to appropriate any lands not yet conceded and titled (Lemarchand 1979; Lumpungu 1981; MacGaffey 1982; Schoepf and Schoepf 1984)—even including those currently occupied. It also means that some officials can increase their incomes by awarding titles. Furthermore, since the state can revoke concessions defined as insufficiently "dynamic" and re-allocate them, security of tenure is linked to continuing political favor. Thus land concessions enter the patrimonial system and the sociopolitical dynamics of class formation. The officials of *Titres Fonciers*, the concession-granting agency, have become enormously powerful (Lumpungu 1981).

Dispossessions are referred to as "*spoliation*". Entire communities are despoiled to make way for plantations and cattle ranches. Between January 1979 and July 1983 more than one thousand new land title petitions were filed at the title registry office for North Kivu (Katuala 1985: 25). Big businessmen, multinational firms, government officials and chiefs have been involved. Repression, including arbitrary arrests, extortion and crop destruction have been employed against peasants who refused to abandon homes and fields. Many have been forced off the land; others now work in exchange for squatters' rights.

There has been significant resistance, as well. During the same period there were 61 formal complaints against despoilment and 116 requests to annul the decisions of "customary" authorities for fraudulent appropriation. A few peasants have used violence against new acquisitors and their agents (Katuala 1985; Newbury 1984b; interviews 1985). In 1983 the lands of some 2,000 families were restituted following mediation by the Catholic bishop and leaders of ACOGENOKI, a federation of livestock producer cooperatives (Katuala 1985). The latter continue to represent members' interests against the "despoilers" despite pressure from officials (interviews 1985).

The current attraction of the Northeastern Corridor for large ranchers is enhanced by the presence of internationally funded herd health projects which provide veterinary coverage and medicines not available from government services. Ranching is a means toward capital accumulation, for as in Shaba (Schoepf and Schoepf 1984) property titles are used as collateral to obtain bank loans; a "gold rush for titles" is the result (Katuala 1985:25). Credit is supplied through local commercial and development banks. Capital obtained in this manner can be used to buy livestock as a hedge against inflation or for other purposes including commerce, the hotel business, etc. Road improvements are being made which will further increase the attractiveness of the area to the bourgeoisie, leading to greater income disparities and adding to the survival problems of the poor (cf Cook 1985 for examples of this elsewhere).

Considerable wealth is being accumulated in the flourishing "irregular" economy of the highlands (cf Bianga 1982; J. MacGaffey 1981; Vwakyanakazi 1982). Traders operating across the borders typically exchange coffee, gold and cattle for scarce consumer durables and trucks with which to move them. While these authors emphasize the absence of the state in connection with this "second economy," numerous officials also are reported to be involved in smuggling, trading on their own account and, for a fee, closing their eyes to the activities of others (Callaghy 1984; D. Newbury 1986; CS/BGS interviews). Ranches, which serve as storehouses for some of this wealth, are adding to the land hunger and the food crisis. The government loses potential tax revenues but the state itself (in the sense of a ruling class organ) is made stronger by the increased flow of resources through the patronage system.

Accumulation involves competition between ascendant locals and members of the state bourgeoisie. Such conflict provides oportunities for self-serving ethnic discourse (C. Newbury 1984b, B. G. Schoepf 1975b). Transformation of conflict over land into ethnic conflict is advantageous for those able to assert "traditional" claims, which in reality date only from the colonial period (D. Newbury 1986). These are used to legitimate new appropriations (Schoepf and Schoepf 1987). Ethnic conflict is a classical political safety valve against class conflict and ethnic solidarities cement patron-client relations. The land question is not only related to clientelist national politics, however. Its international aspect lies in the development finance, policy advice and expertise supplied by western governments giving aid to Zaire. These are linked to patronage networks in all fields, including that of agricultural development and research, where the privatization of government-held resources has become the international buzz-word (cf World Bank 1982).

Land shortage and the crisis of peasant agriculture undoubtedly have fueled massive rural exodus from the region. Highlands towns grow at 8 to 10 percent annually, forming clusters of 40,000 to 100,000 people that look like sprawling villages and live from little else than trade. For many of the dispossessed, hawking, distilling home-brew, digging gold and smuggling present ways to survive and fuel dreams of growing wealthy. These survival strategies and the dreams which few will actually realize also serve as safety valves against growing discontent. Young women who face a bleak future of drudge labor on small farms and plantations leave the countryside with even more alacrity than men despite the dearth of urban employment. Peasant men complain that they cannot find brides. Women predominate in the regional capital, Bukavu, where the administrative census of 1959 and the sample count of 1970 found many more men than women. The census of 1984 enumerated slightly fewer men than women (49:51), a reversal of the general urban sex ratio of 51:49 (GOZ 1984). The census figures indicate that while Kivu's case is extreme, rural women have been departing the villages throughout Zaire. As Staudt (1987) points out, irregular, or "off-the-books" activities by African women are part of their efforts to direct their labor into channels where they can exercise some control over their production and trade.

A Brief Comparison

In a vast, multi-cultural nation, gender opportunities and deprivations cannot be assumed to be uniform. In earlier papers we have examined ways in which an agricultural development project's neglect of the role and status of women contributed to failure to meet project objectives in southeastern Shaba region (B. G. Schoepf and C. Schoepf 1984; B. G. Schoepf 1985b, 1987; also see Newbury and Schoepf 1989). The National Maize Program developed a high-yielding variety and advised peasants to plant increased surfaces with the new maize. Planners had expected that men, whom they viewed as household heads, could direct the labor of other family members. They held to these assumptions despite protests by women that project methods required too much of their labor and interfered with gardening and other tasks (B. G. Schoepf 1975c) Our field study of farming systems and gender relations, conducted in 1976–1978, discovered that most women exercised considerable autonomy in agricultral decision-making. Women's relative independence was supported by their land rights and control income from their cash crops. These rights were reinforced by the local matrilineal ideology, uxorilocal post-marital residence and bride-service. In the case of conflicting demands, children tended to work for mothers rather than for fathers or maternal uncles. Women's concern to preserve a cropping system that yields a steady supply of both vegetable sauce ingredients and cash with which to purchase cooking oil, salt and fish in small amounts throughout the year, limited their collaboration in maize production improvement projects directed at their husbands.

Women in that community were also more able to control their nutrient intake relative to that of men than were the less autonomous women of neighboring groups. A comparative nutrition survey made in 1958 found that, whereas most other women were nutritionally deprived, the women of the Lemba hamlet consumed a slightly greater share of proteins and other essential nutrients than men in proportion to body height and weight (Lambrechts and Bernier 1961). Rather than eating men's leftovers, as is the case in many cultures in Zaire (and elsewhere, cf Rosenberg 1980;B. G. Schoepf Mali fieldnotes 1979, 1984), Lemba women set aside portions of meal and sauce—including animal protein foods—for themselves and for the children eating with them, before serving men. Where women contribute heavily to agricultural work, food processing and preparation, such an allocation is rational in terms of energy replacement, particularly when they reproduce and nourish infants (Palmer 1981; B. G. Schoepf 1985b).

Such change combined with deepening poverty may result in emergence of sex differential nutrition patterns in the future. Further comparative analysis is the subject of other papers (Newbury and Schoepf 1989; Schoepf and Schoepf in preparation). The data presented here indicate that women's status in Zaire is both variable and of central concern when food crisis and food crop production are at issue.

Conclusion

The crisis of peasant reproduction, which has worsened in many parts of Africa during the past decade, has deep roots in the eastern Kivu highlands. It is being exacerbated by changes brought about by the current class formation process as accumulation strategies pursued by dominant classes continue to drain resources from peasant production systems. Explanations of the causes of African food crisis are as diverse as those which attempt to account for the origins of male dominance and female subordination. Although some have proposed "naturalistic" explanations of both phenomena—ecological destruction and overpopulation for the first, biological sex differences for the second—social explanatory paradigms appear to be more powerful in both cases. With Berry (1984) we seek explanations in "changing conditions of access to economic opportunity and productive resources."

This paper offers a dynamic view of struggles over resources in one area of Zaire. From the analysis of gender roles in a local farming system we have proceeded to examine broader issues. We do not claim that the agrarian system around the Mulungu Research Station is typical of Zaire, nor even of the Eastern Highlands. Rather, diversity of ecology and production systems are the area's hallmark. However, viewing the local system in relation to a "macrosystem" with its characteristic sociopolitical relations offers a framework in which other local variants have their special place (Schoepf 1980a). Similarly, Bifuko (1977, 1978) shows how development projects, parastatals and mercantilist activities have contributed to the declining condition of the peasantry in the nearby Ruzizi Valley where quite different ecological conditions prevail.

Many students agree that privatization of societal resources by the state or politico-commercial bourgeoisie is a major function of the contemporary Zairian state. The economy remains primarily dependent on the export of minerals. The imbalance created during the colonial period has been accentuated by technological advances and the organization of international finance over the past two decades. Zaire's copper dependency was increased as a result of the first IMF stabilization program introduced in 1967 and further expansion begun in 1975 (World Bank 1977). In 1985, funds were sought for a third phase of the national copper/cobalt investment program which would allow processing of these raw materials to be completed in Zaire. However, copper prices have remained below World Bank low option projections during the decade, as have cobalt prices with the exception of a sharp rise for two years following the Shaba rebellions. Metals dependency has not only affected government finances; it has also shaped the fundamental pattern of industrialization, urban growth and rural impoverishment (Jewsiewicki 1977; Kabwit 1979; B. G. Schoepf 1975a,b). Industry, commerce and finance remain heavily concentrated under the control of large-scale transnational firms. The classic role of international lending is "to assume the transfer of 'metropolitan' capital to ensure that private capital operations remain profitable and that the global equilibrium" is maintained (Jewsiewicki 1979; 51). However, declining terms of trade and local accumulation strategies combined with continuing foreign domination of technology, industrial production, investment policy and finance have led to economic crisis over the past fifteen years (Gran, ed. 1979; Jewsiewicki, ed. 1984; Nzongola, ed. 1986; Young and Turner 1985). The general crisis has been exacerbated to the point of chaos by pervasive corruption which has been an integral part of international support and of state power during the Mobutist period. One result is declining profitability of transnational enterprise.

Policy shifts have occurred in response to pressure from international lending agencies which have gained trememdous leverage as a result of the massive public foreign debt. These "structural adjustments" include devaluation, an end to foreign exchange controls, free repatriation of profits, an end to parastatal monopolies and decontrol of many food prices. Debt service payments have necessitated stringent budget cuts. During the past five years the central government has provided few resources to peripheral areas. Consequently local administrations have imposed new taxes on peasants and traders, while partial decontrol of rural producer prices has benefited mainly the traders. Devaluation and inflation have raised prices of tools and consumer goods; terms of trade have become even more unfavorable for peasant households, particularly for those located at some distance from large marketplaces (B. G. Schoepf 1985a).

One result of this "economic stabilization policy" is increased pressure on peasant production systems. Peasants are pressured to produce more, to sell more and to do so on less land. They also must consume less and thus have less health and energy. Within peasant households the unequal gender division of roles and responsibilities and male dominance in resource control may further jeopardize the family food suply. At the same time the ideology and practice of male dominance lead many men to a relative sense of superiority, and some to alcoholism and family violence. These and other safety valves noted above limit the ability of poor men and women to focus on the underlying causes of their common, but different, exploitation. When peasants are the losers in such circumstances, women and children are the first and foremost sufferers. Since women are also the major food producers, the crisis of peasant reproduction and women's special burdens are fundamental to contemporary food crisis.

As noted above, only 28 percent of Kabare *Collectivité* households whose fields were measured had more than one hectare. Yet more and more peasant lands are being despoiled by the politico-commercial class in the guise of "land reform." Without genuine land reform which provides adequate resources to peasant households—particularly to women—and agriculture-based industrialization to provide jobs at a living wage, the subsistence needs of the poor majority cannot be met. Those who remain on the land need new technology to improve the productivity and reduce the drudgery of labor, particularly women's labor (Palmer 1981; B. G. Schoepf 1980b). This might include needs already identified by women in Eastern Kivu: higher bean yields, improved water supplies, better tools for land preparation and weeding and manioc processing technology and ways of restoring or maintaining soil fertility which are realistic in terms of labor time. Agricultural research in Zaire needs to be applied especially to reducing the burdens of poor rural women. However, as we have argued, class forces operating in the regional, national and international arenas are unlikely to respond positively to these needs.

The state continues to be an arena of intense struggle over which classes will control the amount and forms of surplus accumulation. With Newbury (1984b, 1986) we find that some important changes in the nature of this struggle are currently taking place. As international lending has dwindled, the entry gates into the state bourgeoisie have narrowed. This has had repercussions on the clientelist redistribution system. Commercial agriculture is a safety valve institution in which entrepreneurial capital can, with help from subsidies legitimated by international support or "privatization," find avenues for profit-making. This process contributes to the maintenance of state power by providing new resources for reinforcing patron-client relations in the face of increasing scarcity.

New pressures are being generated by shifting alliances between commercial and industrial interests, expatriates and Zairians (cf Bemba 1982 for an example). While these groups press their demands for economic reforms and probity, there is little likelihood that they will alter the nature of dominant class and state relations with the peasantry. Nor will they alter the fundamental pattern of what Verhagen (1984) terms "technological imperialism," by which the transnational firms continue to dominate and drain the national economy.

In the absence of solutions to the agrarian crisis, food production will continue to fall short of national needs and the condition of poor urban and rural families will worsen. Female rural exodus will continue. Yet Zairian women will be unable to provide even current levels of education for their daughters—a solution suggested by Guyer (1984) for women in other areas faced with discriminatory patterns of agricultural change. Without diplomas and special skills to help them compete in the oversupplied formal sector job market, young women will join the crowded ranks of petty traders. As we show elsewhere, these activities are less and less viable; more than ever, women are constrained to offer sexual services in exchange for subsistence (Schoepf 1988; Walu and Schoepf forthcoming). In the past, poor women with multiple sexual partners and their children encountered substantial health risks (Schoepf and Schoepf 1981). In the present period, the burgeoning AIDS pandemic has turned what formerly was a survival strategy into a death strategy.

Bibliography

Ames, Peter, Brooke G. Schoepf and others 1981 Zaire Country Environmental Profile, Phase II. Washington DC: USAID.

Barrell, R.A.E. and M.G.M. Rowland 1979 Infant Foods as a Potential Source of Diarrhoeal Disease in Rural West Africa. Transactions of the Royal Society of Tropical Medicine and Hygiene, 73, 1:85–90.

Bashizi Chirhagarhula 1978 Processus de Domination Socio-Economique et Marché du Travil au Bushi (1920–1945). Enquétes et Documents d'Histoire Africaine (Lubumbashi): Pp. 1–29.

Bemba Salona 1982 Les Entreprises Privées au Zaïre: Leur Role et leur Probleémes. Zaïre-Afrique (Kinshasa) 163:133–142.

Berry, Sara S. 1984 The Food Crisis and Agrarian Change in Africa: A Review Essay. African Studies Review 27, 1:59–112.

Bezy, Ferdinand, J. P. Peemans and J. M. Wautelet 1981 Accumulation et Sous-Développement au Zaïre, 1960–1980. Louvain-la-Neuve: Presses Universitaires de Louvain.

Bianga Warusi 1982 Peasant, State, and Rural Development in Post-Independent Zaire: A Case Study of 'Réforme Rurale' and its Implications. Ph.D. dissertation, University of Wisconsin-Madison.

Bifuko Baharanyi 1977 The Study of Management of Rural Development in Zaire: The Cases of the ONAFITEX and the Agro-Pastoral Project in the Ruzizi Valley 1969–1975. MA Thesis, University of Dar-es-Salaam.

———— 1978 Development Theories and the Study of Rural Development in the Uvira Zone in Eastern Zaire: From Colonial Times to the Post-Independence Experience. Paper presented at the Annual Meeting of the U.S. African Studies Association, Baltimore, November.

van Binsbergen, Wim and Peter Geschiere, eds. 1985 Old Modes of Production and Capitalist Encroachment: Anthropological Explorations in Africa. Boston: Routledge and Kegan Paul.

Boserup, Ester 1970 Woman's Role in Economic Development. New York: St. Martin's Press.

Bosmans, R. P. 1981 Des Vivres ou des Cultivateurs: Il Faut Choisir. In Comité Anti-Bwaki 1981:51–56.

Bucyalimwe Mararo 1984 Une Rationalisation? Les Migrations Rwandaises au Kivu, Zaïre. In Ambiguiteés de l'Innovation: Sociétés Rurales et Technologies en Afrique Centrale et Occidentale au XXéme Siécle. B. Jewsiewicki and Jean Chretien, eds. Pp. 39–54. Quebec: Safi.

Callaghy, Thomas M. 1984 The State-Society Struggle: Zaire in Comparative Perspective. New York: Columbia University Press.

Comité Anti-Bwaki, (CAB) 1971 Analyse de la Malnutrition au Bushi: un Probléme Economique et Médico-Social. Bukavu, Zaïre: Oeuvre pour la Lutte Contre le Bwaki et la Protection de l'Enfance.

———— 1975 Rétrospective 1965–1975 et Rapport Annuel 1974–1975. Bukavu, Zaïre. 1983–1984 Comptes-Rendus des Reunions Generales (mimeo).

Cook, Cynthia C. 1985 Social Analysis in Rural Road Projects. *In* Putting People First: Sociological Variables in Rural Development. Michael M. Cernea, ed. Pp.297–321. Washington, DC: Oxford University Press for The World Bank.

Etienne, Mona 1980 Women and Men, Cloth and Colonization: The Transformation of Production-Distribution Relations Among the Baule. *In* Women and Colonization: Anthropological Perspectives. M. Etienne and E B. Leacock, eds. Pp. 214–238. New York: Praeger.

Governement du Zaïre 1984 Combien sommes-nous? Recensement Scientifique de la Population. Kinshasa: Département du Plan.

Gran, Guy, ed. 1979 Zaire: The Political Economy of Underdevelopment. New York: Praeger.

Guyer, Jane 1984 "Women in the Rural Economy: Contemporary Variations"*In* Women South of the Sahara, M. J. Hay and S. Stichter, eds. London: Longman.

Hart, John A. 1978 From Subsistence to Market: A Case Study of the Mbuti Net Hunters. Human Ecology 6, 3:325–353.

Hecq, Jacques 1958 Le Systéme de Culture des Bashi (Kivu, Territoire de Kabare) et ses Possibilités. Bulletin Agricole du Congo Belge 9, 4:969–997.

Hecq, Jacques and A. Lefébvre 1959 Eléments de la Production Agricole au Bushi (Kivu, Territoire de Kabare): Recherche de la Superficie Nécessaire par Famille. Bulletin Agricole du Congo Belge 50, 1:285–293.

———— 1961 Rotations au Kivu. Bulletin Agricole du Congo Belge 52, 1:1–8.

Hochegger, Herman 1973 La Division du Travail entre l'Homme et la Femme chez les Buma. *In* Agriculture et Elevage dans l'Entre Kwango-Kasaï (République du Zaïre). H. Hochegger, ed. Pp. 20–52. Bandundu (Zaïre): Centre d'Etudes Ethnographiques.

Inonga Lokongo L'Ome 1976 Le Nouveau Régime Foncier Zaïrois, Revue Juridique du Zaïre, (Lubumbashi). Numéro Spécial:41–62.

Jewsiewicki, Bogumil 1977 Unequal Development: Capitalism and the Katanga Economy, 1919–40. *In* The Roots of Poverty in Central and Southern Africa. R. Palmer and N. Parsons, eds. Pp. 317–344. Berkeley and Los Angeles, CA: University of California Press.

———— 1979 Zaire Enters the World System: Its Colonial Incorporation as the Belgian Congo, 1885–1960. *In* Zaire, the Political Economy of Underdevelopment. Guy Gran, ed. Pp.29–63. New York: Praeger.

———— 1984 Introduction to Zaire Symposium. Canadian Journal of African Studies 18, 1:8–12.

Joye, Pierre and Rosina Lewin 1961 Les Trusts au Congol Brussels: Société Populaire d"Editions.

Kabala Matuka 1976 La Conservation de la Nature au Zaïre. Kinshasa: Lokele.

Kabare Zone, Kivu Region, Zaire 1981 Annual Report, Affaires Politiques.

Kabwit, Ghislain 1979 The Growth of Internal and External Opposition to the Mobutu Regime. *In* Zaire: The Political Economy of Underdevelopment. Guy Gran, ed. Pp. 283–295. New York: Praeger.

Katuala Kaba-Kashala 1985 le Phénoméne de 'spoliation': le Terme et le Fait dans la Sous-Région du Nord-Kivu. Grands Lacs (Information Bulletin of the CEPGL) 15:24–30.

Lambrechts, A. and Georges Bernier 1961 Enquéte Alimentaire et Agricole dans les Populations Rurales du Haut-Katanga. Lubumbashi: Centre d'Etudes des Problémes Sociaux Indigénes. Mémoires II.

Lele, Uma 1975 The design of Rural Development: Lessons From Africa. Baltimore: Johns Hopkins University Press.

Lemarchand, René 1979 The Politics of Penury in Rural Zaire: the View from Bandundu. *In* Zaire: The Political Economy of Underdevelopment. G. Gran, ed. Pp. 237–260. New York: Praeger.

Lumpungu Kalambay 1977 Land Tenure Systems and the Agricultural Crisis in Zaire. African Environment 2, 4 and 3, 1:57-71.

———— 1981 Le Nouveau Droit Foncier Zairois. Cahiers Economiques et Sociaux (Kinshasa) XIX, No. 1-2:100–110.

MacDonald, William 1967 (1962) Kristo Alipenda Kanisa. Bunia (Zaire): Editions Evangéliques.

MacGaffey, Janet 1986 "Women and Class Formation in a Dependent Economy: Kisangani Entrepreneurs." *In* Women and Class in Africa C. Robertson and I. Berger, eds. New York: Africana.

MacGaffey, Wyatt 1982 The Policy of National Integration in Zaire. Journal of Modern Africa Studies 20,1 (March): 87–105.

McCormack, Jeanne, Martin Walsh and Candace Nelson 1986 Women's Group Enterprises: A Study of the Structure of Opportunity on the Kenya Coast. Boston: World Education Inc.

Mamdani, Mamoud 1973 The Myth of Population Control: Family, Caste and Class in an Indian Village. New York: Monthly Review.

Mateso, M. 1977 La Pharmakina et son Incidence Sociale dans le Bushi. Mémoire de Licence en Sociologie Rurale, UNAZA, Lubumbashi, Département de Sociologie/Anthropologie.

Merlier, Michel 1962 Le Congo de la Colonisation Belge á l'Indépendance. Paris: Maspéro.

Moeller de Ladersous, A. 1930 Extrait d'une lettre envoyée au CNKi, 21 March 1930. Enquétes et Documents d'Histoire Africaine (Lubumbashi) 1978:32–38.

Newbury, Catharine A. 1984a Ebutumwa Bw'Emiogo: the Tyranny of Cassava: a Women's Tax Revolt in Eastern Zaire. Canadian Journal of African Studies, 18, 1:35–54.

———— 1984b Dead and Buried or Just Underground? The Privatization of the State in Zaire. Canadian Journal of African Studies, 18, 1:112–114.

—— 1986 Survival Strategies in Rural Zaire: Realities of Coping with Crisis. *In* The Crisis in Zaire: Myths and Realities. Nzongola-Ntalaja, ed. Pp. 99–112. Trenton, NJ: Africa World Press.

Newbury, Catharine A. and Brooke G. Schoepf 1989 "State, Peasantry and Agrarian Crisis in Zaire: Does Gender Make a Difference?" *In* Women and the State in Africa. J. L. Parpart and K. A. Staudt, eds. pp. 91–110. Boulder, CO: Lynne Rienner.

Newbury, David 1986 "From 'Frontier' to 'Boundary': Some Historical Roots of Peasant Strategies of Survival in Zaire." *In* The Crisis in Zaire: Myths and Realities. Nzongola-Ntalaja, ed. Pp. 87–97. Trenton, NJ: Africa World Press.

Ngirabakunzi Kaberuka 1976 Modes de Production et Rapports Socio-culturels dans la Zone de Rutschuru. Mémoire de Licence en Anthropologie, UNAZA, Lubumbashi.

—— 1983 Pastoralisme, Toparchie et Petite Production Paysanne dans la Zone de Rutshuru. Annales, No. 14:33–53. Lubumbashi: Centre d'Etudes Politiques pour l'Afrique Centrale (CEPAC).

Packard, Randall 1980 "Social Change and the History of Misfortune Among the Bashi of Eastern Zaire." *In* Explorations in African Systems of Thought, I. Karp and C. Bird, eds. pp. 237–267. Bloomington: Indiana University Press.

Palmer, Ingrid 1981 Seasonal Dimensions of Women's Roles. *In* Seasonal Dimensions of Rural Poverty. Robert Chambers, Richard Longhurst and Arnold Pacey, eds. Pp. 195–201. London: Frances Pinter.

Rogers, Barbara 1979 The Domestication of Women: Discrimination in Developing Societies. New York: St. Martin's Press.

Rosenberg, Ellen M. 1980 Demographic Effects of Sex Differential Nutrition. *In* Nutritional Anthropology: Contemporary Aproaches to Diet and Culture. Norge W. Jerome, Randy F. Kandel and Gretel H. Pelto, eds. Pp. 181–203. Pleasantville, N.Y.: Redgrave.

Rowland, M.G.M., A. Paul, A. M. Prentice, E. Muller, M. Hutton, R. A. E. Barrell and R. G. Whitehead 1981 Seasonality and the Growth of Infants in a Gambian village. *In* Seasonal Dimensions of Rural Poverty, R. Chambers, R. Longhurst and A. Pacey, eds. Pp. 164–175. London: Frances Pinter.

Schoepf, Brooke G. 1975a Villes et Campagnes dans le Haut-Shaba: Perspective sur le Developpement Inégal au Zaïre. Colloquim, History Department, National University of Zaire, Lubumbashi, February.

—— 1975a Rural Development in Zaire: Conceptual Models and Historical Perspective. Paper presented at the joint meeting of the U.S. and Netherlands Societies for Applied Anthropology, Amsterdam, April.

—— 1975c Family Farming and Green Revolution in the Lufira Valley, Research Proposal submitted to Rockefeller Foundation, Social Science Division.

—— 1980a Macrosystem Factors in Farming Systems Research, discussion paper. *In* Proceedings of the Second Workshop on Sahelian Agriculture. R. Morris and K. White, eds. Purdue University: Department of Agricultural Economics.

—— 1980b Women and Development: Overcoming the Colonial Legacy in Africa. Interview, Exchange Report. Mid-Decade NGO Conference. Copenhagen, July.

———— 1985a Macroeconomy, Microeconomy, Women's Roles and Introducing Agricultural Change. Pp. 11-35 of 'Priorité des Priorités': Zaire Assessment Team Report. African Food Systems Initiative. Peace Corps. Washington, D.C.

———— 1985b Food Crisis and Class Formation in Shaba. Review of African Political Economy 33:33–43.

———— 1985c The 'Wild,' the 'Lazy' and the 'Matriarchal'. Michigan State University, Women in International Development, Working Paper No. 96. East Lansing, MI.

———— 1986 Food Crisis and Class Formation in Zaire: Political Ecology in Shaba. *In* The World Recession and the Food Crisis in Africa. Peter Lawrence, ed. Pp. 189–212. London: James Currey.

———— 1987 Social Structure, Women's Status and Sex Differential Nutrition in the Zairian Copperbelt. Urban Anthropology, 16, 1:73–102.

———— 1988 Women, AIDS and Economic Crisis in Central Africa. Canadian Journal of African Studies 22,3:625–644.

———— In prep. That Ethereal light . . . The Invention of Marx in Africa. Paper for colloquim on Rethinking Marxist Anthropology, African Studies Association, Nov. 1989.

Schoepf, Brooke G. and Claude Schoepf 1981 Zaire's Rural Development: Problems and Prospects. *In* The Role of U.S. Universities in International Agricultural and Rural Development (243–257), ed. B. G. Schoepf. Tuskegee Institute.

———— 1984 State, Bureaucracy and Peasants in the Lufira Valley. Canadian Journal of African Studies 18, 1:89–93.

———— 1987 Food Crisis and Agrarian Change in the Eastern Highlands of Zaire. Urban Anthropology, 16, 1:5–37.

———— 1988 "Land, Gender and Food Security in Eastern Kivu, Zaire." *In* Agriculture, Women and Land: The African Experience, Jean Davidson, ed. pp.106–130. Boulder, CO: Westview.

Schoepf, Claude 1982a Results of Base-Line Survey in Four Localities near INERA Mulungu Station, Kivu Province. Report for MASI and USAID/Kinshasa.

———— 1982b Soybean Production and Consumption in Southern Kivu Province. Report for MASI and USAID/Kinshasa.

Schulz, M. et al. 1982 Vulgarisation Agricole Visant le Petits Exploitants de la Zone de Kabare. Analyse de Situation et Proposition de Projet. German Technical Cooperation (mimeo).

Sosne, Elinor 1979 Colonial Peasantization and Contemporary Under-development: A View From a Kivu Village. *In* Zaire: The Political Economy of Underdevelopment. Guy Gran, ed. Pp. 189–211. New York: Praeger.

Staudt, Kathleen 1987 Uncaptured or Unmotivated? Rural Sociology 52,1: 37–55.

Steward, Julian, Robert Manners, Eric Wolf, Elena Padilla, Sidney Mintz and Raymond Scheele. 1956 The People of Puerto Rico. Urbana: University of Illinois Press.

Verhagen, Benoit 1984 Paradoxes Zaïrois. Canadian Journal of African Studies, 18, 1:73–79.

Vuysteke, Dr. 1981 Fonds Social du Kivu, Hopital de Walungu, Comité Anti-Bwaki 1981:41–49.

Vwakyanakazi Mukohya 1982 African Traders in Butembo, Eastern Zaire 1960–1980: A Case Study of Informal Entrepreneurship. Ph.D. Dissertation, University of Wisconsin-Madison, Dept. of Anthropology.

Walu Engundu and Brooke G. Schoepf "Women's Contributions to Households Budgets in Kinshasa." *In* Systéme D: The Second Economy in Zaire. J. MacGaffey, ed.

White, Benjamin 1973 Demand for Labor and Population Growth in Colonial Java. Human Ecology 1:217–236.

World Bank 1977 Economic Conditions and Prospects of Zaire. Report, April 13. Eastern Africa Regional Office. Nairobi: World Bank.

――――― 1982 Zaire: Review of Agricultural Projects. May 22. Report. Nairobi: World Bank Eastern Africa Regional Office.

Young, Crawford and Thomas Turner 1985 The Rise and Decline of the Zairian State. Madison, WI: University of Wisconsin Press.

Profiles of Men and Women Smallholder Farmers in Malawi

Anita Spring

Professor of Anthropology and African Studies
Department of Anthropology
University of Florida
Gainesville, Florida 32611 USA

INTRODUCTION

Focus on the Household

In order to disentangle the factors that contribute to the African food crisis or to food self-sufficiency, a focus on the household level of production is beginning to come to the fore. Joyce Moock notes that large scale agriculture has occupied the attention of development planners and she argues instead for a farming systems approach that focuses on smallholder agriculture at the household level in order to bridge the gap "by providing a realistic assessment of the conditions under which different types of production units operate" (J. Moock 1986:2). Undoubtedly, any comprehensive examination of Africa must include both the commercial and the smallholder agricultural sectors, the latter especially so because African agriculture is extensively practiced by the rural population. The commercial sector is often under the auspices of government, parastatals, or private control. By contrast, the smallholder sector, although influenced by pricing policies to a greater or lesser extent, has a certain degree of autonomy and self-sufficency.

In discussing food self-sufficiency in Sub-Saharan African, Hyden (1986) argues that capitalist and socialist models that have been used elsewhere often cannot apply as well or provide as much predictive value in assessing African smallholder production, because the "invisible economy" or "economy of affection" of the smallholder agricultural household must be considered. The economy of affection "denotes networks of support, communications and interactions among structurally defined groups that are connected by blood, kin, community or other affinities" and in which "the needs and dynamics of micro- rather than macro-structures" are important, especially because producers still farm their own land (Hyden 1986:26). This type of agriculture is based on farming systems that usually are highly locale-specific where the results may not be linked only to productivity (i.e., yield), because off-farm activities and family priorities may take precedence. For Hyden, this family system cannot be easily manipulated or "captured" by governments for development purposes. By contrast, other researchers argue that individual smallholders are sensitive to profit motives (Guyer 1986) and/or that rural elites can gain control over some segments of the smallholder population in order to limit productivity or "severely compromise the equity goals of rural development schemes" (Lemarchand 1986:31).

In looking at the smallholder sector, a system approach is often used. The farming system in an area may be characterized by the crop and livestock enterprises and how these relate to the market- place and to the people's food needs, there is increasing recognition given to non-farm activities as they link up with the system. The household is usually taken as the unit of any approach that deals with the farming system because it is concerned with production and consumption. The household is seen as the bounded unit in which the distinction between the external factors that are outside the control of the household decision-maker(s) and the internal factors that are within the control of its members may be distinguished (Guyer 1986:93). A standard approach has been to examine the household as an aggregate unit rather than to look at its constituent parts. Usually this has meant that male household heads (MHHs) have been the center of attention and they have been selected to "represent" the household. However, researchers, who have studied the dynamics of the African household, point to problems with the household as the unit because of the semiautonomous nature of its members where "men and women . . . separately control productive resources, take partly independent decisions, manage personal incomes, assume different responsibilities and favor different investments" (Guyer 1986: 93).

Many writers now recognize the different resource bases and dif-

ferent responsibilities of individuals within the household, and the
separate incomes and expenditures of men and women and of husbands and wives (Gladwin et. al. 1984; Guyer 1984; McMillan 1986;
Rogers 1980; Spring 1986a, 1986c, 1993). These authors state that
farming households in Africa may be characterized as overlapping but
semiautonomous production and consumption units and that women are
not simply embedded within households, but are rather semi-autono-
mous persons who often have a great deal of independence in terms of
food production and distribution. Male and female household heads
have been compared by some authors (Due and White 1986; Spring,
Smith and Kayuni 1983a, 1983b; Spring 1984), although Peters remarks that this may "divert" attention away from the role of . . .
women as farming wives, sisters and daughters" (1986:143). Two
major concerns are how to disentangle the complicated labor and
remuneration patterns in African households in terms of their individual constituents and how to relate this to overall household productivity and societal food self-sufficiency.

Perhaps an important question to be asked is why should a consideration of women's roles or of gender issues at the level of household
or the individual assist in an understanding of issues of Africa's food
security. One answer is that African rural women have farming, food
preparation, and food distribution defined as part of their roles in
society, and the majority of people in the countryside are women
farmers because of extensive male out-migration in many areas. Additionally, although Africa is rapidly urbanizing, industrialization is
less rapid and farming will remain the major means of livelihood for
a large percentage of the population for some time. Including women
in research and extension activities improves the ability of African
countries to produce food for family production and for sale in rural
and urban areas.

The Invisibility of African Women Farmers

In general, African women have tended to be economically invisible.
Their contributions to subsistence or cash agriculture as unpaid family
workers are not accounted for separately because standard labor force
statistics usually refer to activities in which cash or kind is the intended outcome. This excludes many workers from labour force statistics because they are not paid wages for what they produce, though

the work is critical to the production processes and to food self-sufficency. Work frequently performed by rural women workers (who constitute an essential part of the agricultural work force doing planting, weeding and harvesting, food processing and storage, tending small animals, and working in dairying and other livestock enterprises) tends to be unrecognized. Often these activities are not monetized, resulting in gross underestimates of women's contributions to the household and to the agricultural economy. Women are also under-counted in agricultural employment statistics (this is also true for some men). Furthermore, surveys of the agricultural labor force may be conducted during slack agricultural periods and inquire about work performed recently (in the last week or month). Since, rural women tend to work more during seasonal peaks, they are more likely to be statistically misclassified as non-workers in these surveys. The labor force approach bypasses self-employed people as well and may there-fore omit women who are market vendors and food distributors. Sta-tistics on economic activities in many countries classify a large proportion of women as "economically not active" and therefore the data bases on women either as heads of households or as members of male-headed households (that are used in planning for development activities) are inadequate (Dixon 1985).

Programs for women usually focus on their domestic and reproduc-tive capacities rather than on their productive activites such as agri-culture, but their domestic and child rearing activities are generally not valued for national income accounting (even though they produce the labour force). The result of all of this is that failure to consider the factors affecting women in agriculture and their input to home production affects the ways in which women are prepared for their tasks, the tools and techniques they are given, and the efficiency of their efforts. Women often have been excluded from learning new technologies and participating in capital-intensive schemes. It is sug-gested here that this has contributed to a decrease in food production and to the current food crisis in Africa.

The Contribution of African Women Farmers

Boserup (1970) pointed to the importance of women in African agri-culture. (She distinguished between male and female systems of farm-ing and identified the features of each.) She argued that in Europe, the Middle East, and some Latin American societies, male systems of farming are predominant. In Africa and some parts of Southeast Asia, female systems or male-assisted female systems are the mode. Boserup documented how colonial powers, followed by the newly independent governments, dismissed the female system of farming as unimportant. Cash crops and new technologies were introduced to men, while women were discouraged or bypassed in agricultural training, credit, extension, and land reform programs. Research focused on extractive agricultural enterprises rather than on local food. Although some women moved into commercial production, most women farmers responsible for their family's food supply were disadvantaged in many ways.

Although Boserup's work is now dated and has been criticized for undervaluing women's agricultural work in some areas, for not considering women's reproductive roles along with their productive roles, for believing that education for women was the panacea, and for not realizing that employers would exploit women as well as men in agribusiness and industry, she did point to Sub-Saharan Africa as one area where farming is part of the definition of women's role in society (Beneria and Sen 1981). In addition, she and subsequent researchers have documented that African women contribute 60 to 80 percent of the labor and management in food production in many places on the continent, although in other regions their contribution is only 30 to 50 percent (Dixon 1985; Rogers 1980). Currently it is estimated that a third of rural African households are headed by women who are frequently the sole decision-makers for the household.

Women tend to focus on food crops, but cereal and other food crops are often grown for both food and cash, and it is difficult to say that women are not involved in cash enterprises. In households that produce for the market, women's participation is usually much greater than realized (Clark 1975; Guyer 1984). Women participate in a variety of farm activities with other family members or on their own. Some aspects of their work such as harvesting and food processing are better recognized and accounted for than others such as land preparation, planting, and weeding. Researchers have extended Boserup's work on the female system of agriculture in Sub-Saharan Africa in the last two decades by documenting women's contributions to food production, processing and preparation, and distribution (e.g., Bukh 1979; Butler 1982; Clark 1975; Dey 1981, 1984; Due et. al.

1985; Fortmann 1978, 1984; Gladwin et. al. 1984; Guyer 1984; Spring et. al. 1983b). In addition, the ways in which development strategies include or bypass women have been studied (Brain 1979; Due and Summary 1982; Fortmann 1981; Palmer 1985; Rogers 1980; Spring and Hansen 1985; Spring 1986c, 1993; Staudt 1975–76).

Boserup noted that men's smaller contribution and women's self-sufficiency in female systems of agriculture means that men may easily leave their families in the rural areas while they seek employment on plantations, in mines, or in the urban sector. (By contrast, in areas with male systems of farming, the entire family must move together, since women are unable to provide food for themselves and their children.) Extensive male migration occurred in Africa initially because of the colonial imposition of taxes; migration continues because of a variety of "pull" factors such as the desire to obtain income, consumer goods, and more experience as well as "push" factors such as poor agricultural conditions, drought, wars, and military recruitment. Women cannot leave the rural areas as easily as men, since there are few urban jobs for them other than prostitution or petty trade. In addition, land is under continuous cultivation in many parts of Africa and there is no new land to clear; this means that the agricultural tasks that men performed in clearing and preparing land are no longer needed, making it easier for men to leave their families in the rural areas and to leave the farming to the women.

Researchers studying the people left at home report that with a high rate of labor out-migration, the sexual division of labor in farming systems is often modified and accentuated. Women do their usual work, and do the men's work also. Men rarely do any of the tasks that are considered "women's work." At the same time, women are more bound to the homestead, sometimes waiting for remittances that never come or that are too little or too late for the agricultural season. Hence, instead of the anticipated intensification in food production to match increased population and a more modern economy, rural households struggle to produce for household food security.

The Sexual Division of Labor

The sexual division of labor in African agriculture is usually described as men and women being each responsible for certain discrete tasks. Standard descriptions of crop enterprises state that men clear and prepare the land (and plow it, if the society uses the plow), while women plant, weed, harvest, process, and store the crops. However, careful studies show that a variety of labor and cultivation patterns exist, and that these patterns have been changing in the past fifty to one hundred years. In one pattern, men and women cultivate similar crops on separate plots of land and/or have separate livestock holdings. In a second pattern, men and women cultivate different crops. In a third, women and men do different farming operations on the same plots or with the same animals (this is the so-called "standard" sexual division of labor). In a fourth pattern, there is no division; men and women perform the same farm operations on the same plots. Finally, in rural female headed households, women are responsible for all agricultural production.

In societies that are pastoral or that have mixed agricultural systems, men· usually care for the larger animals while women may be responsible for small ruminants and poultry. Men generally obtain the income from sales and women control the allocation of milk between the needs of the herd and the family. Other patterns may exist out of expediency with women and men sharing livestock care, doing different tasks, or with all the care falling to women in men's absence. In some areas, women are beginning to own cattle, and as the care of large animals moves from the range to the village, as in stall-feeding projects, women become more important in cattle production (Spring 1986a).

In aggregate terms, women's agricultural labor in the smallholder agricultural sector in many areas is comparable to or greater than men's and has been increasing since the colonial period. A number of studies show that women spend as much time on farm work as they do on domestic activities (Boserup 1970; Clark 1975; FAO 1983, 1990). Agricultural development projects often increase the amount of agricultural work, in terms of hours per day and days per year, for both men and women (Clark 1975; FAO 1983). Whether in areas undergoing development changes or those that are not, gender influences how tasks are carried in some areas and in some households. Often, the so-called traditional sexual division of labor gives way to expediency as women have to perform certain tasks because they may be the only adults left on the farm. In some areas, women are involved in all aspects of farming such as land clearing, plowing and applying fertilizer, either routinely or when male labor is unavailable. Women work on both food and cash crops and do many farm operations that are commonly believed to be done only by men, such as spraying cotton and planting tobacco (Clark 1975; Spring et. al. 1983).

In Malawi, the subject of this chapter, all the work patterns mentioned above co-exist at the present time. There is variation by area and, within an area, by household (Agro-Economic Surveys 1968-1983; NSO 1982). Women contribute the majority of labor in smallholder agriculture, and they make agricultural decisions in many rural households (Spring et. al. 1983; Spring 1985, 1993). Labor and cropping patterns are variable, but women are usually involved in all aspects of farming, especially in the cultivation of the staple crops of maize, cassava, and rice. In subsistence areas, women have the responsibility for food crop production and have the greatest labor input. Women work with a variety of cropping patterns from mixed subsistence to cash crops such as peanut (groundnut), rice, tobacco, cotton, and smallholder (as opposed to estate-produced) coffee and tea. In some groundnut growing areas surveyed, men and women put in similar amounts of time, but do different tasks. In other areas, groundnuts are considered a "women's crop," and women do most of the work. Rice production areas are variable in terms of the allocation of labor. In some places, men are responsible for its cultivation, while women only assist because of their work on other food crops.

Tobacco is largely considered a crop that men grow, but women and children often help in farm operations. In other areas, the household head, either male or female, is responsible for the rice or tobacco crop. Labor on oriental tobacco in male headed households is distributed evenly between men and women. In all areas, men are in charge of the cotton crop but women contribute significantly to various operations. Cultivation of the crop in some areas would not be possible without adult female labor. In smallholder coffee and tea production, many tasks are shared between the sexes except that men are responsible for pruning. Where tasks associated with cash crops become particularly labor intensive, women's labor in certain tasks increases relative to men's (Agro-Economic Surveys 1968–83; Spring et. al. 1983; Spring 1985).

Furthermore, various researchers (Chaney and Lewis 1980; Guyer 1984; Kydd 1982a, 1982b; Rogers 1980) argue that smallholder agriculture is becoming more "feminized" as more work becomes carried out by women. Women are taking an even greater responsibility for farming as men are doing part-time farming only, because men have other off-farm activities or have left farming entirely due to local employment or to migration out of the area. Sex ratios of working-aged people in rural areas of many countries show that there are more women than men, and that the numbers and proportion of female headed households are increasing. In some areas of Zimbabwe, there are special programs to intensify male participation in agriculture to counteract male migration from rural to urban areas. However, approximately one third of rural households in Malawi, two thirds in Lesotho, and forty-five percent in Kenya are now headed by women (NSO 1982; Butler 1982; FAO 1990).

Households headed by women may be of different types and the diversity of land and labor configurations may have consequences for production and distribution. This diversity of female household heads (FHHs) includes (1) women who have never married (and it makes a difference as to whether or not these women reside with their own relatives who take care of them as opposed to being on their own); (2) married women whose husbands are away for long or short times; (3) married women who have been abandoned by their husbands; (4) separated women; (5) divorced women; and (6) widows. Households headed by women, especially those where there are no remittances being sent back, are likely to be associated with labor constraints, simpler farming systems, food deficits and the lack of agricultural services (Due and White 1986; Spring 1984; Spring et. al. 1983a, 1983b, 1993). Households in which absent husbands provide the land to cultivate, own livestock, and send remittances and/or return at intervals are more similar in their farming systems to comparable male headed households. Although the data show that both male and female headed households are to be found among the ranks of low and high resource farms, there is a tendency for more of the FHHs to be low resource farmers and for more of the high resource farmers to be males. It is not so much differences in farming abilities that produces these differences as it is differences in access to labor, land holdings, credit and training programs, and mechanization. These differences in resources may place the female headed households at a disadvantage and contribute to their lower productivity which in turn leads to household food insecurity and to a lack of surplus for market sales.

New Technologies Bypass Women

Rogers (1980) argues that western stereotypes about women's "natural" place in society influence the design of development endeavors. Consequently, programs developed for women in the colonial and post-independence period continue into the development agenda and focus on domestic activities such as embroidery, sewing, cooking, crafts, and hygiene; women become accustomed to seeing this type of curriculum for themselves. All over Africa, the development curriculum for boys and girls and for men and women is gender-specific (Spring 1983a, 1986a, 1993). Women are often considered gardeners, instead of farmers, so women's agricultural extension curriculum includes only instruction in small-scale poultry and vegetable production, rather than on major staple crops and large livestock. Extension advice and loans for mechanization (in the form of plows and tractors) and inputs (seeds and fertilizers) are given to men. Mechanization of women's work either in the field or in food processing lags far behind. Similarly, whether it is land reallocation or registration, new varieties or breeds, cash or export commodities, or credit or input programs, men as heads of households are targeted and it is assumed that information or inputs will "trickle-over" and that all household members will benefit. Few development planners understand the economic semi-autonomy of many African household members, or recognize the prevalence of households headed by women. Few planners realize that increased income and leisure often benefit men much more than women, as shown, for example, by research in the Central African Republic where men average two hours more rest and sleep a day than do women (FAO 1983). The efficiency of agricultural intensification is jeopardized by this failure to appreciate women's needs and interests.

Sometimes women learn about new technologies in spite of the lack of formal instruction and they may purchase inputs themselves instead of getting them on credit (P. Moock 1976; Guyer 1984). Other times women become more dependent on men, as in the Gambia when a rice scheme allocated all the land and inputs to men (Dey 1981). Various studies show that many women are interested in new technologies and want to take advantage of development services, but are handicapped by the way training or other programs are established. In some places women's agricultural productivity outstrips men's in spite of the lack of services (P. Moock 1976; Staudt 1975-76). Currently, there is enough information from various parts of the continent to show that when women are given the opportunity to receive credit, agricultural training and inputs, their agricultural performance becomes similar to the better male farmers in the area (Spring et. al. 1983; Dey 1984).

Men and Women Farmers in Malawi

Case Study of Male and Female Household Heads

This chapter is a case study that investigates the demographic, socio-cultural, and agronomic aspects of agricultural development under conditions of planned agricultural change. It seeks to answer questions about the nature of food security among smallholder agriculturalists in Africa and, in particular, about what happens at the household level in terms of male and female participation in farming. The analysis here attempts to differentiate the agricultural practices in households where women are the main decision-makers (i.e., those that they head) from those in which they farm with their husbands, who are considered the household heads. In order to do this, the article reports the findings from several large surveys conducted in rural Malawi. The purpose of this analysis is threefold: (1) to ascertain the effects of a development project on the farming systems of men and women smallholder farmers; (2) to study the similarities and differences in farming practices between male-headed and female-headed households; and (3) to study differences in farming practices between men and women in the same households.

This research was part of the Women in Agricultural Development Project in Malawi (WIADP) that was funded by the United States Agency for International Development, Office of Women in Development, and functioned as a nationwide project through Malawi's Ministry of Agriculture. The project has a series of research, training, and policy-oriented components that accomplished the following tasks (Spring 1985, 1986a, 1986b, 1988a, 1988b, 1993).

1. The collection of data on men and women smallholders in terms of their farming practices, development project services addressed to

them, and output and results in terms of farming (Spring, et. al. 1983b; Spring 1984; Spring 1984a)

2. The establishment of mechanisms to disaggregate data by gender in collection, analysis, and monitoring phases (Spring 1985).
3. The execution of a series of Farming Systems Research and Extension trials (Spring 1986b, 1988, 1993).
4. Leadership training and retraining of extension staff, including discussion of women's issues and the legitimization of male extensionists to work with women farmers (MOA 1983; Spring 1983).
5. Work with policymakers and planners to target women as farmers in national development plans (Spring 1983a; Spring, et. al. 1983b).

The data on farming practices and project services that are the focus of this analysis come from the Lilongwe Rural Development Project (LRDP) funded since 1968 by the World Bank. This is one of a series of integrated rural development projects designed in the 1960s and 1970s to improve rural standards of living and to make the process of development self-sustaining (Lele 1975). Such projects focus on rural production, but also include infrastructural components such as roads, water, and markets, as well as components that address health and education.

As an integrated rural development project, the LRDP includes extension services, infrastructure, political development, crop and livestock development, and the monitoring of these activities for their success. The LRDP is located to the west and south of the city of Lilongwe, the capital of Malawi, in an area of gently undulating plains. The area has an altitude of 1090 to 1230 m, a temperature range of 15 to 23 degrees Celsius, and rainfall ranging from 640 mm to 1090 mm between November and April. The farmers in the area grow maize, tobacco, groundnuts, and some beans and sweet potatoes under rainfed conditions, often in pure stands. Only 11% own cattle; some own goats and chickens. Land holding size averages about 1.5 hectares. About one-fifth, or 20% of the households, are headed by women.

The information analyzed here comes from two formal diagnostic surveys: one is the National Sample Survey of Agriculture (NSSA) funded by the World Bank and carried out by the Ministry of Agriculture; the second is a survey of developmental indicators carried out by the WIADP and the Farming Systems Analysis Section of another

USAID project. According to the literature, a number of authors have attempted to identify key indicators of development (Castro, et. al. 1981; Kydd 1982b). Indicators that have been suggested include such aspects as demography (e.g., household size and composition, education, migration, urban and international experiences), land (control, types, land tenure, and acquisition), productive resources (such as capital equipment, farm equipment, and dwellings, cropping patterns (crops planted, use of inputs, experience cultivating improved varieties, and farming practices), yields, local people's perceptions of development and their knowledge of development services (including their perceptions of change as a result of the project and their adoption of innovation), the contact with extension staff, and wealth and income of the farmers. The WIADP survey attempted to include these indicators in the design of its survey instruments.

The NSSA survey had a sample of 520 randomly selected households, while the WIADP survey had approximately 20% (101) of these same households. Statistical determinations showed that there are no significant differences between the two samples in terms of the population. Different questions were asked in the two surveys, and information from both surveys are utilized here to discuss the indicators of development.

Survey Results

The characteristics of farmers in the LRDP are presented here in terms of specific development indicators. This discussion represents a summary of the findings; statistical support material may be found in Spring (1984, 1988a, 1993).

Demography Table I sums up the findings regarding the demographic features of the households surveyed. A fifth of the households are headed by women and of these 39% are married, but their husbands are away from the family farm. The sex of the household head may change over time because of male migration, divorce and remarriage, and death. The WIADP queried the stability of the female headed households (FHHs) over time. At first glance, the numbers appear stable since the data show that there were 58 of them in 1980/81 and 61 in 1981/82. On closer examination, 12% of the 58 FHHs in 1980/81 became male-headed households (MHHs) in 1981/82. Similarly, of the 61 households headed by women in 1981/82, 16% were

Table I. Demography

Indicator	Finding
Sex of household head	−MHHs 80%, FHHs 20%
	−FHHs: 39% are married, 31% are widows
	−16% of FHHs changed to MHHs and 12% of MHHs changed to FHHs in one year
Household size	−Average = 5.3
	−MHHs = 5.5
	−FHHs = 4.2—one less person
Natality	−No differences in number of children for FHHs and MHHs
	6.9 pregnancies
	4.0 children
Education:	
Adult	−MHHs > Wives > FHHs
Children	−boys > girls
	−Children of MHHs > children in FHHs

headed by men during the previous survey year. Therefore, in only one year, one sixth of the households changed. (Given the available data, it is not possible to know what the changes are over a longer period of time; see Hansen 1988).

Families average 5.3 persons, but those headed by women have one less person. An examination of age, sex, and relationship to the household head shows that the difference is primarily that of an adult male (husband), since the average number of women and children does not differ between the two types of households. Women in both types of households have similar reproductive experiences (and average 6.9 pregnancies and 4.0 living children). Parents have less education than their children; children in FHHs and girls in both types of households have less education than boys. Women have less education and most are illiterate compared with men whose education, literacy and migration experiences are greater.

Land The majority of gardens cultivated are rainfed while streamside gardens are at a premium; little land is under fallow. Land for gardens may be acquired through inheritance, gift, loan, purchase, or by clearing. Each sex tends to obtain land from a relative of the same sex, mostly through gifts or inheritance. The households headed by women have fewer gardens, because there is only one adult bringing in

Table II. Land: acquisition, types and holding size

Indicator	Finding
Acquisition:	–Much acquired from relative of same sex through inheritance and gifts.
Length of time held:	–No difference
Garden types:	–Seepage: MHHs > FHHs –Total: MHHs > FHHs
Range:	–FHHs have a smaller minimum (0.18 ha) and a larger maximum (5.6 ha) than MHHs (0.4 ha and 4.84 ha). However, there is only 1 FHH having over 2.5 ha. Standard deviation is smaller for MHHs (0.9) than for FHHs (1.2).
Mean:	–MHHs > FHHs, but the means are closer together as the number of FHHs in sample increases.

	MHHs	FHHs	
Sample 1	1.83	1.53	(n.s)
Sample 2	1.83	1.27	
	(sigT(99) = 2.58 p < 0.1)		

Distribution of	–MHHs tend to have larger holdings (1.0 ha–2.5 ha) while the FHHs tend to have smaller holdings (less than 1 ha). Most farmers, however, are in the middle range.

	MHHs	FHHs
< 1 ha	18%	50%
1 ha–2.5 ha	60%	48%
> 2.5 ha	22%	2%

land. Since only one third of the FHHs are married, the remainder do not have the option to acquire land through the husband's relatives. Table II shows that the average holding size for MHHs is 1.83 hectares (ha) and for FHHs is 1.27 or 1.53 ha depending on which sample is used. The majority of the farmers have between 1.0 and 2.5 ha, but 22% of the MHHs have more than 2.5 ha compared with only 2% of the FHHs. Half of the FHHs cultivate less than 1.0 ha compared to only 18% of the MHHs. There are no differences between households in terms of the average hectarages of each crop grown, but FHHs tend to grow fewer different crops.

Cropping Patterns An examination of the cropping patterns (Table III) shows that all households grow unimproved or "local" maize and then add other food or cash crops. The most common second crop is

Table III. Cropping pattern

Indicator	Finding		
	Both MHH and FHH grow food and cash crops		
Innovative* and	More MHHs are growers of tobacco, hybrid maize, sweet potato, green bean, and mixed bean		
Non-innovative crops	No difference in the number of growers for local maize, groundnuts, synthetic maize, ground bean		
	MHHs—22 patterns, FHHs—11 patterns		
	Most frequent patterns		
		FHHs	MHHs
	Local maize and groundnuts	53%	34%
	Local maize, groundnuts, tobacco*	10%	14%
	Local maize	12%	8%
*Innovative crops are hybrid/synthetic maize and tobacco.	Local maize, groundnuts, hybrid maize*	3%	6%
	Other 18 patterns (Includes *)	18%	38%
	TOTAL	100%	100%
Cropping patterns and wealth	–Innovative farmers own more wealth items than non-innovators		
Cropping patterns and hectarage	–Farmers growing innovative crops have more total land than non-innovators. (2.41 ha compared to 1.28 ha)		
Hectarage and type of crop	–No difference in the mean hectarages for crops		

groundnuts followed by hybrid maize and tobacco. Innovative crops were introduced into the farming system by the LRDP and include tobacco, hybrid maize, and synthetic maize. Although the data here divide the cropping patterns into a two-fold scheme (innovative and non-innovative crops), twenty-two patterns are identifiable (Hansen and Ndengu 1983). The non-innovative, or traditional crops, include combinations such as local maize, groundnuts, sweet potatoes, green beans, and fallow. The most frequent patterns consists of local maize

Table IV. Wealth items (farm equipment, housing, consumer goods)

Indicator	Finding
Farm equipment	–No difference in basic implements (hoe, ridgers, plow)
	–MHHs have more water cans, ox carts
Housing	–MHHs have more glass windows, latrines
Consumer goods	–MHHs have more bicycles, tables, lamps, chairs, radios
Hectarage	–Farmers with more land own more wealth items
	$r = .31, p < 0.1$
Cropping pattern	–Innovative farmers have more items than non-innovative
(innovators versus	farmers
non-innovators)	$r = .32, p > .01$

and groundnuts with over half of the FHHs and 38% of the MHHs having these patterns. The houses headed by women grow cash as well as food crops, although fewer of the FHHs than the MHHs grow tobacco and hybrid maize. Tobacco in particular is thought to be a crop grown by men and the technical aid goes to men. It is therefore intriguing that women manage to grow it at all, but almost one fifth of the FHHs do so. Farmers growing innovative crops have twice the amount of land (2.41 ha) as those with traditional patterns (1.28 ha). One conclusion is that the availability of land is the most significant variable in innovative cropping patterns, although contact with extension services is also important (see below).

Productive Resources Most households rely on the basic agricultural tool, the hoe, and have few improvements to their houses. Consumer goods such as tables, lamps, chairs, radios, and bicycles are not owned by most, but the MHHs have more items than the female household heads and the innovative farmers have more wealth items including farm equipment than the non-innovative (Table IV). Few farmers have improved houses with baked bricks or cement floors, but more of the MHHs have glass windows compared with FHHs. A main housing improvement that requires labor rather than cash input is the latrine. Female heads of households have fewer of these, probably because they lack male labor to build them.

Labor Table V sums up the information concerning labor showing that the male have more units of labor than the female household heads and the farmers growing innovative crops have more labor than the non-innovative farmers. The WIADP used two different methods to

Table V. Labor

Indicator	Finding		
	Mean: MHHs > FHHs		
		MHHs	FHHs
Size of labor force	"Standard"		
	mean	2.95	2.35
	minimum	1.67	0.67
	maximum	6.80	6.80
	"Equalitarian"		
	mean	3.34	2.76
	minimum	1.60	0.80
	maximum	7.30	7.50
Cropping patterns	Innovative farmers (MHHs and FHHs) have more labor units than non-innovative farmers (3.4 and 2.9 units) $f(1) = 4.6$, $p < .03$		

calculate the labor units available in a household. The method common in the literature (called "standard" here), counts male labor as 1.0 and female labor as 0.67 for comparable activities. A second method, devised by the WIADP, is more "equalitarian" and counts men and women's labor as equal, but distinguishes people by age. The analysis shows that the male heads have more labor units than the female heads in both cases. The results of these labor configurations and yields (see below) are reflected in the consumption units and amount (volume) of stored maize. Innovative farmers have both more labor and land which is directly related to the household's ability to feed more people. However, the increased labor available in the MHHs affects total production due to the cultivation of additional land and not necessarily to cultivating their land more efficiently. The lack of significant differences in yields for both unimproved and hybrid maize in the two types of households (see below), indicates that the labor tasks performed by the women are those most affecting efficiency of output.

Consumption Households growing innovative crops have more consumption units (that is, individuals who eat the food) and more stored maize (Table VI). Households that produce more can allow more people to stay with them. One farmer defined "development" for the WIADP staff as follows: "Development is when you don't have to

Table VI. Consumption units

Indicator	Finding
Units and cropping pattern	Households growing innovative crops have more consumption units.
Units and hectarage	Households with more consumption units have greater hectarage. (r = .26, p < .001)
Stored maize per consumption unit	Households growing innovative crops have more stored maize per consumption unit. (significant for all HHs and MHHs, but not for FHHs) 1.8 versus 1.1, p < .02
Stored maize per consumption unit and hectarage	Households with more stored maize per consumption unit have more hectarage. (r = .34, p < .001)
Total volume stored maize	Higher mean for innovative households (1.84) than for non-innovative households (1.13). Innovative FHHs have a much higher mean (2.9) than non-innovative FHHs (1.1).

send your children away because you can take care of them by feeding and clothing them properly.''

There are also correlations between the amount of land, consumption units, and stored maize. The greater the land holding size (hectarage), the greater the number of consumption units and the more stored maize. These correlations illustrate again the importance of land holding size. In addition, the correlation between innovative cropping pattern and consumption units demonstrates that innovative farmers have more land and store more maize. This is especially true for the FHHs growing innovative crops where the mean volume is 4.9 cubic meters compared to 1.1 cubic meters for those female heads growing non-innovative crops.

"Cultural" Practices and Knowledge of Improved Practices Actual farming practices such as time of planting, plant spacing and populations, weeding, and fertilizer usage were examined as well as farmers' use of improved technologies and their knowledge of improved farming practices. Male and female farmers are alike in terms of when they prepare their land and when they plant their crops, unless they have been contacted by extension and have adopted those newer recommended practices. Extension recommendations stress early land preparation, early planting (including dry planting), and specific plant populations (in terms of seeds per station and spacing between stations and ridges). Because extensionists tend to focus on

Table VII. **Cultural practices knowledge of improved practices**

Indicator	Finding
Cultural practices	–No difference in time of land preparation, planting, or weeding –No differences in plant populations
Knowledge of correct cultural practices	–MHHs > Wives > FHHs
Use of fertilizer	–MHHs slightly more in "good" years and much more in scarce years
Knowledge of types and prices of fertilizers	–MHHs > FHHs > Wives know types and prices
Knowledge of correct usage	–Few farmers know correct usage MHHs > Wives > FHHs
Application of fertilizer	–MHHs know correct application; but many farmers have incorrect application (method and timing)

men, more men than women know and use the new recommendations, and the ways that women and men farm become more differential.

Women, whether they are in male headed households or are farm managers themselves, know less than men about types of fertilizers and applications, credit and its procedures, time of planting, spacing, plant populations, time of weeding, and disease and pest management. They also have less access to improved seed and technologies (Table VII). For example there is a difference between household types in terms of knowledge of fertilizer usage. Fertilizers need to be applied at planting time and again when the plants are small, but most farmers think that fertilizers should be applied later in the growth cycle. The men correctly apply the fertilizer in greater frequencies than the female heads (66% versus 47% for 1980 and 42% versus 11% for 1981). The incorrect information correlates with both stated and observed application. It is therefore not surprising that yields are low, because maize plants cannot absorb the nutrients late in the growth cycle. The number of farmers who apply fertilizer too late in the growing cycle is large and constitutes a major constraint to improving yields and to having a cost effective system.

Extension The majority of people receive no extension contacts, but of those who do, most see the extension worker at group meetings and personal visits, but contact is always much higher for men than

Table VIII. Extension

Indicator	Finding
	For those receiving advice:
Amount of Advice	–Majority receive none
	–Men receive twice as much as women
	–MHHs (45%), Wives (26%), FHHs (25%)
Source of advice*	–Group meetings is main method
	MHHs > FHHs > Wives
	66% > 49% > 44%
	–Extension workers visits is second method
	MHHs > Wives > FHHs
	41% > 28% > 23%
Club membership	–MHHs > Wives > FHHs

*For those receiving advice

for women (Table VIII). Men tend to be the members in farmers' clubs and therefore eligible for credit; fewer wives are members, but even they are more likely to be members than the FHHs.

Yield Differences in yields probably have less to do with real differences in farming skills (because both men and women seem equal in this respect), than they have to do with growing innovative crops, having increased hectarage, and having access to inputs and extension information. The data demonstrate that women produce yields comparable to men's on a kg/ha basis with less available labor and with fewer inputs (Table IX). Local, unimproved maize yields are significantly lower (MHHs = 1419 kg/ha; FHHs = 1252 kg/ha) than those for hybrid maize (MHHs = 3676 kg/ha; FHHs = 3921 kg/ha). Only 25% of the local maize plots are fertilized and only half of these plots show the increased yields as a result of fertilizer usage, probably because of improper usage. Hybrid maize yields are also undifferentiated by sex of farmers although many more of the MHHs than FHHs grow the crop; virtually all farmers who grow the crop fertilize it. More of the FHHs than the MHHs continue to apply their fertilizers too late because they have received no information on correct usage, demonstrating that both men and women need more information on time of fertilizer application to prevent its late application. The differences between the two types of households become apparent when total production that accounts for land holding size is calculated. There are no

Table IX. Yield

Indicator	Finding
Local maize	
Mean yield	No significant differences between MHHs and FHHs (1419 kg/ha and 1252 kg/ha).
Fertilizer use	25% of farmers use fertilizer (no difference between MHHs and FHHs) but only half obtained higher yield.
Hybrid maize	
	More MHHs than FHHs grow the crop.
Mean yield	No significant differences between MHHs and FHHs (3676 kg/ha and 3921 kg/ha).
Fertilizer use	Almost 100% (no differences between MHHs and FHHs)
Hectarage	MHHs with higher yields of local maize have a greater hectarage. r = .26, p < .01
	No correlations between yield of hyrid maize and hectarage.

differences in local unimproved maize, but with hybrid maize, the MHHs with their greater hectarage have twice the production of the FHHs (4609 kg versus 2704 kg). Because the female heads have less land and labor than the male heads, they are not able to grow as much food and/or cash producing crops and their total yields are lower.

Change and Development The LRDP began in 1968, although not all farmers in the various surveys have lived in the project area nor have had infrastructural and other resources available to them for the entire length of time. Farmers were asked how they felt about various aspects of their agricultural production such as food self-sufficiency and utilization of infrastructure and services over the years. Farmers see hybrid maize and credit as the main services that the project has brought to them (Table X). They note marketing facilities as a main change as a result of the LRDP, but more male than female household heads mention that the markets have helped them. Fifty-four percent say they have more income as a result of the project, but only 40% of all households believe there is more food. Another 40% believe there is less food, and 44% mention they have less income since LRDP came into existence. The FHHs in particular feel less impact of the LRDP in terms of inputs, marketing, and credit (Table X).

Income All households require cash income, and most obtain their money from agricultural sources (Table XI). Once again, differences in types of crop sold are apparent between the two types of house-

Table X. Change and development

Indicator	Finding
Major impact Impact of project	–Hybrid maize and credit
Changes in food self-sufficiency	–50-60% of all farmers say there is more food; 38% say there is less food
Income	–54% have more income –40% have less income. Of these, FHHs (53%) and Wives (51%) > MHHs (41%)
Inputs seeds, fertilizer, machinery	–Greater usage, MHHs (86%) > Wives (78%) > FHHs (59%) –No change or use FHHs (41%) > Wives (21%) > MHHs (15%)
Credit	–Most farmers see use of credit as big change but MHHs > FHHs
Marketing and transport	–Most MHHs (83%) and Wives (70%) see increase, but most FHHs (56%) note no change

Table XI. Income

Indicator	Finding
Crops and livestock	–Most households sell groundnuts FHHs (93%), MHHs (76%)
Frequencies of households	–MHHs derive more income from tobacco, chickens, and hybrid maize –FHHs derive more income from bananas, eggs, and local maize –Wives similar to MHHs but derive more income from sweet potatoes
Relative amounts from crops and livestock	–MHHs income: 1) maize, 2) tobacco, 3) groundnuts –FHHs income: 1) groundnuts, 2) maize
Non-agricultural income	–FHHs and Wives—beer brewing –MHHs some construction, artisan work, but agricultural income is main source for all

holds. Men gain cash from tobacco and hybrid maize, commodities that tend to generate substantial income while women rely on groundnut sales that provide more modest returns. The male household heads also gain income from produce from streamside (naturally irrigated) gardens. In terms of non-agricultural income generation, women rely on beer brewing while men are more likely to find off-farm employment that is higher paying.

Conclusion

Because of increasing male mobility, the basic smallholder farm unit in Malawi is the woman and children (although many children may be in school and unavailable for farm work). Most households still have the husband present for most of the year and as a result have increased land, labor, access to resources, and extension services compared with households without adult males. When labor and resources are constrained, compensations in the farming system must be made. A female headed household simplifies its farming system by generally growing fewer crops, especially innovative crops such as tobacco and hybrid maize. As a result, there may be a return to (or a continuation of) a more traditional cropping system that generates little or no income, as access to improved seed, fertilizer and advice is reduced or nil.

Women work as farmers in households headed by men or by themselves. They actively manage the farm if husbands are not there or if they have no husbands. Since some men prefer to leave the farm for employment, farming responsibilities then fall to their wives. Some of the men do not return or return sporadically; others use their off-farm cash income to develop their farms. Marriages may be strained by male mobility, and unions in this area are capable of dissolving easily. Women may be married one farming season and separated, divorced, or widowed the next. Men have the option of having more than one wife and household, thereby being only a part-time participant in each household. Women, therefore, at different points in the life cycle may find themselves managing the farm alone.

Yet, there is diversity within the male and the female headed households. Some of the FHHs are impoverished and have a reduced farming system, fewer resources, and less possibility of educating their children. Although fewer than the male heads, some women heads-of-households cultivate larger hectarages with improved technologies and use their remuneration for improved housing, consumer goods, and children's education. The continuum of the MHHs likewise ranges from impoverished to affluent, but there are more male than female household heads in the latter category. It should be pointed out that an initial examination of the data concerning the two household types of men and women would show that the MHHs cultivate more land than the FHHs and that more of the MHHs cultivate hybrid maize or tobacco. As a result, some researchers and extensionists have argued that the MHHs are therefore "worthier" of attention, extension services, credit, and so forth, than the FHHs. Some have also concluded that men are better farmers than women, because average holding size or (total) yields are higher for them. However, access to inputs, technical advice, and resources need to be considered as well. The MHHs' increased ability to grow innovative crops allows them to take advantage of extension recommendations and new technologies, while contact with extension increases their ability to use these new technologies. Under distress conditions, any category of individuals that lacks access to training or new technologies would be disadvantaged and the female headed households with fewer entitlements would fall into this category.

In a set of trials carried out by the WIADP and the Farming Systems Analysis Section elsewhere in Malawi, farmers selected by extension personnel as participants had different characteristics and these tended to differ by gender (Spring 1988, 1990). The men selected were mostly younger, high-resource farmers with adequate family labor and extension training; as cattle owners their lands were fertilized with manure. The women selected were mostly older, female heads of households, who were low-resource farmers with little family labor and no extension contacts or cattle. They came from households that were not food self-sufficient and often sold their labor of food. The results of these maize trials have been subjected to scrutiny including a quantifiable series of tests known as a modified stability analysis (Hildebrand and Poey 1985; Hansen 1986). The results show that the high-resource farmers had good environments (soils and management) so that an improved variety (cultivar) did better there, while in the poor environments of the low-resource farmers, the unimproved cultivar was superior. There would be potential failure if the low-resource farmers tried to use improved technologies in their poor environments. The analysis by gender demonstrated that most, but not all of the women selected, tended to fall into the poor environment situation because they were low-resource farmers with land shortages, lack of extension information, and lack of family labor (Spring 1988). Although there are men who are low-resource farmers as well, they were not selected by extension personnel, nor were the few high-resource women farmers. In this case, lack of access to land and capital as well as differences in training and extension contacts separated men and women farmers. To begin to target low-resource women who had been bypassed by extension services, new strategies, including credit smaller packages, leadership training, and extension contacts were needed to increase the food self-sufficiency in the area in which 35% of the households are female headed. Fortunately new methods to give credit and more appropriate input packages to these households were devised, and an entire group of people (in a limited area) were moved up the scale in terms of the "entitlement bundle" of food (Sen 1981).

As Boserup noted almost 20 years ago, gender is (and continues to be) an important issue in African systems of food production (Boserup 1970). It is a particularly important issue in studies of household dynamics and smallholder agriculture, because of women's multiple roles. Rural African women are both consumers and producers, and are increasingly recognized as decision makers in both realms. However, the invisibility of women farmers noted by Boserup has been only partially corrected, and extension services and planned agricultural change still frequently show a male bias. This bias can only be detrimental to long-term food security.

In Malawi, the data from both the NSSA and the LRDP Survey, as well as from the field trials, show that men and women do not differ in basic farming skills and practices. However, differences in resources, exposure to new technologies, and access to services have consequences for the outcome of production, income, and the quality of life. By examining the data at the household level, rather than looking only at project production yields or numbers of participants in a program, it is possible to discern the characteristics of smallholders and the impact of the exogenous factors on the farming system. By disaggregating the household into types and into the individual adult members (male and female), it is possible to understand household differences in the level of resources and knowledge and in the access to development project services. Finally, by using a household focus, it is possible to link features of the farming system to food supply and household food self-sufficiency. Understanding these links is an essential first step in alleviating the current food crisis.

References

Agro-Economic Surveys (AES). 1968-83. (51 Reports) Lilongwe, Malawi: Ministry of Agriculture.

Beneria, L. and G. Sen. 1981. Accumulation, reproduction, and women's role in economic development: Boserup revisited. *Signs* 7:279–299.

Boserup, E. 1970. *Woman's Role in Economic Development.* New York: St. Martin's Press.

Brain, J. 1976. Less than second-class: Women in rural settlement schemes in Tanzania. In *Women in Africa,* ed. by N. Hafkin and E. Bay. Stanford: Stanford Unversity Press. pp. 265–284.

Bukh, J. 1979. *The Village Woman in Ghana.* Uppsala: Scandanavian Institute of African Studies.

Butler, L. 1982. *Review of Social and Cultural Documents and Annotated Bibliography.* Maseru, Lesotho: Ministry of Agriculture.

Castro, A., N. Hakansson, and D. Brokensha. 1981. Indicators of rural inequality. *World Development* 9(5):401–27.

Chaney, E. and M.W. Lewis. 1980. *Women, Migration, and the Decline of Smallholder Agriculture.* Washington, DC: Office of Women in Development, USAID.

Clark, B. 1975. The work done by rural women in Malawi. *Eastern Journal of Rural Development* 8(2):80–91.

Dey, J. 1981. Gambian women: Unequal partners in rice development projects? *Journal of Development Studies* 17(3):109–122.

———— 1984. *Women in Rice-Farming Systems: Focus: Sub-Saharan Africa.* Rome: FAO.

Dixon, R. 1985. Seeing the invisible women farmers in Africa: Improving research and data collection methods. In *Women as Food Producers in Developing Countries,* ed. by J. Monson and M. Kalb. Los Angeles: UCLA African Studies Center and African Studies Association. pp. 19–36.

Due, J. and R. Summary. 1982. Constraints to women and development in Africa. *Journal of Modern African Studies* 20(1):155–166.

Due, J. and M. White. 1986. Contrasts Between Joint and Female-Headed Farm Households in Zambia: *Eastern Africa Economic Review* 2:1:94–98

Due, J. and T. Mudena, with P. Miller and M. White. 1985. *Women's Contributions to Farming Systems and Household Income in Zambia.* Women in Development Series Working Paper No. 85. Ann Arbor: Michigan State University.

FAO (Food and Agriculture Organization). 1983. *Time Allocation Survey: A Tool for Anthropologists, Economists, and Nutritionists*. Expert Consultation on Women in Food Production, December 7–14. Rome: FAO, Food Policy and Nutrition Division. ESH:WIFP/83/17.

―――― *Women in Agricultural Development: FAO's Plan of Action*. Rome: FAO.

Fortmann, L. 1978. *Women and Tanzanian Agricultural Development*. Economic Research Bureau Paper 77.4. Dar-es-Salaam, Tanzania: Economic Research Bureau, University of Dar-es-Salaam.

―――― 1981. The plight of the invisible farmer: the effect of national agricultural policy on the women in Africa. In *Women and Technology Change*, ed. by R. Dauber and M. Cain. Boulder, Co.: Westview Press and AAAS pp. 205–214.

―――― 1984. Economic status and women's participation in agriculture: A Botswana case study. *Rural Sociology* 49(3):452–464.

Gladwin, C., K. Staudt, and D. McMillan. 1984. Reaffirming the agricultural role of African women: One solution to the food crisis. *Proceedings of the Association of Faculties of Agriculture in Africa. Fifth General Conference on Food Security*. Manzini, Swaziland.

Guyer, J. 1984. *Family and Farm in Southern Cameroon*. African Research Studies No. 15. Boston: African Studies Center, Boston University.

―――― 1986. Intra-household processes and Farming Systems Research: perspectives from anthropology. In *Understanding Africa's Rural Households and Farming Systems*, ed. by J. Moock. Boulder, CO: Westview Press. pp. 92–104.

Hansen, A. 1986. Farming Systems in Phalombe, Malawi: The limited utility of high yielding varieties. In *Social Sciences and Farming Systems Research: Methodological Perspectives on Agriculture and Development*, ed. by J. Jones and B. Wallace. Boulder, CO: Westview Press. pp. 145–196.

―――― 1988. Correcting the underestimated frequency of the head-of-household experience for women farmers. In *Gender Issues and Farming Systems Research and Extension*, ed. by S. Poats, M. Schmink, and A. Spring. Boulder, CO: Westview. pp. 111–126.

Hansen, A. and J.D. Ndengu. 1983. Lilongwe Rural Development Project Cropping Patterns: Information from the National Sample Survey of Agriculture. Chitedze Agricultural Research Station, Farming Systems Analysis Section. Mimeo.

Hildebrand, P. and F. Poey. 1985. *On-Farm Agronomic Trials in Farming Systems Research and Extension*. Boulder, CO: Lynne Rienner Press.

Hyden, G. 1986. The invisible economy of smallholder agriculture in Africa. In *Understanding Africa's Rural Households and Farming Systems*, ed. by J. Moock. Boulder, CO: Westview Press. pp. 11–35.

Kydd, J. 1978. Lilongwe Land Development Programme Farm Management Survey 1969/70 to 1971–72. Report No. 1. Labor Allocation and Crop Labor Requirements 1969/70. Mimeo.

―――― 1982a. The Lilongwe Rural Development Project Farm Management Surveys, 1969/70 and 1978/79: An Initial Comparison of the Baselines. Paper presented at the

Conference on Socioeconomic Research in Rural Lilongwe. Chitedze Agricultural Research Station (January 23).

———— 1982b. *Measuring Peasant Differentiation for Policy Purposes: A Report on a Cluster Analysis Classification of the Population of the Lilongwe Land Development Programme, Malawi, for 1970 and 1979.* Zomba, Malawi: Government Printer.

Lele, U. 1975. *The Design of Rural Development: Lessons from Africa.* Baltimore: Johns Hopkins Press.

Lemarchand, R. 1986. The political economy of food issues. In *Food in Sub-Saharan Africa,* ed. by A. Hansen and D. McMillan. Boulder, CO: Lynne Rienner. pp. 25–42.

McMillan, D. 1986. Distribution of resources and products in Mossi households. In *Food in Sub-Saharan Africa,* ed. by A. Hansen and D. McMillan. Boulder, CO: Lynne Rienner. pp. 260–273.

Ministry of Agriculture (MOA). 1983. *Reaching Female Farmers through Male Extension Workers.* Extension Aids Circular 2/83. Lilongwe, Malawi: Ministry of Agriculture (written by A. Spring).

Moock, J. 1986. Introduction. In *Understanding Africa's Rural Households and Farming Systems.* Boulder, CO: Westview, pp. 1–10.

Moock, P. 1976. The efficiency of women as farm managers: Kenya. *American Journal of Agricultural Economics* 58(5):831–5.

NSO (National Statistical Office). 1982. *Preliminary Report of the National Sample Survey of Agriculture for Customary Land 1980/81.* Zomba, Malawi: Government Printer.

Palmer, I. 1985. *The Nemow Case: Case Studies of the Impact of Large-Scale Development Projects on Women.* A Series for Planners. International Programs, Working Paper No. 7. Washington, DC: USAID (1979). Reprinted in West Hartford, CT: Kumarian Press.

Peters, P. 1986. Household management in Botswana: cattle, crops, and wage labor. In *Understanding Africa's Rural Households and Farming Systems,* ed. by J. Moock. Boulder, CO: Westview Press. pp. 133–154.

Rogers, B. 1980. *The Domestication of Women: Discrimination in Developing Societies.* London and New York: Tavistock.

Sen, A. 1981. *Poverty and Famine: An Essay on Entitlement and Deprivation.* Oxford: Clarendon Press.

Spring, A. 1983a. *Priorities for Women's Programmes.* Report for the Ministry of Agriculture, Malawi, and Office of Women in Development. Washington, DC: USAID.

———— 1983b. Disaggregating National Agricultural Data by Sex in Malawi: Progress to Date and a Proposal. Paper presented at the Association for Women in Development Conference, Washington, DC (October 15).

———— 1984. *Profiles of Men and Women Smallholder Farmers in the Lilongwe Rural Development Project, Malawi.* Final Report. Washington, DC: Office of Women in Development, USAID.

———— 1985. The Women in Agricultural Development project in Malawi: Making gender free development work. In *Women Creating Wealth: Transforming Economic*

Development, ed. by R. Gallin and A. Spring. Washington, DC: Association for Women and Development. pp. 71–75.

———— 1986a. Men and women participants in a stall feeder livestock program in Malawi. *Human Organization* 45(1):154–162.

———— 1986b. Trials and errors: Using Farming Systems Research in agricultural programs for women. In *Applying Social Sciences in Farming Systems Research,* ed. by J. Jones and B. Wallace. Boulder, CO: Westview Press. pp. 123–142.

———— 1986c. Women farmers and food in Africa: Some considerations and suggested solutions. In *Food in Sub-Saharan Africa,* ed. by A. Hansen and D. McMillan. Boulder, CO: Lynne Rienner. pp. 332–348.

———— 1988. Using male research and extension personnel to target women farmers. In *Gender Issues in Farming Systems Research and Extension,* ed. by S. Poats, M. Schmink, and A. Spring. Boulder and London: Westview Press. pp. 407–426.

———— 1988. Putting women in the development agenda: Agricultural development in Malawi. In *Anthropology of Development and Change in East Africa,* ed. by D. Brokensha and P. Little. Boulder and London: Westview Press. pp. 13-42.

———— 1993. *Agricultural Development and Gender Issues in Malawi.* Lanham, MD: University Press of America.

Spring, A. and A. Hansen. 1985. The underside of development: Agricultural development and women in Zambia. *Agriculture and Human Values* 2(1):60–67.

Spring, A., C. Smith, and F. Kayuni. 1983a. An Evaluation of Women's Programmes in Lilongwe ADD: How LADD Sections and Projects Can Incorporate More Women Farmers in Their Programmes, WIADP, April 30 (Mimeo).

———— 1983b. *Women Farmers in Malawi: Their Contributions to Agriculture and Participation in Development Projects.* Report to the Ministry of Agriculture, Malawi, and Office of Women in Development. Washington, DC: USAID.

Staatz, J. and C. Eicher. 1986. Agricultural development ideas in historical perspective. In *Food in Sub-Saharan Africa,* ed. by A. Hansen and D. McMillan. Boulder, CO: Lynne Rienner. pp. 43–63.

Staudt, K. 1975-76. Women farmers and inequalities in agricultural services. In *Rural Women: Development or Underdevelopment?* ed. by A. Wipper. *Rural Africana* 29:81–94.

Part II

STRATEGIES FOR INCREASING FOOD SECURITY

Curriculum Development
in the Study of African Food Issues
at a U.S. Land Grant University

Della E. McMillan

Department of Anthropology and Center for African Studies
University of Florida 32611

Introduction

It is increasingly obvious that any long-term solution to the root problems of poverty and hunger in Sub-Saharan Africa will require the collaborative efforts of scholars, researchers, politicians, and civil servants to go beyond existing models of food policy and food policy analysis. While the production and extension of suitable technology is obviously a key aspect of this process, there is increasing recognition that the policy environment in a particular country can be of equivalent or even greater importance (Bates 1981; Busch 1981; World Bank 1981; F.A.O. 1982; Timmer, Falcon and Pearson 1983; Pinstrup-Anderson, Berg and Forman 1984; Eicher 1984; Murphy 1983; U.S.D.A. 1984; Bryant et al. 1985; MacNamara 1985; O.T.A. 1985; Mann 1986; Asante 1986; Fleuret and Fleuret 1986; Hansen and McMillan 1986; Lemarchand 1986; Mellor 1986).

To date, however, the traditional approach of U.S. universities to research and instruction on African agriculture has been fragmented (Russell 1982). Agricultural scientists in fields such as agricultural engineering, agronomy, horticulture, forestry, and soil and animal science have focused on technical problems of production while issues of distribution, nutrition and the wider policy environment have been left to the agricultural social scientists (sociology, economics, home economics and increasingly political science and anthropology). Each discipline has generally carried out its work independently of the others. A similar subdivision is apparent in textbooks and until recently the majority of technical assistance programs.

While specialization *is* an essential part of agricultural research and training, it is, by its very nature, associated with the loss of a certain "generalist" perspective. This generalist perspective includes the capacity to see how new interventions relate to one another and to the wider ecological, economic, political, and social environment within which agriculture takes place.

If U.S. land grant universities are to equip students with academic backgrounds that will enable them to make intelligent, rational, and sensitive decisions regarding the policies that affect world food supplies and the more specific food problems that face African and other Third World developing countries, they must design a curriculum that will give to students specializing in the agricultural sciences the intellectual framework necessary for articulating their technical expertise within the wider development picture (York 1984). At the same time this curriculum must provide students in the agricultural, social and policy sciences with some basic understanding of the technical issues that are involved in ameliorating food production and consumption.

There is also the need to address the more specific concerns of individual target groups.[1] One target group includes the African students pursuing graduate training in U.S. universities. A second target group is U.S. graduate students who have chosen to concentrate on Africa. A third target group includes faculty who are involved in the teaching and the administration of the University's overseas development projects. A fourth target group that is less directly affected includes students who are involved in Bachelors, Masters and Ph.D. training programs in the African universities with which a particular U.S. university may have joint development projects.

What we are faced with, then, is a series of questions about the tradeoffs between academic training that promotes technical specialization versus a more generalist understanding of African food policy. Is there any way that both concerns can or should be addressed within the framework of a single university curriculum?

The present chapter argues that the concept of a thematically focused interdisciplinary center or program can be usefully employed to bring about a more integrated program of university involvement in training and research on African food issues. The point is raised, however, that any long-term success of such a program must be linked to the development of a strong base of department and university-level support for interdisciplinary research on developing country agriculture. The study focuses on the analysis of a specific case. More specifically, the chapter provides a brief history of the University of Florida's involvement in overseas agricultural projects, the growth of direct university involvement in African agriculture, and early attempts by the African Studies Center to develop an area focus on African food issues in the late 1970s and early 1980s. In the final section, I present a list of practical suggestions for the design of similar types of interdisciplinary programs on developing country agriculture and the more specific development problems of Sub-Saharan Africa.

African Studies and Development Research at the University of Florida

Background Interest in Developing Country Agriculture

The University of Florida has a strong tradition of interdisciplinary collaboration in overseas agricultural development focused primarily on Latin America and the Caribbean. In 1976, the Office of International Programs in the College of Agriculture (the Institute of Food and Agricultural Sciences or IFAS) was instrumental in the development of a formal Certificate in Tropical Agriculture in which students could follow a recommended curriculum of technical and social science courses related to tropical agriculture. This Certificate was awarded in conjunction with a masters or Ph.D. degree in an agricultural science or social discipline. This was followed by the development of an informal network of faculty and students interested in small farm development programs in 1977. As part of the formation of this group, meetings were held with Deans and Department Chairs to develop a list of interested faculty and relevant courses. The faculty-student group became known as SAFS (Social, Agricultural and Food Sciences) and continues to meet bi-monthly for informal bag lunch seminars on rural development.[2]

Although SAFS's development is very specific in that it did not include the creation of any formal institutional or academic structures, the activities of the group did contribute to the development of a separate Farming Systems Research and Extension (FSR/E) Program. The Farming Systems Program began in 1979 with an initial focus on

North Florida. Since then the program has developed a core course on farming systems research and extension methods and a follow-up course on development administration. Students also have the option of earning a minor degree in Farming Systems. The FSR/E program has maintained a high level of faculty involvement through a network of interested faculty from the social and agricultural sciences who serve as student advisors. The program was given a tremendous boost in 1982 when Florida signed a Memorandum of Understanding with the USAID—funded Farming Systems Support Project (FSSP) and joined an international group of Farming Systems Associates.

A more specific area of cross-disciplinary concern in developing country agriculture relates to the special needs and constraints of women food producers. Although there was a strong interest in Women in Development issues at the University throughout the 1970s, an independent program did not develop until 1984. In that year, the University of Florida Women in Agricultural Development Program (WIAD) began a bi-monthly speakers program that met opposite the SAFS speakers. Unlike SAFS, the WIAD program developed a formal administrative structure that included both a steering and advisory committee. The program was also successful in seeking outside funding for special activities including speakers, bibliographic materials development, and a major international conference on gender issues in farming systems in 1986.

A number of related interdisciplinary University programs and speaker series were started during the same time period of the late 1970s and early 1980s. These include the Humanities and Agriculture Program, (with support from the W. K. Kellogg Foundation), the Certificate of Pest Management and Plant Protection, the Center for Tropical Animal Health, the Agroforestry Seminar Series, the International Health and Nutrition speaker series, and various tropical studies curriculum and networking groups. One example of these programmatic changes can be found in anthropology where an Anthropology and Agriculture Program was created that recognized the right of the student to organize an interdisciplinary committee, and to take courses in agriculture, and later encouraged them to pursue a degree minor in one agricultural discipline. The period was also associated with an increase in the number of agricultural and social science courses dealing with tropical agriculture, Third World development and food policy.[3]

Growth of Interest in Africa

In the wake of the 1972-1974 drought, there was a substantial growth in development assistance of all sorts for Sub-Saharan Africa. In response to this, the IFAS Office of International Programs made a deliberate decision to shift from their earlier focus on Latin America and the Caribbean to bid on large African projects. The four projects they received involved agricultural research, teaching, and extension as well as the coordination of an international farming systems network of scholars and training programs (Table I). Although each of the grants was very different in terms of goals and funding, the four projects share certain characteristics in terms of their relationship to curriculum, faculty, and student development. In each case, the UF/USAID (United States Agency for International Development) projects have been associated with some amount of graduate training for faculty, researchers and administrators from the affiliated African institutions (this was especially the case for the University's collaborative programs with the Ministry of Agriculture in Malawi and the University Centre at Dschang in Cameroon). In only one case, the University Centre at Dschang, however, did a UF/USAID project actually work with curriculum development in an African university setting. In the case of the Malawi and Cameroon projects, there were opportunities for faculty travel in connection with supervising students. All four projects involved faculty—many of whom had never been to Africa before—in short-term technical assistance and consulting. Other funds from USAID through the Title XII program provided opportunities for University of Florida faculty and students to engage in research related to the development of future Africa contracts. Travel funds through the Center for African Studies, as well as spe-

---

Table I. Major USAID funded projects in the College of Agriculture at the University of Florida

1. Malawi Research and Extension Program (1979 planning; 1980–1986 funded)
2. The UF/USAID/Cameroon Agricultural Project (1980 planning; 1982–1991 funded)
3. USAID Farming Systems Support Project (FSSP) (1982–1987 funded, 50% of activities in Africa)
4. UF/USAID/Heartwater Research Project (Zimbabwe) (1985–1992 funded)

cial grants from USAID, the Ford Foundation, the United States Information Agency (USIA)/Fulbright, and the American Association of University Women were also used.

It was in recognition of this growing level of departmental and interdisciplinary involvement in research and teaching on African agriculture and food issues, that the Center for African Studies shifted the emphasis of its programs to rural development in 1981. The Center was started as an area research center within the College of Liberal Arts and Sciences in the late 1960s to coordinate university-wide research, teaching and extension activities related to Africa. The Center does not award a degree but offers a Certificate in African Studies in recognition of an area concentration on Africa in conjunction with a Bachelor's, Master's or Ph.D. degree. As such, the Center for African Studies, like the other area studies centers at the University of Florida—the Center for Latin American Studies and the Asian Studies Program—provides a mechanism for area studies coordination across the administrative boundaries between budgetary units. At Florida these include the three budgetary units that receive separate funds from the State Board of Regents: the Institute of Food and Agricultural Sciences (IFAS), the Health Center, and the General Education Budget. By the late 1970s there were numerous faculty from different colleges, schools, departments, and programs in each of these three funding units with Africa-related research and teaching activities as well as funded projects with participants from two or more units.

The Center's development of a programmatic focus on development included a deliberate attempt to attract faculty and students through public events programs. In addition, Center funds from the University, the Department of Education Title VI Foreign Language and Area Studies Program, and other sources provided administrative and financial support for visiting African and U.S. scholars. Center funds were also used to "seed" new faculty positions and to sponsor special conference, workshop, and publication projects.

In 1982 the decision was made to focus the spring interdisciplinary seminar in African Studies on rural development. The course included readings from a wide range of disciplines as well as four guest lectures from visiting African scholars. In 1983 there was a dramatic change in the organization of the course into a faculty-student seminar with a series of weekly guest lectures by faculty involved in overseas research on African agriculture and food policy. As such, the seminar provided a focus for the emerging multi-disciplinary concern with African food issues on campus. There were a number of spinoffs from the seminar including rekindling an active research and teaching interest in faculty who may have worked in Africa in the past but who had more recently been involved in domestic agriculture. One of the more immediate responses was the organization, with Center support, of an August 1983 conference, "Overcoming Constraints to Livestock Production in Africa" and the publication of an edited volume by the same name (Simpson and Evangelou 1984). The book includes contributions by African, European and U.S. scholars from agricultural economics, economics, anthropology, animal science, and range management as well as veterinary medicine. The development seminar was repeated in 1984 and 1985. By 1985 when many of the guest lecturers were presenting for the third time, the presentations had evolved into a series of 25 page chapters and recommended readings. It is this group of solicited chapters/guest lectures, recommended readings, reprinted and revised articles that was produced in the text *Food in Sub-Saharan Africa* (Hansen and McMillan 1986).

The Food in Africa Program (FIA) was initiated in 1983 to "integrate, consolidate, and provide leadership for the growing number of Center-sponsored and University activities dealing with African food issues." The leadership of FIA was vested in a steering committee of fifteen members from the Colleges of Agriculture, Liberal Arts and Sciences, Medicine, Veterinary Medicine and the School of Forest Resources and Conservation. The activities of FIA within the Center can be grouped into six areas including leadership, faculty and student development, curriculum, curriculum materials development, and conference organization (Table II).

Workshop on Curriculum Development

By fall 1984 it was increasingly apparent that any comprehensive plan for the development of disciplinary and interdisciplinary research and teaching programs on African food issues would require a more solid base of support within individual departments and colleges. It was to address this issue that the Food in Africa program organized a spring workshop on curriculum development in April 1985.[4] Letters were sent from the appropriate Deans to Chairs of departments with a his-

Table II. Activities of the Food in Africa Program,
Center for African Studies, University of Florida

1. *Leadership.*
   Providing leadership for integrating the different faculty and students involved in on and off-campus programs dealing with African food issues.
2. *Faculty and Student Development.*
   a. organizing the faculty-student interdisciplinary seminar on African food issues each spring.
   b. publicity of the activities and coordination with different speakers programs sponsored by S.A.F.S., W.I.A., the Center for Tropical Agriculture, F.S.S.P., the Farming Systems Program and the Agriculture and Humanities Program.
   c. utilization of the resources of the University, the Center for African Studies and the Center for Tropical Agriculture to encourage supplementary training by non-agriculturalists in agricultural fields as well as relevant travel and research in Africa by agriculturalist and non-agriculturalists faculty and students to study and learn about food problems.
3. *Curriculum*
   a. organizing the one semester faculty-student seminar which students could take for credit.
   b. stimulating the revision of existing courses and the development of new courses.
   c. circulation of information about relevant courses in different departments.
4. *Curriculum Materials Development*
   Encouraging faculty to participate in joint projects to develop more extensive and better quality texts and text supplements for courses.
   a. Texts developed include, *Overcoming Constraints to Livestock Production in Sub-Saharan Africa* (Simpson and Evangelou 1985) and *Food in Sub-Saharan Africa* (Hansen and McMillan 1986).
   b. Text supplements include the production of two pilot audio-visual modules based on seminar presentations that relate to book chapters in *Food in Sub-Saharan Africa.*
      1. African Landscapes as a Background to Agriculture in Africa (David Niddrie and Bob Hesterman, Geography)
      2. Overcoming Constraints to Livestock Production in Sub-Saharan Africa (James Simpson, Agricultural Economics)
   c. Orientation Notebooks on African Countries for technical assistants based on materials developed with country experts (Patricia Kuntz, Series Editor and Center Outreach Coordinator)
5. *Networking.*
   Encouraging inter-university linkages as well as ties with overseas institutions and universities through the seminar and SAFS lunch program and by inviting guest speakers from outside the University.
6. *Conference and Seminar Organization.*

toric interest in Africa including student training and direct involvement in overseas programs. Chairs were responsible for organizing department review teams and team leaders. Each team then prepared a report that examined opportunities and constraints to address African food issues within the departments' requirements for undergraduate and graduate students, and faculty requirements for teaching and publication.

The internal workshop on African food issues provided each University department, college and school a chance to publicly review the opportunities and constraints for students to address African food issues within their existing programs. As such, one of the major accomplishments of the workshop was to increase University and departmental awareness of faculty participation in Center-sponsored activities as well as faculty research, publication, and teaching on African food issues. Moreover, there was a better understanding on the part of Center for African Studies administrators of the relatively distinct constraints that face faculty and students in certain departments and colleges, in particular the College of Agriculture with its split faculty appointments in research, teaching and extension and the Colleges of Medicine and Veterinary Medicine with their legislature-mandated restrictions on the enrollment of students from outside the United States.

One of the important conclusions of the workshop was that questions of student development cannot be addressed independently of questions of faculty development. Without faculty appreciation of the need to examine the area-specific nature of African development problems, there is little recognition or encouragement of student work in this area. In the absence of administrative recognition for the validity of research and publication on international development as far as time assignments and tenure and promotion decisions, there is further support for the idea that too extensive an involvement in overseas activities before achieving the rank of Professor is ''academic suicide.'' However, it would be too facile an argument to lay all of the blame for the lack of an integrated and recognized curriculum on Third World development and African food issues onto University administration. There was in fact a very willing participation in and support of the spring workshop at every level of administration, especially in the Agriculture College. Both faculty and administration revealed a strong interest in finding out about Africa-related activities on campus; the number, background, and research interests of U.S. and African students interested in African agriculture; and a desire to have information on the relevant interdisciplinary degree and certificate options within the University more widely distributed.

Recommendations for the Design of Future Programs

In sum, the early interest in African food issues at the University of Florida shows a steady increase in the scale of research and teaching activities over the last six years. It should be emphasized, however, that no single development project, person, or monetary input was responsible. Rather, there was a series of independent but related decisions by the Office of International Programs in Agriculture, the African Studies Center, and individual faculty, to move away from the earlier focus of the University's development interests on Latin America and the Caribbean. The receipt of several large grants from USAID to coordinate projects in Africa fed into the existing structures of a strong interdisciplinary African Studies Language and Area Resource Center and an established Center for Tropical Agriculture to ensure programmatic and curricular continuity in the Africa programs. New faculty who were brought in through directed department and Center hiring decisions reinforced this momentum.

A recurrent theme in the development of cross-disciplinary curricula at the University of Florida was a movement away from informal faculty-student interest groups focused on topical areas like women in development, interdisciplinary small farm research, and African Studies, to the institutionalization of these interests in college and cross-college programs and centers. It should be emphasized that very few of the interdisciplinary centers or programs had line faculty positions and only the Latin American Studies Center offers a separate degree. Most of the other cross-disciplinary programs were construed as degree minors or certificates to be awarded in conjunction with one of the established Bachelor's, Master's or Ph.D. degrees. One of the main characteristics of successful (e.g. longstanding) interdisciplinary programs at Florida, has been their ability to work within the existing structure of departments and colleges to "institutionalize" their cross-disciplinary perspective through the modification of existing or introduction of new courses, public events programs, seed money for faculty and student travel, and assistance with special projects.

Course Development

Specific suggestions for faculty, student, and curriculum development include the use of interdisciplinary courses to provide a central focus for interdisciplinary faculty and student participation. Consideration should be given to involving faculty from a wide range of disciplines as guest lecturers and in the design of course readings as a mechanism for insuring that the cross-disciplinary focus of the course is not a simple window dressing. One successful example of this is the Food in Africa course which was listed as a special seminar by the African Studies Center during the first three years it was offered. By the fourth year, the course was moved to permanent course status with a joint listing in the catalogue under General Agriculture and African Studies. In Spring 1987 the course was team taught by five faculty, one each from the fields of agronomy, animal science, and political science, and two from anthropology.[5] There was a strong consensus among the faculty attending the spring workshop that the University did not need a proliferation of interdisciplinary development courses, but only one course for each of the major program areas. Experience has shown that when sequential interdisciplinary courses in the same area have been tried, they were usually less than successful in attracting enrollments and filling a meaningful place in the curriculum.

Second, the expressed need for interdisciplinary courses should not be used as an excuse for departments to abdicate their responsibility to increase the African content in pre-existing development courses within their established curriculum. One of the results of the workshop was the reactivation of several courses that had been listed but not taught in recent years.

Third, efforts to increase the African content and the relevance of African materials presented in existing and new courses must address the need to develop course materials with which to teach. The experiences of the FSR/E, FIA, and Tropical Animal Health groups in developing interdisciplinary texts, suggests that these projects can provide an important rallying point and basis for interdisciplinary communication with faculty from different fields. However, textbooks in the absence of teaching aids such as slides will not be of much assistance to instructors on topics outside their areas of specialization.

Faculty Development

Fourth, questions of student development cannot be addressed apart from questions of faculty development in terms of encouraging faculty to remain current on African research. It was suggested that one very fruitful avenue for the development of faculty strength on Africa is to provide faculty with opportunities to pursue graduate courses in areas outside their original fields of training.

One of the unresolved issues that emerged repeatedly was the cost to faculty in terms of lack of publication in the major refereed journals of their discipline when involved in extensive overseas and interdisciplinary research. In view of this, every effort should be made to facilitate and publicize faculty attendance at interdisciplinary conferences and professional meetings sponsored by groups like the African Studies Association, the International Farming Systems network, and Association of Women in Development, and to encourage their publication of research results in the major refereed interdisciplinary journals.

Student Development [6]

Fifth, an important recommendation with regard to the formal training of the African students who are funded for graduate degrees was that some allowance should be made in the initial outline of their graduate programs for them to enroll in at least one interdisciplinary or disciplinary course outside their major discipline. This was considered to be an important constraint on the African students' participation in complementary development courses and programs since many of them were only funded to complete their degree requirements within an absolute minimum time period with little allowance for electives.

Sixth, if disciplinary and cross-disciplinary course enrollments are to be encouraged, it is necessary to increase the publicity for course offerings in different departments. Moreover, department administrators should be made aware of the need for courses that include a large percentage of cross-disciplinary enrollments, to be offered on a regular basis so that they can be incorporated into two and three year course plans for student schedules. Sample courses that attract cross-disciplinary enrollments at the University of Florida include upper division courses on African ethnography, politics and geography, tropical soils, agronomic field methods and farming systems research and extension.

Public Events

Seventh, public events programs that sponsor speakers, workshops and conferences have an important role in program development. Efforts should be made, however, to coordinate the timing of events so that students and faculty are not swamped. Conscious efforts to coordinate with pre-existing speakers' programs increase faculty and student participation, as do efforts to solicit suggestions for speakers from faculty and student groups. For speaker programs to be successful over time, there needs to be some recognition of the limitations on volunteerism, with provisions made for either recognizing and/or compensating the faculty and student time involved in organizing these events. In the absence of some concrete provision for administrative duties, this type of program can quickly become a burden to key faculty and student organizers.

To conclude, the question of curriculum development in the study of African food issues requires teamwork and a high level of intra-institutional collaboration. At the level of individual faculty, it involves an early recognition of the limitations of one's own knowledge and a willingness to acquire basic literacy in a wide range of related fields. Without this type of concrete broadening of our academic skills and training beyond that of passive ''concern'' and ''sensitivity'' to the issues, no individual researcher or instructor is likely to have much effect on a university's curriculum, much less on the university's overseas projects. For social and agricultural science departments to be effectively involved, it requires a conscious decision to move beyond a verbal acquiescence to the importance of developing country agriculture, to the creation of faculty incentives, courses, and opportunities for student and faculty networking (Russell 1982). For universities, it requires that they reinforce these departmental endeavors through allotments of staff, fellowships, material support, and faculty time.

This review of curriculum options at the University of Florida has focused on the potential role of an interdisciplinary area studies center in giving direction and momentum to the University's research and instruction on African food issues. The analysis of this experience, however, suggests that the mere existence of an interdisciplinary area studies center is not enough. Any more long-term success with curriculum development in the study of African food issues must be built on a strong base of faculty, student and administrative support for the concept of interdisciplinary research and teaching on developing country agriculture, and an appreciation of the Africa-specific nature of certain types of development problems. Moreover, this complementary support must necessarily both begin and end within the traditional structure of departments. In almost every case where one of the Florida programs has attempted to work around this departmental base through a proliferation of interdisciplinary institutes, seminars, and autonomous support, this has proven to be only a short-term and non-permanent solution that disappeared when special funding or the persona of a charismatic leader was withdrawn.

An additional point relates to the fact that although there can be no substitute for volunteerism in the initial development of a cross-disciplinary program, it is a currency that is quickly drained. A large part of the Center for African Studies' success in institutionalizing its position within the University of Florida, can be attributed to the fact that it *did* have independent sources of university and non-university support at key points in the development of the program. What is important here is the question of balance. Although the Center for African Studies did have independent funds with which to support faculty, student and curriculum development, it did not have line faculty positions. The Center was therefore forced to rely on and indeed cultivate the voluntary participation of faculty whose salaries were paid from different departments and budgetary units.

Although it is unlikely that any one university's programs on developing-country agriculture can ever achieve an optimum balance between volunteerism and institutionalization in the development of interdisciplinary research and teaching programs, I suggest that the balanced model I have outlined should remain an administrative ideal.

It is an ideal that exists today, in partial form, in many land grant universities. Moreover, there is a strong need for additional research that compares and contrasts the curriculum models of different universities and university consortia.

Notes and Acknowledgements

The author wishes to thank R. Hunt Davis, Jr., Art Hansen, and Chris Andrews at the University of Florida, and Larry Busch, Larry Burmeister, Mary Powell and Billie DeWalt at the University of Kentucky for their comments on earlier drafts of this paper.

1. Since the mid-1980s, questions of curriculum design for target groups in African agricultural development have been an important theme in discussions at Winrock International (recently merged with the Agricultural Development Council), the Ford Foundation, and U.S.A.I.D. (Crawford 1982; Nygaard et al. 1985; Busch 1986; Flora 1985; Mann 1986; Blase 1986; USAID 1985a, 1985b). Issues raised in the literature range from general questions concerning the relevance to the U.S. land grant university model for developing country agriculture, to more specific issues of textbook development, curriculum and funding for graduate and post-graduate training (Hinderink and Sterkenberg 1983; Gruhn 1984).

A problem which is frequently discussed is the fact that, at least during the past, a high number of the returning African students were quickly promoted to administrative posts with daily work that had little or nothing to do with their graduate education. Therefore, it is maintained, there is a strong need for graduate programs to build in from the start some awareness of the wider economic, social and political setting within which the technical training a student receives will be used. It has also been observed that students will sometimes receive training in research techniques and equipment to which they will not have access when they return to their home countries. This is then used to argue that there is a strong need to adopt the research methods, topics and geographical areas where the graduate students conduct their research to the situations the students will face when they return. Others have argued conversely there is an inherent danger in efforts to modify curricula in that African students might begin to receive a second class education. Would we then be setting in motion a pattern of institutional underdevelopment in these university systems? For most it is a question of choice—whether to train students to be at the cutting edge of a technical discipline or to adapt the students' training to the research facilities that will be available to them in their home countries when they return and the opportunities and constraints of the limited resource smallholders who constitute from 60-85 percent of the total population in most African countries. For an excellent review of the literature on different training models for research and extension workers from less developed countries see Swanson (1974).

2. In any given year from 30–50 percent of the SAFS and WIAD (see later discussions) presentations were on Africa. Other presentations though not specifically focused on Africa touch on issues which have direct relevance to the continent.

3. Social science courses in geography, economics, anthropology and political science have tended to focus on theoretical models of development including food policy. In the agricultural science courses in agronomy, soil science, vegetable crops, animal science, and entomology the emphasis was placed on the expansion of existing or introduction of new courses on tropical livestock and cropping issues.

4. Planning for the workshop began in Fall 1984. Meetings between the leadership of the Food in Africa program and the appropriate Deans of the different colleges involved were scheduled in November. In addition to the departmental reviews which were circulated in advance, individual team members were expected to provide a list of critical issues which students, faculty and administrators concerned with Third World food issues, and more specifically, African food issues, needed to become acquainted. On the morning of the second day of the workshop the department teams were recombined into issue related groups that crossed disciplinary boundaries on the general topics of livestock, plant sciences, economic policy, special interdisciplinary minor and certificate programs, physical and environmental sciences, health and food sciences and social sciences. Each interdisciplinary group prepared a short report that examined the opportunities and constraints to address these themes with the existing fund of resources on campus. The proceedings volume distributed to administrators and faculty participants includes an edited version of the presentations by guest speakers, a synthesis of the position papers on critical issues, and final reports of the departmental and interdepartmental groups.

5. Each faculty member was responsible for the design of one three to four week unit and shared responsibility for the course outline, testing, and grading procedures. The course units are expected to shift every year according to the areas of expertise of the faculty involved in team teaching. The five units in spring 1986 were: (1) environmental and human systems; (2) crop and forestry systems; (3) livestock and wildlife systems; and (4) long-term policy options. Students were expected to leave the course with: an understanding of basic food and fiber research issues; (2) the vocabulary necessary to understand and integrate possible or potential solutions originating in and/or affecting different academic disciplines; (3) a general understanding of the research and policy concerns of the four disciplines involved in team teaching and the interrelationship of these disciplinary concerns to one another; and (4) contemporary food and policy options for national and international development agencies.

6. A third unresolved issue that was hotly debated concerned the admission of graduate students from non-English speaking areas. Some faculty suggested that in many cases the University's language requirements exclude foreign students who are able to catch up once they begin formal training. Other faculty noted that the potential problems caused by admitting gradu-

ate students without the proper qualifications far exceed any benefit to be had from lower admission requirements. This remained an open topic of discussion.

References

Asante, S.K.B. (1986). Food as a Focus of National and Regional Policies in Contemporary Africa. In, *Food in Sub-Saharan Africa*. Eds., Art Hansen and Della E. McMillan. Boulder, CO.: Lynne Rienner Publishers, Inc.

Bates, Robert (1981). *Markets and States in Tropical Africa: The Political Basis of Agricultural Policies*. Berkeley: University of California Press.

Belshaw, Deryke and Thomas, Ian (1984). The Rural Development Challenge to the Universities: Safety in Theory or Danger in Practice? *Journal of Modern African Studies* 22,1: 109–132.

Blase, Mel (1986). Evaluating Institution Building Projects. Paper presented at Workshop on Agricultural Universities and Rural Development. December 17, 1985. Paper submitted to Dr. Gary Hansen. Washington, D.C.: USAID/PPC/CDIE.

Bryant, Carol A., Courtney, Anita, Markesbery, Barbara A., Dewalt, Kathleen M. (1985). *The Cultural Feast: An Introduction to Food and Society*. St. Paul, Minnesota: West Publishing Company.

Busch, Lawrence (1981). *Science and Agricultural Development*. Osmun: Allanheld.

Busch, Lawrence (1986). Evaluating Agricultural Research Institutions. Paper presented at Workshop on Agricultural Universities and Rural Development. December 17, 1985. Paper submitted to Dr. Gary Hansen. Washington, D.C.: WSAID/PPC/CDIE.

Crawford, Paul R. (1982). AID Experience in Agricultural Research: A Review of Project Evaluations. AID Program Evaluation Discussion Paper, No. 13. May. Washington, D.C.: Office of Evaluation, Bureau for Program and Policy Coordination, USAID.

Eicher, Carl (1984). International Technology Transfer and the African Farmer: Theory and Practice. Working Paper 3/84. May. Paper presented at a conference of the Association of Faculties of Agriculture in Africa (AFAA), Manzini, Swaziland, 22–27 April, 1984.

Food and Agriculture Organization (F.A.O.) (1982). Famine in Africa: Situation, Cause, Prevention, Control. Rome: Organization of African Unity, F.A.O.

Fleuret, Anne. (1986). Survey of Nutrition in East Africa. In, *Training Manual in Nutritional Anthropology*. Eds., Sara A. Quandt and Cheryl Ritenbaugh. A Special Publication of the American Anthropological Association. No. 20. Pp. 90–97.

Fleuret, Anne and Fleuret, Pat. (1986). Nutrition and Development. In, *Training Manual in Nutritional Anthropology*. Eds., Sara A. Quandt and Cheryl Ritenbaugh. A Special Publication of the American Anthropological Association. No. 20. Pp. 82–89.

Flora, Cornelia (1985). Lessons from the U.S. Land Grant Experience for Creating Agricultural Colleges. Paper presented at Workshop on Agricultural Universities and

Rural Development. December 17, 1985. Paper submitted to Dr. Gary Hansen. Washington, D.C.: USAID/PPC/CDIE.

Gruhn, Isebill V. (1984). Towards Scientific and Technological Independence? *The Journal of Modern African Studies* 22,1:1–17.

Hansen, Art and McMillan, Della E. (1986). *Food in Sub-Saharan Africa.* Boulder, CO.: Lynne Rienner Publishers, Inc.

Hinderink, J. and Sterkenburg, J.J. (1983). Agricultural Policy and Production in Africa: the Aims, the Methods and the Means. *The Journal of Modern African Studies* 21, 1:1–23.

Lemarchand, Rene (1986). The Political Economy of Food Issues. In, *Food in Sub-Saharan Africa.* Eds., Art Hansen and Della E. McMillan. Boulder, CO.: Lynne Rienner Publishers, Inc.

MacNamara, Robert S. (1985). The Challenges for Sub-Saharan Africa. Sir John Crawford Memorial Lecture. November 1, 1985.

Mann, Charles (1986). The Role of the University in Improving National Food Policies. Paper presented at Workshop on Agricultural Universities and Rural Development. December 17, 1985. Paper submitted to Dr. Gary Hansen. Washington, D.C.: USAID/PPC/CDIE.

McMillan, Della E. and Hansen, Art (1985). Proceedings of a Workshop on Curriculum Development in the Study of African Food Issues. Gainesville, FL.: Center for African Studies, University of Florida.

Mellor, John (1986). Agriculture on the Road to Industrialization. International Food Policy Research Institute (I.F.P.R.I.), Reprint No. 83. Washington, D.C.: I.F.P.R.I.

Murphy, Josette (1983). Strengthening the Agricultural Research Capacity of the Less Developed Countries: Lessons from A.I.D. Experience. A.I.D. Program Evaluation Report No. 10. Washington, D.C.: USAID.

Nygaard, David F., Makhambera, Peter T.E., Mrema, Geoffrey C., Bonnen, James T. and Panagides, Stahis (1985). Training Agricultural Scientists for Southern Africa. Southern African Development Coordination Conference. Unpublished report submitted to the Ministry of Agriculture, Harare, Zimbabwe. July. Distributed through the Agricultural Development Council and Winrock International, Morrillton, Arkansas.

Office of Technology Assessment (O.T.A.) (1984). *Africa Tomorrow: Issues in Technology, Agriculture, and U.S. Foreign Aid: A Technical Memorandum.* Washington, D.C.: Congress of the United States, Office of Technology Assessment.

Ongla, Jean (1985). Training Experts for Africa—What They Should Know. Paper presented, Workshop on Curriculum Development in the Study of African Food Issues. April 17–19, 1985. Gainesville, FL.: Center for African Studies.

Pinstrup-Anderson, Per, Berg, Alan and Forman, Martin (1984). *International Agricultural Research and Human Nutrition.* Washington, D.C.: International Food Policy Research Institute.

Russell, Martha Garett, ed. (1982). *Enabling Interdisciplinary Research: Perspectives from Agriculture, Forestry and Home Economics.* St. Paul, Minnesota: University of Minnesota, Agricultural Experiment Station, Miscellaneous Publication 19–1982.

Simpson, James R. and Evangelou, Phylo, eds. (1984). *Livestock Development in Subsaharan Africa.* Boulder, CO.: Westview Press.

Swanson, Burton Eugene (1974). Training Agricultural Research and Extension Workers from Less Developed Countries: An Examination of Training Approaches Used by the International Rice Research Institute and the International Maize and Wheat Improvement Center. Ph.D. thesis, University of Wisconsin. Madison, Wisconsin.

Timmer, C. Peter, Falcon, Walter P., and Pearson, Scott R. (1983). *Food Policy Analysis.* Baltimore: The Johns Hopkins University Press for the World Bank.

United States Agency for International Development (USAID) (1985a). Education for Agriculture: Proceedings of the Symposium on Education for Agriculture. Manila: International Rice Research Institute (Available through USAID reprint service).

United States Agency for International Development (U.S.A.I.D.) (1985b). Plans for Supporting Agricultural Research and Faculties of Agriculture in Africa. Washington, D.C.: U.S.A.I.D., Bureau for Africa, Bureau of Science and Technology. Office of Agriculture.

United States Department of Agriculture (U.S.D.A.) (1984). Sub-Saharan Africa: Outlook and Situation Report. Washington, D.C.: U.S.D.A., Economic Research Service. RS-84-10. July.

World Bank (1981). *Accelerated Development in Sub-Saharan Africa: A Joint Program of Action.* Washington, D.C.: The World Bank.

York, E.T. (1984). A Major International Dimension for U.S. Colleges of Agriculture—An Imperative. Seaman A. Knapp Memorial Lecture presented at the Annual Meeting of National Association of State Universities and Land-Grant Colleges. Washington, D.C.: United States Department of Agriculture, Extension Service.

Towards A Participatory Evaluation Methodology: The Southern African Pilot Learning Process

Ann Seidman[1]

Department of International Development
Clark University
Wooster, MA 01610–1477

> "You only get really self-reliant
> development when the people themselves
> raise questions and examine the causes of
> the difficulties they face and look for new
> answers. You can't push projects down
> their throats."—A participant in the
> Gwebi Learning Process Workshop,
> August, 1985.

Introduction

In the 1980's, despite extensive aid, independent African states confronted a crisis. Food shortages, mounting debt, rising prices, and falling per capita incomes plagued the continent. Members of grassroots development projects in remote rural areas experienced growing difficulties that hindered their attempts to improve their incomes and living standards. Many aid agencies, as well as social scientists, puzzled over the reasons why.

In 1984, Oxfam America initiated the Southern African Pilot Learning Process to involve grassroots project members themselves in

---

[1] This paper is based on a book, jointly edited by Denny Kalyalya, Khethiwe Mhlanga, Ann Seidman, and Joseph Semboja, entitled *Aid and Development? A Pilot Southern African Learning Process.* Trenton, NJ: Africa World Press. (1987)

a search for some answers to the problems engendered by development.[2] For two years, researchers from three southern African universities worked together with representatives of intermediary agencies and members of 14 grassroots projects in Zambia, Zimbabwe, and Tanzania to evolve a participatory problem-solving methodology. They not only aimed to strengthen project members' capacity to discover the causes of the difficulties they confront. They sought, too, to create a participatory methodology which would empower the project members themselves to devise better strategies for attaining self-reliant development. This paper aims to 1) outline the Pilot Learning Process and its goals, 2) explain the three theoretical foundations on which it rests—participation by project members, a problem-solving methodology, and use of national researchers, and 3) summarize the findings of the Pilot Learning Process.[3]

The Aim Of The Pilot Learning Process

The Pilot Learning Process aimed to involve the project members of the 14 sample projects, together with selected aid agency staff members, in a novel program for assessing their projects. This program concentrated on the behaviors and decision-making processes of project members, rather than of donor agencies or professional project staff. By involving the actual project participants in a study of how their project worked, the Learning Process organizers hoped to gain insights into reasons for success or failure of their projects. This learning process would give participants a method for evaluating future projects. It would therefore help participants and aid organizations to achieve better results in the future.

To clarify the limited aim of the pilot process, Figure 1 pictures the several actors in the aid process. International private voluntary orga-

---

[2] Other agencies that participated in the learning process included the Catholic Relief Services, the American Friends Service Committee, the Canadian Universities Service Organization, and the Community Development Trust Fund of Tanzania. The Ford Foundation, as well as several individual donors, contributed generously to making the pilot learning process possible.

[3] The process and the findings are described at much greater length in Kalyalya, et al. 1987.

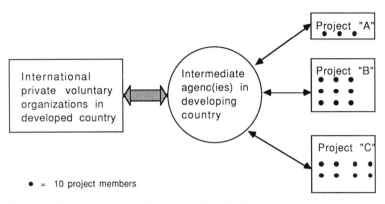

● = 10 project members

Figure 1. The several actors in the transfer of aid

nizations, intermediary agencies, and projects all have their own perspectives and goals. These may not always coincide. They also have their own internal decision-making structures. The outcome of any given project is the cumulative result of actions taken all along the line. While grassroots project members have little control over the decision process at higher levels, they can learn to evaluate that process at the level of their own project. This was the level at which the pilot process was designed to operate.

Understanding the conflicting goals and pressures of the different actors in the aid process is an important step in removing the obstacles to development.[4] International private voluntary organizations, like other bureaucracies, may respond not only to the concerns of third world rural inhabitants, but to the pressures of donors and their own internal structures. Further (Figure 1), international private voluntary organizations frequently transfer resources through a variety of intermediary organizations in the differing socio-economic contexts of particular third world countries. These intermediaries may include the international organizations' field offices, or the field offices of other international agencies with similar perspectives. They may also include non-government groups of nationals (religious or secular) who

---

[4] Frances Korten (1981) discusses the obstacles to donor agency support for participatory project development. The arguments are summarized in Kalyalya, et al. (1987: Chapter 1).

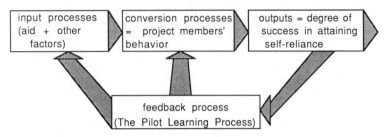

Figure 2. A model of the role of the learning process in the transfer of aid

seek to stimulate rural development, or local development agencies with fairly close ties to government. Each of these intermediaries has its own priorities and methods of work.

Finally, the projects receiving aid may each have their own goals which may differ implicitly, if not explicitly, from those of the intermediaries and donors. Their individual members, too, may have conflicting needs and demands which the projects' internal decisionmaking structures may or may not adequately mediate.[5]

The Pilot Learning Process focused on how projects affected the way that members utilized aid in their efforts to achieve the project's stated goals. Figure 2 adapts a decision-making model to illustrate the way the Learning Process sought to provide feedback to project members and aid agency staff. The model depicts the way decision-makers behave in a particular institution or process of resource transfer.

In the case of development projects, the model depicts three sets of activities to produce outputs: 1) the input processes, that is, the transfer of aid along with other resources to the project; 2) the conversion processes, that is, the way project holders work together to utilize the resources; 3) the feedback process, which provides information influencing the decision-maker's behavior, suggesting how it might be improved to achieve the desired goals. If the outputs do not correspond to the goals stated in the initial project document—and they almost never do—the feedback process should help to explain why,

---

[5] Korten (1981) examines several obstacles which may hinder participatory organization of community structures.

and should lay the basis for decisions leading to improved future performance.[6]

The model focuses on the way project members respond to their range of choices in using the resources transferred to them by the aid agency. Although it provides no insight into the factors determining the donor agencies' decision-making processes, improved information as to how the project members are likely to behave in response to the new opportunities created by the transfer of resources should enable the agencies to devise aid strategies which better meet the project members' needs.[7]

While the Pilot Learning Process concentrated on improving project performance, it also aimed to relate theory to practice. It did this by systematically examining how project members functioned to attain stated goals. To illustrate, most private voluntary organizations generally hold that their aid empowers project members to attain self-reliant development. Admittedly, "self-reliance" remains poorly defined, both as concept and as theory. However, systematic evaluation of projects that receive aid should help the project members and aid agency staff to identify both the patterns of behavior—institutions— and resource allocation that affect attainment of self-reliance. By increasing their understanding of the constraints and resources, the process should empower the project members to deal more effectively with their environment.

At the same time, the process should help further define the concept of self-reliance and develop the theory explaining it. The collapse of a bridge raises questions not only about its plan and construction, but also the underlying theory of mechanics on which its design rested. So, too, by comparing the predicted results of the transfer of aid with the actual consequences, evaluation research should test and help to improve, not only specific plans, but also the underlying theory.

---

[6] Baratz and Bachrach (1970) criticized Dahl's model as static. The model as used in the learning process attempts to introduce a dynamic character by emphasizing decision-making activities or processes.

[7] The model may be easily adapted to consider the role of feedback in aid agencies by substituting them (and their internal staff structures) for the project members in the conversion process: the input and feedback processes define the factors likely to influence their decisions; and the outputs constitute their transfer of particular resources to projects.

Thus, the Pilot Learning Process sought to utilize an approach to evaluation which would contribute to empowering project holders to attain self-reliant development. Three primary features constitute the theoretical foundations of the learning process: Participation by the project holders together with donor and intermediary agencies; a problem-solving methodology; and the role of qualified facilitators, preferably nationals.

The Theoretical Foundations

1. The Participation Of Project Members.

In recent years, more and more evaluators have emphasized the advantages of involving those whose work is being assessed in the evaluation process.[8] Designers of the Learning Process aimed to test the proposition that through participation in an improved evaluation process, project holders can learn to analyze and overcome the obstacles thwarting their efforts to attain self-reliance. A considerable body of theory undergirds this proposition.[9] The southern African pilot project sought to adapt that theory to the process of evaluating aid projects. To plan aid, donors must anticipate how project holders will behave within the constraints and resources of their environment.

The argument for project members' participation in the Learning Process rests on two premises. First, common sense argues that no one can better describe those constraints than the project members themselves. By creating an environment in which the members can

---

[8] E.g., see Korten (1980) for a review of some case studies illustrating the advantages of increased participation in project design and evaluation; also see comments in Kalyalya, et al. (1987:Chapter 1).

[9] See Korten (1980). An international participatory research network has been established, with participants from Africa, Asia, and Latin America, which has been experimenting and developing the theory and practice of participatory research. Its head office is in Canada. The African component started in Tanzania and has spread into a number of African countries. In 1986, Deryk Malenga of the University of Zambia became the president of the African Participatory Research Network.

participate in the evaluation process, the voluntary agencies can tap their special knowledge about the causes of their problems.

Second, by engaging in a systematic evaluation of the obstacles hindering their progress, the project members may acquire a better understanding of their own behavior, as well as the constraints and resources within which they hope to attain their objectives. In the process, they should learn to formulate more self-reliant strategies for the future.

Robert Seidman (1978) suggests that seven categories of factors will likely influence the behavior of project members in their efforts to attain their goals (see Chambliss and Seidman 1971). These factors are:

Rule. Like any law or norm, the project document typically prescribes the changed behavior required to achieve the stated goal. The members must work together in certain specified ways to sew uniforms, to plant, harvest, and sells crops, etc.

Opportunity. By transferring specified resources, aid aims to create the opportunity for the members to use them, together, with other resources, to achieve their goals.

Capacity. Unless they have the necessary skills, members will likely miss their goals. In addition to the ability to sew, or knowledge about the growing and marketing of crops, they must have bookkeeping and management skills (or the transfer of resources must help them to acquire these skills). They must also have internal institutions which enable them the make appropriate decisions and settle disputes.

Communication. For the project members to behave in appropriate ways, they must have received and understood information about the project goals and processes. Communications theory underscores the advantages of engaging members in a two-way face-to-face dialogue to insure this.

Interest. Members are unlikely to behave in appropriate ways unless convinced that the project serves their interests.[10]

---

[10] Unlike mainstream economic theory, which focuses on interest as the single most important influence affecting behavior, this approach includes interest along with six other factors.

Process. Members are more likely to change their behavior to carry out the project as planned if they have participated in the decision-making process. Since evaluation constitutes a crucial feature of the decision-making process, project holders should participate in evaluation as well as in the initial planning process.

Ideology. If project goals or process contradict the community's values and attitudes, project members will probably not behave in appropriate ways to achieve the goals unless, through participation in an evaluation process, they consciously decide to adopt different values and attitudes.[11]

These seven factors provide an agenda or a checklist for evaluation research designed to explain the project members' behavior in utilizing aid. These factors all lie within the environment of the project members, who therefore possess special knowledge concerning them. For these reasons, the Learning Process focused on creating the opportunity for grassroots project members to participate in analyzing them. By involving the project members in the design and implementation of the process, it aimed to help them to understand and view evaluation as essential to their own interests.

Furthermore, the final category, ideology, suggests that project members' own values may impose a major constraint on their development efforts; unless they change these values, they may behave in ways that impede attainment of their stated goals. For example, many southern Africans, accepting the traditional belief in women's inferiority, exclude them from project decision-making. However, depending on where they live on the continent, women grow 40 to 80 percent of the food crops. Unless women understand and participate in formulating plans for projects to grow food crops, those projects may fail.[12] If, by participating in the Learning Process, the project members themselves discover that their traditional exclusion of

---

[11] These categories are adapted from an analysis of the factors likely to influence a role-occupant's behavior in response to new norms embodied in law. The mnemonic, ROCCIPI, may help to remember them (R. Seidman 1978, Chambliss and Seidman 1971).

[12] The governments of Tanzania, Zambia, and Zimbabwe have all initiated programs to help insure that women have the opportunity to participate fully in development projects.

women from decision-making blocks their progress, they will more likely seek ways to include them.

In sum, the pilot Learning Process aimed to enable project members to strengthen their capacity to plan and improve their own efforts to achieve self-reliance. At the same time, the process sought to create a mechanism for channelling their findings to the private voluntary agency community to enable it to improve its contribution to their efforts (Yin and Yates 1975).[13] This analysis may help to explain not only the disillusionment with outsiders' evaluations, but also why many projects fail to attain their goals. First, without the members' participation, evaluators can discover only with difficulty the causes of problems encountered. Second, unless the members participate, they themselves may never understand the causes. As Mamdani (1985) put it:

"(A)ny strategy that claims to be a solution must seek to revive the creativity and initiative of the people. Central to this must be educating people about the relations that make them disaster-prone. This education must be based on investigation, concrete and independent. And it must lead to organization, both popular and around concrete issues."

2. A Problem-Solving Methodology.

Achieving meaningful project member participation in the evaluation process requires an appropriate methodology that fosters learning through doing. That is, the methodology should empower the project members themselves to take part in the process of examining the constraints and resources affecting their attainment of self-reliant development. Such a methodology should strengthen their capacity to formulate more effective development strategies. For this purpose, the Southern African Pilot Project adopted a problem-solving approach.

The problem-solving methodology provides a framework for engaging the decision makers in systematically analyzing the causes of the difficulties they confront. It seeks to identify the resources on which they may rely, and the obstacles—including institutions and values— which may constrain their efforts. Thus it lays a basis from which they may identify strategies to overcome the institutional and resource

---

[13] See Lisa Peattie (1985) for a criticism of the ladder concept as simplistic.

constraints that might otherwise obstruct their implementation of self-reliant development strategies.

Adapting the problem-solving methodology to evaluating the impact of aid requires a recognition that aid itself constitutes only a proposed partial solution to the problem of underdevelopment as conceived by its designers—whether they constitute the aid agency, its intermediary, the project members, or all of them together. Like all human enterprises, development (whether on the national or the grassroots level) is an ongoing process involving many interacting factors. Projects necessarily have limited goals, and no planned strategy ever succeeds perfectly. Both internal factors and changing external circumstances inevitably impede progress. Underdevelopment persists because of these circumstances. To conclude that projects have failed because they encounter difficulties in achieving their initially stated goals reflects an inadequate understanding of the development process. Instead, the project members, together with those who assist them, must continually monitor the results of implementing aid strategies. In this process, they will inevitably discover new difficulties. They must then analyze the causes of these new difficulties as the basis for revising their old strategies or formulating new ones. Gradually the project holders themselves will improve their capacity to use their own resources to achieve self-reliant development.

There are five basic steps that comprise the problem-solving methodology. Designers of the Pilot Learning Process sought to adapt these steps to their proposed participatory process for evaluating aid. They aimed to engage the project holders together with donor and intermediary agency representatives to:

1. *Identify the problem.* Define the nature and scope of the difficulties or problems that hinder project members from attaining their goal. The Learning Process involved the project holders themselves, since, as the ones most affected, they know the most about the problems they confront.

2. *Consider the full range of explanations.* Formulate all possible explanations of the problems into logically consistent sets of propositions capable of being tested in light of objective information available from the project. All too often, donor agencies and project holders assume they "know" what causes the difficulties. Their conventional wisdom tends to take society's values and insti-

tutions as given. In contrast, systematic considerations of all possible explanations will more likely uncover unsuspected causal factors. The attempt to formulate the candidate explanations as a set of logically consistent propositions, capable of being tested against the facts, facilitates determination as to which ones deserve further analysis. Involvement of the project members in this exercise will enable them to learn how in the future to better analyze the causes of their problems.

3. *Test the explanations against the facts.* Involve the project members in gathering evidence to test which of the alternative possible explanations coincides most closely with the evidence as to the causes of the difficulties which the project confronts. Social science cannot "prove" the truth of a proposition, but it can determine which candidate explanation seems most consistent with the available evidence. The formulation of explanations as testable propositions simultaneously suggests which relevant facts project holders should gather to test them. It is critical to engage project holders in gathering relevant information to evaluate the validity of the alternative explanations. In the process, they will acquire more knowledge of the resources available to them, as well as the constraints likely to thwart their efforts.

4. *Propose solutions.* Discovery of the explanation most consistent with the available data helps to empower project members to devise better strategies for solving their problems. It exposes the causes of the difficulties which they must address. Having participated in the first three steps, the members should have acquired the new understanding needed to devise more suitable strategies to overcome them.

5. *Monitor implementation of the new strategy.* Since the new or revised strategy will inevitably encounter new or further difficulties, the problem-solving approach emphasizes the necessity of institutionalizing an on-going participatory feedback mechanism. Having taken part in the first phase, the members will have acquired the skills for this exercise. In other words, participation in the problem-solving evaluation process will help to empower them to conduct an on-going evaluation of their next steps, a vital foundation for building self-reliance.

The problem-solving methodology outlined here differs in several respects from the ends-means approach employed by many evaluators to assess aid projects (Banfield 1973). The ends-means approach typically takes the goals of the project as given. Frequently, this implies stating the goals in quantitative terms. Examples of such terms are: In a given period, the plowing of so many acres and the production and sale of so many bags of maize (or cotton or beans or other crops); the sewing and sale of a stated number of school uniforms; the digging of a specified number of boreholes. The evaluators then assess the means that led to the success or failure as measured by the extent to which the project achieved those quantitatively formulated goals.[14]

The ends-means approach stems from the widely used but seldom explicitly stated theoretical framework which pervades conventional decision-making (i.e., positivism). By its very nature, the ends-means approach cannot serve voluntary agencies' requirements. It identifies ends with values, about which people may debate, but which publicly available data cannot serve to validate. This approach tends to take values and even institutional structures as reflecting "society's" goals. As a corollary, ends-means proponents argue that, except by surveying opinion, evaluators cannot even conduct empirical research concerning values, and therefore, goals. This frequently implies that a project can only encompass incremental change, leaving intact the basic institional behaviors and attitudes of society often interwoven into and sustaining the fabric of underdevelopment.[15]

As a logical consequence of its underlying premises, the ends-means approach limits decision-making to the mobilization of bias; those with the power to make decisions—whether on a national, a village, or a project level—may impose their values on the less powerful. For example, with the best will in the world, a private voluntary organization may simply adopt conventional wisdom as to what

---

[14] E.g., the World Bank Evaluation of an El Salvador site-and-service housing project established indicators of housing standards, family satisfaction, and economic value, measured against a pre-determined scale. See Bamberger, et al. (1982).

[15] This view of ends-means capsizes the conventional argument that problem-solving—usually equated with pragmatism—encompasses only incremental change, whereas ends-means alone permits radical change. However, introduction of a problem-solving approach within the context of a broader analysis of the causes of underdevelopment fosters consciousness-raising concerning the need for more basic change.

project members should do to achieve self-reliant development. Since it has the power to give or withhold aid, it may thus shape the project's goals.

At the level of the project, members may accept the leaders' decisions because, for whatever reasons, the community institutions give these leaders power. But the members who disagree may implement the resulting decisions in a perfunctory manner. As the swath of failed aid projects in the development field attests, an ends-means approach that neglects the role of members' values and institutions cannot fulfil the aid-givers' dreams.

Unlike the ends-means approach, the problem-solving methodology outlined here provides an agenda for integrating on-going evaluation into the design of every grassroots project, each of which constitutes a part of the overall complex, contradictory process of development. The problem-solving methodology provides all those engaged in transferring aid to grassroots projects with an opportunity to understand the factors hindering self-reliant development for the rural population. It also gives that population concrete tools for improving the impact of aid. In this sense, the methodology provides a systematic framework for involving all the actors in the transfer of aid in an ongoing "learning process."[16]

3. The Use Of National Researchers.

Conducting a participatory evaluation of aid projects does not imply simply bringing the project holders together in a workshop, explaining the process, and leaving them to implement it. Rather, it requires the creation of a group dynamic which enables the participants to work together to find solutions to their problems. Creating that dynamic requires the participation of a trained facilitator.

An experiment with self-evaluation in Zimbabwe illustrates the difficulties of simply encouraging project members to undertake a self-

---

[16] By incorporating the problem-solving methodology, this approach attempts to further systematize the first of the three basic steps identified by David Korten (1980) as central to a participatory approach to development: 1) embracing (not rejecting) error; 2) planning with the people; and 3) linking knowledge-building with action.

evaluation. Prior to the introduction of the pilot Learning Process, one intermediary agency sought to encourage the members of some of the same group of projects to conduct a self-evaluation. A staff member met with the leaders of the projects, explained the purpose of the exercise, and left them with a questionnaire to fill out with the information they gathered. Examination of the "answers" provided revealed that few, if any, of the project leaders had really understood the aims of the exercise, far less learned anything from it. They merely listed some incomplete facts about the background of the participants of the projects.[17]

The seven factors listed earlier (ROCCIPI) can serve as a framework for examining the need for a facilitator skilled in a problem-solving methodology. Without the on-going participation of such a facilitator, participatory evaluation is likely to fail.

Rule. The pilot project proposed that those engaged generate statements of difficulties, explanations, and proposals for solution.

Opportunity. The Learning Process provided the opportunity for implementing the project.

Capacity. The problem-solving methodology requires the ability to formulate and test the full range of possible explanations of the causes of rural poverty and underdevelopment which aid aims to empower the project members to overcome. The causes of problems affecting projects may exist at several levels: 1) the lack of management capacity, even with all the technical skills that aid may help to provide; 2) factors hindering the democratic participation of all the project members in project decision-making; and 3) externally imposed constraints, ranging from government policies to the consequences of the international recession. An understanding of the multiple causes of underdevelopment calls for a fairly high level of social science education denied to most rural dwellers the world around.

Communication. A workshop involving the project members would not suffice to communicate to them all the necessary understandings and skills required to produce meaningful explanations and proposals for solution. That would require an on-going, learning-

---

[17] Brian Smith (1983) found similar results.

by-doing kind of process throughout a prolonged period, facilitated by someone capable of assisting them to tease the relevant explanations out of their complex environment.

Interest. Some donor and intermediate agency staff members, not to mention some project leaders, might not find it in their interest to explore all the relevant explanations. It might turn out that their own negative role causes the difficulties. To leave the evaluation process to those who may seek to utilize aid for their own ends in these circumstances would likely prove counterproductive.

Process. Under the best of circumstances, bringing donor staff and project members together in a participatory process is difficult. Each has unconscious attitudes and patterns of behavior that may constitute blocks to effective participation. Without an outside facilitator, these may remain as obstacles to implementation of a truly participatory process.

Ideology. The attitudes and values of the project holders themselves, as well as donor and intermediary staff members, may thwart behavior changes needed to implement the proposed learning process. For example, if project holders' attitudes exclude women from making decisions concerning a food-crop project, that same bounded rationality may hinder them from recognizing that exclusion as a major cause of failure. A sympathetic outside facilitator might help them to discover and perhaps overcome this constraint.

Widespread criticism of aid agencies' employment of expatriate evaluators constitutes an important factor leading to the design of the pilot Learning Process.[18] In part, this criticism may reflect the non-participatory style of those evaluators, as much as the fact that they were expatriates. In part, however, it reflects a two-fold concern. First, expatriate evaluators frequently lacked sufficient familiarity with the culture of the region. Second, exclusion of national researchers from the evaluation process denied them the opportunity to learn from, as well as contribute to, grassroots rural development. As the Nigerian ambassador to the United States observed (1985), if aid

---

[18] Smith (1983) argues that trust is an important element in institutions and network building, which thorough evaluations, especially by North Americans, may undermine.

agencies do not include African researchers in finding solutions to underdevelopment, they may become part of the problem.

In the early years of independence, because of colonial neglect of education, donor agencies could argue with some justification that not many Africans had acquired the needed skills to conduct the kinds of evaluation they sought. However, by the 1980's, over a quarter of a century after the first African states had achieved independence and begun to build up their own educational institutions (including universities), that argument was no longer valid. Africans constituted a high proportion of the social science staff in most southern African universities. Exceptions to this generalization were Mozambique and Angola, which inherited illiteracy rates of 90 to 95% from prolonged rule by the Portugese, one of the most underdeveloped European countries.

Given that development of a participatory evaluation process, at least at the outset, requires a perspective and facilitation from outside the project, engaging African nationals as facilitators, rather than bringing in foreign "experts," has significant potential benefits. First, African researchers are more likely to speak the project members' language and to have knowledge of their cultures and traditions. They can work closely in a participatory process with the members, helping them to strengthen their capacity to analyze and find solutions to their problems. [19]

Second, as staff members of national research or teaching institutions, national facilitators can integrate the results of the information gathered in the course of the evaluation process into the expanding national body of critical thought needed to ensure more effective planning at the grassroots, national, and regional levels. Over time, through participation by their staff in the Learning Process, national research and teaching institutions may obtain valuable grassroots evidence to test the broad range of development theories. This should contribute to improving those theories as possible guides for the formulation and implementation of national plan strategies. This should also help to reduce national as well as small rural projects' depen-

---

[19] The Bagamoyo project in Tanzania supports this proposition; see Swantz and Jerman (1977).

dency on outside aid.[20] Thus the participation of national researchers in the participatory learning process should strengthen the national capacity (as well as that of project members) to analyze the causes of poverty and underdevelopment.[21]

Given the fairly recent origin of southern African institutions of higher education and research, this proposition may be more true here than in Asia or Latin America. First, in Africa, many of the national researchers come from rural backgrounds that enable them to empathize with and understand peasants' problems. Second, the relative scarcity of high level personnel has limited the division between teaching and research that characterizes institutions of higher learning in some other regions. This means that researchers will more likely introduce the lessons of the learning process into classes that they teach. They may also integrate the learning process methodology into teaching curricula, helping to reduce rather than widen the gap between theory and practice, and between the lives of rural people and the teaching and research community.

The pilot Learning Process involved an effort to work closely with the national research and teaching institutions to select as facilitators researchers who not only possessed relevant academic qualifications, but who empathized with and understood the villagers and their problems.

The Pilot Process

An outline of the pilot process may clarify the way it introduced a participatory, problem-solving methodology. In July, 1983, representatives of the 14 projects, selected intermediary agency staff members, and three national university researchers from Tanzania, Zambia, and Zimbabwe met in Lusaka, Zambia, for a week-long workshop

---

[20] See Ann Seidman (1972) for a further analysis of alternative possible national development strategies. The 1980's crisis that engulfed African and other third world rural populations bears witness to the importance of these issues.

[21] Strengthening national research capacity was also an aim of the Bagamoyo project (Swantz and Jerman 1977).

to design the learning process. During the week, the workshop participants discussed the nature of the problems confronting the projects, possible explanations as to their causes, and how to involve the project members in collecting information to assess which explanation most effectively coincided with the evidence. This workshop not only laid the foundation for carrying out the process; it constituted an important learning experience for the participants about their respective roles in it.

On their return to their home countries, the researchers together with the intermediary staff members, arranged national workshops. These involved project representatives, together with carefully selected university students, in analyzing how the participatory problem-solving methodology might best be used in the projects in each country. The students, coming from the project areas, understood the language and the culture of the project members. In fact, in Tanzania, the participants conducted the workshop in Swahili. During the workshop, the students learned how to work together with the project members to gather evidence to assess candidate explanations as to the causes and possible solutions for the difficulties they confronted.

The students then went with the project representatives back to the projects during their long vacations (six to eight weeks). There, they lived and worked with the project members, helping them to gather, record, and systematize relevant information for identifying the constraints and resources encountered in their efforts to build self-reliant projects. The students' primary responsibility lay in assisting the project members' own efforts to analyze their situations. The university researchers supervised the students' work, where possible visiting them and meeting at least once during the long vacation to discuss and improve their use of the methodology.

Following the prolonged period of work with the projects' members, the students wrote up the members' findings. The project representatives and the students then met for a final national workshop with the university researchers and the intermediary staff members to compare and analyze their findings, and to discuss the strategies the members proposed for overcoming the obstacles they faced. The workshop participants discussed how, in the future, both national and international private voluntary agencies and university staff members might assist in implementing more self-reliant project strategies.

Finally, in August, 1985, the original Lusaka workshop participants reconvened in a final regional workshop in Gwebi, Zimbabwe, to assess the overall findings and their implications for increasingly self-reliant grassroots project activities. It is impossible, in this brief paper, to do more than summarize the main hypotheses emerging from their findings as to some of the seemingly systemic tendencies toward difficulties experienced by members of most grassroots projects. By acquiring a greater understanding of these tendencies during the learning process, the participants found themselves able to devise more effective strategies to overcome them.

The systemic tendencies identified by the pilot Learning Process include:

1. Unless community members participate in designing and implementing aid projects, they may have, at best, a peripheral impact on surrounding communities.
2. Unless the project design includes programs to ensure that all members acquire the skills and knowledge required to implement the project (including book-keeping and management skills), elitism and stratification may thwart effective community participation in and benefit from it.
3. Unless project members engage in formulating strategies appropriate for dealing with government officials, they may find themselves unable to gain access to resources necessary for increasing community self-reliance.
4. Unless community members participate in formulating the project design in terms of their own needs, donor agency rules and policies may foster increased, rather than decreased, dependence on donor agency staff.
5. Unless national and international agencies implement policies that strengthen national self-reliance, grassroots projects may find themselves vulnerable to external forces over which they have no control, but which foster chronic difficulties in obtaining essential inputs and marketing outputs.
6. Unless both women and men in the community realize the importance of overcoming attitudes and customs that thwart women's effective participation, projects will suffer and may fail as a result of not benefitting from women's essential contribution. Community

attitudes and practices render efforts to organize and implement women's projects particularly vulnerable to the previous five tendencies.[22]

At the end of the Gwebe workshop, the participants underscored their belief that holding a series of workshops and working with national researchers, first to design and then to assess the results, constituted an important feature of the learning process. They declared their intention to attempt to institutionalize the learning process as a way of strengthening grassroots, national, and regional cooperation for formulating and implementing more self-reliant development strategies.

Summary

The Southern African Pilot Learning Process Project aimed to design a participatory, problem-solving methodology. It created a framework within which members of rural projects, together with national researchers and donor agency representatives, could evaluate the consequences of aid for the project members' efforts to improve their use of available resources to achieve sustained improvements in their incomes and living conditions. Viewed this way, the Learning Process constitutes more than an insightful "window on the project" for the donor agency. It contributes to the creation of new decision-making structures, which empower project members to deal more effectively with their environment and to attain self-reliant development. Supposedly, after all, that is what aid is all about.

Literature Cited

Bamberger, M., E. Gonzalez-Polio, and U. Sae-Han. 1982. *Evaluation of Sites and Service Projects: The Evidence from El Salvador.* World Bank Staff Working Papers #549. Washington, DC.

---

[22] The workshops debated but did not finally agree on whether it was preferable to organize women into projects separately from or as part of larger community projects involving both men and women.

Banfield, E. C. 1973. Ends and means in planning. In *Planning Theory*. ed. by A. Faludi. New York: Pergamon Press. pp 139–149.

Baratz, M. and P. Bachrach. 1970. *Power and Poverty*. New York: Oxford University Press.

Chambliss, W. J. and R. B. Seidman. 1971. *Law, Order, and Power*. Reading, MA: Addison-Wesley Pulishing Co.

Kalyalya, D., K. Mhlanga, A. Seidman, and J. Semboja. 1987. *Aid and Development? A Pilot Southern African Learning Process*. Trenton, NJ: Africa World Press.

Korten, D. C. 1980. Community organization and rural development: a learning process approach. *Public Administration Review* 40:480–503.

Korten, F. 1981. Community participation: a management perspective on obstacles and options. In *Bureaucracy and the Poor: Closing the Gap*. ed. by D. C. Korten and F. B. Alfonso. New York: McGraw Hill International Book Co. pp. 181–200.

Mamdani, M. 1985. Disaster prevention: defining the problem. *Monthly Review* (October).

Nigerian Ambassador 1985. Key-note speech, Northeast Regional Meeting, National Council for International Health, Boston, MA.

Peattie, L. 1985. Participation in developing countries: a Peruvian case. Paper presented at Collegiate Schools of Planning Conference, Atlanta, GA.

Seidman, A. 1972. *Planning for Development in Sub-Saharan Africa*. New York: Praeger and Tanzania: Tanzanian Publishing House.

Seidman, R. B. 1978. *Law and Development*. London: Croom-Helm.

Smith, B. H. 1983. *U.S. and Canadian Nonprofit Organizations (PVO's) as Transnational Development Institutions*. New Haven: Program on Non-profit Organizations, Institute for Social and Policy Studies, PONPO Working Paper 70, and ISPS Working Paper 2070.

Swantz, M-L, and H. Jerman. 1977. *Jipemoyo: Introduction to its General Aims and Approach*. Dar es Salaam: Ministry of National Culture and Youth.

Yin, R. K. and D. Yates. 1975. *Street-Level Governments*. Lexington, MA: Lexington Books/D.C. Heath.

Development Alternatives And The African Food Crisis

David A. Cleveland

Center for People, Food and Environment
344 South Third Avenue
Tucson, Arizona 85701, U.S.A

Introduction

Sub-Saharan Africa is the only major geographical area which has experienced a decline in per capita food production during the last quarter of a century[1] (Christensen et al. 1981; USDA 1984). Although the last two years have seen a slight rise in per capita production, the total food deficit is still large (USDA 1986). Billions of dollars in development aid, the introduction of numerous technologies, and a multitude of studies of the social and physical environment have been applied to the food problem in Africa during this period. Why has this effort failed? What are the alternatives?

My objective in this paper is to broaden the discussion of sustainable solutions to the agricultural and food crisis in Africa. The argument has five major parts.

1) Value systems form the basis for different views of the cause of the crisis in the African food system of the best solution. The Western establishment views development as based on the economics of production in a world system which it dominates. It sees the cause of Africa's food crisis within Africa, and the solution in transferring the industrial agriculture model and in greater integration with the world system. Opposing views place greater emphasis on direct benefits of

---

[1]Agricultural statistics for sub-Saharan Africa are undoubtedly quite inaccurate and undue emphasis is given to minor differences in time and place (see Berry 1984). Yet the over-all failure of production to keep up with nutritional need cannot be denied.

development for Africans, see the cause of the problem outside of Africa, and frequently see as the solution the support of traditional African food systems. I use the term development to mean improvement in well-being based on equity, local control, and economic, environmental and social sustainability.

2) As "development", industrial agriculture has had a mixed record even in the U.S. Though it has been remarkably successful in increasing production, it is also associated with social disruption, economic inequity and inefficiencies, and environmental degradation. Its record in Africa is similar, with the exception that it has not had an overall impact on production.

3) Traditional African agriculture has been shown to be socially, economically and environmentally valuable in terms of equity and sustainability, at least in the past. However, there is evidence that under present circumstances it is associated with environmental degradation, social disruption, and hunger.

4) In response to failures of industrial and traditional agriculture, a growing number of people in both the U.S. and Africa are promoting and experimenting with sustainable agriculture based on the best features of industrial and traditional agriculture.

5) An important contribution of anthropologists and other social scientists is to play the role of objective observers, orienting discussion toward underlying values and the structure[2] of the world food and agricultural system within which a solution to Africa's food crisis must be found.

What Is Development?

The most revealing part of the international debate on hunger and poverty in Africa is the apportioning of the blame. [Ndumbu 1986:10]

There are many different definitions of development. All of them are based on value judgments (de Kadt 1985), including those about the nature of "human nature" itself (Howard 1983:469). While this

---

[2]I use the terms structure and structural to refer to relationships of control over resources which determine the observed patterns of resource distribution in the food and agriculture system.

relativistic approach is familiar to anthropologists and other social scientists, its absence from most discussions of African development may jeopardize their usefulness. Here I discuss what I refer to as the "establishment" and the "opposing" viewpoints of African development. For the sake of the argument they will be painted in broad, bold strokes. The definition of development chosen greatly affects the way in which specific problems of development are themselves defined and approached in the context of development programs and projects.

African Development from the Viewpoint of the Western Establishment

The specialized farm represents the final and most advanced stage of individual holding in a mixed market economy. It is the most prevalent type of farming in advanced industrial nations. . . . the provisions of food for the family with some marketable surplus is no longer the basic goal. Instead, pure commercial "profit" becomes the criterion of success, and maximum per hectare yields derived from man-made . . . and natural resources become the object of farm activity. [Todaro 1985:309]

Production and commercial profit are the basic values of industrial agricultural development in the U.S. Emphasis on increasing land and labor productivity, at the expense of decreasing capital and energy productivity, reflects values nurtured by an era of cheap energy and abundant capital in the West. The primacy of production economics as the goal of development does not mean that the establishment denies the importance of "social values" in development, although they are to be considered secondary to increased production, and not to be achieved at the expense of breaking establishment economic rules (Cooper 1981; Please and Amoako 1984).

Indeed, U.S. development aid is justified to the taxpayers as leading to greater U.S. exports to the Third World (Avery 1985; Council 1984; OTA 1984:22–24; Todaro 1985:450). It is also used to promote "economic stablity . . . democracy . . . access to strategic facilities . . . countering Soviet influence . . . [and] cooperation with the U.S. on international issues" (OTA 1984:24). It is also noted that Africa contains minerals which have "vital industrial and military applications" for the U.S. (ibid.).

In the view of many development and relief agencies, most influentially the World Bank and the United States Agency for International Development (USAID), the African food crisis is the result of environmental, technical, agronomic, managerial, and economic problems *within* Africa (Avery 1985; Brady 1985; McPherson 1985; USDA 1981; Wisner and Nourbakhsh 1985; World Bank 1981, 1983, 1984).

What is good for the Western-dominated world economic system[3] is usually *good* for the hungry African. This establishment interpretation of the problem has dominated efforts at improving the food situation in Africa, through increasing productivity on the Western model, for some time. Examples include projects that try to target the most "progressive" farmers in a community, increase farm size and commercialization, promote export crops because of so-called "comparative advantage", develop hybrid crop varieties dependent on high inputs of water, chemicals (often imported) and efficient, centralized infrastructure, and build large dams and irrigation systems.

While Western-centric economics has remained the underpinning of the establishment definition of development and the analysis of the problems and the solution to them have remained essentially the same, they change slightly through time in response to changing world economic conditions, new information about Africa, and changing political ideologies.

For example, the evolution over the last several decades of the African farmer from a hide-bound traditionalist into an economically rational actor in the eyes of the Western development establishment is no doubt an improvement over the ethnocentric notion of irrationality that prevailed before. However, when farmers do not respond in ways which can be interpreted as the economically rational pursuit of profit maximization, it is seen as the fault of market imperfections, inadequate infrastructure, or African government meddling, and not that

---

[3]Space does not permit consideration of the "communist" approach to development, though not so dissimilar perhaps to that of the "capitalists" both in form and content. While the capitalists insist on economic determinism for all while supporting a system where a few, the state and big business, control more and more of the productive resources, the centrist Marxist states promote development which eulogizes participation by all while the state reserves the total power of coercion and mobilization (de Kadt 1985).

African farmers might have different "values", different "rationality", or different "economics" (see Berry, S. 1984:71–72; Levi and Havinden 1982; Nair 1983:116).

The discovery of economic man in Africa, along with the worsening world economic situation (Hart 1982:155), the failure of large scale projects, and the realization that the small scale farmer was not going to disappear into an industrial work force in the near future, led in the 1970s to an establishment position more directly involving the poor, small-scale farmer in development to meet "basic needs" (Hoben 1980; Richards 1985:37–38).

Whether in fact such policies were ever able to overcome bureaucratic inertia to affect any change (see e.g. Hoben 1980:357–363), or whether any real change was intended by those in charge (see e.g. Reyna 1985) seems doubtful. In addition, drought and famine struck in the 1970s and per capita food production continued to decrease. The world economic situation also began a decline toward the end of the decade and a politically conservative administration moved into the U.S. White House. There has been a turning away from "New Directions", basic needs, and small farmer involvement, and supply side economics now rules at the World Bank and USAID (Derman 1984; Schultheis 1984), with government bureaucrats "scurrying for projects which promote private sector initiative" (Gellar 1985:26). While the small-scale farmer cannot now be ignored, actions in this area are to be "selective", "targeting" those areas which provide "for rapid payoff from additional investment", while also emphasizing large private farms, and multinational "agro-industrial enterprises" (World Bank 1981:52). No consistent or objective analysis is offered to explain these changes in the establishment position.

Opposing Views of African Development

"Does the white man understand our custom about land?"
"How can he when he does not even speak our tongue? But he says that our customs are bad; and our own brothers who have taken up his religion also say that our customs are bad. The whiteman. . . . has put a knife on the things that held us together and we have fallen apart." [Achebe 1959:162]

Definitions of development in opposition to the establishment have in common a value system based on control of African development by Africans. Of course, the question arises as to *which* Africans should be in charge, and exactly what form should this kind of development take.

Opposing views generally agree that the food crisis has its roots outside of Africa, in exploitation and destruction by European colonialists, and that it is perpetuated by the current state of affairs in which many African states are hostage to the technical and economic policies of the industrial countries. Proposed solutions flowing from this analysis of the problem range from a total reordering of the world economic system, placing control of Western style industrial agricultural development in the hands of Africans, to the primacy of indigenous forms of agricultural development with emphasis on local community control and self-reliance.

I will discuss the indigenous agricultural development approach, since it is popular in Africa and among some Western intellectuals, and because it contrasts most with the establishment view. It is an approach based on supporting and strengthening traditional systems that have provided a successful way of life for centuries, until destroyed from the outside.

From this point of view, indigenous systems that balanced food, population, and environment and insured a relatively egalitarian distribution of resources were destroyed by the slave trade, and by military, political, economic, and cultural subjugation (see Berry, L. 1984:106–108; Goody 1980:139; Wangari and Koivukari 1986). Sometimes included are public health measures which decreased mortality and, in the context of weakened traditional social demographic regulators and the absence of any substitute, led to rapid rates of population growth (e.g. Cleveland 1986).

Establishment "solutions" are seen as part of the problem. They promote dependence on the West, discourage community self-reliance, and devalue African culture. Organizations like USAID are perceived not simply to "promote" stability and "democracy" in the greater interest of all, but to actively coerce African governments to adopt policies which maintain and extend U.S. control over African economic and political processes to maintain and promote U.S. hegemony in Africa (see Cokorinos and Mittelman 1985; Morand 1986; Ndumbu 1986). These policies also reduce communal decision-making in favor of individualized decision-making within the parameters of an externally controlled economy. What is good for the

Western-dominated world economic system is usually *bad* for the hungry African.

While free markets and comparative advantage are the basis of establishment agricultural development for Africa, it is asserted that they are not applicable to Africa because, just as in the U.S., the basic assumption of perfect competition is quite unjustified (see Berry 1984:65–66). The market responds not to needs (nutritional, social or physiological), but to money (economic power, or "effective" demand), and the poor can never win in a system controlled by the rich for their own ends (Cokorinos and Mittelman 1985; de Kadt 1985; George 1984; Lappé 1985; Latham 1984).

A Working Definition

I will use the term development here to refer to the process of improving the subjective and objective well-being of the poor majority through economically, environmentally, and socially sustainable means which are equitable, and in which the poor farmers themselves have freedom of participation and power of decision-making (see de Kadt 1985:551; Gellar 1985; Howard 1983; Lappé and Collins 1978; Latham 1984; Perelman 1977). This is not to deny the necessity for profit, production which makes efficient use of resources, or the usefulness of markets. It is simply to say that they are not the highest goals of the food system, and indeed that they should serve higher goals. In the following sections I will examine industrial agriculture and traditional African agriculture in terms of their promise for solving the African food crisis and promoting development.

Industrial Agriculture For African Development: The U.S. Model

. . . when our country became independent in 1961, our ambition was to "modernize" our economy. We did not work this out very thoroughly; but it appeared to us that if you wanted a productive agriculture, you had a mechanized agriculture, and you used chemical fertilizers, chemicals insecticides, and—to be completely up to date—even herbicides. That, at least, was our vision of American and Canadian agriculture—and we were often told that America is the most productive agricultural country. [Nyerere 1983]

U.S. agriculture is often held up as a model for agricultural development in Africa, and Land Grant University (LGU) agriculturalists are in demand by USAID and other development agencies as experts. Agriculture in the dry, western U.S. is seen as especially relevant for the dry savanna areas of Africa, which include much of the region hardest hit by drought and famine. Yet the negative effects of industrial agriculture in the industrialized countries is seldom discussed when this model is urged on Africa. So, before assessing the applicability of this model to Africa we first have to examine its economic, environmental and social record at home.

Industrial Agriculture at Home

U.S. agriculture in the four decades since WW II has experienced a "dramatic transformation" characterized by increasing production per unit of land and labor and decreasing production per unit of capital input, decreasing number and increasing size of farms, increasing concentration of production and assets among the biggest farms, substitution of capital goods (chemicals and machinery) for human and animal labor, increasing use of water (about 80% of all water used in the U.S. in 1977), and increasing importance of farm exports to the U.S. and world economy (see Schertz 1979).

While these trends are often interpreted by the establishment as the inevitable or natural result of economic progress, and the necessity to feed a larger and larger population, they may in fact be the result of particular environmental, social and cultural circumstances. The predominance of large farms in U.S. agriculture, for example, is primarily the result of factors other than increased technical efficiency (Miller et al. 1981). Large size has been nurtured by the "past focus of public research on such things as large scale equipment and technology based on inexpensive energy and inexpensive capital" (USDA 1981:67). The capital resources and backing of large farms make them financially capable of adopting expensive cost-reducing technology, thus increasing minimum efficient operating size even further. Tax and other laws in the U.S. also work to the advantage of the large-scale farm (Davenport et al. 1982). Abundant fossil energy has made an energy-intensive agriculture seem economical only when its replacement costs or environmental impacts are not considered (Pimentel and Pimentel 1979; Steinhart and Steinhart 1974).

Another form of subsidy for agriculture is the sizeable proportion of research done at LGUs which supports large scale, energy-intensive agriculture more beneficial to large corporate rather than small, family farms, farm workers, or consumers (Friedland 1982; Hightower 1978; Johnson and Jesse 1979; Vogeler 1981). The development and adoption of the mechanical harvester and electronic sorting unit in the California process tomato industry is a case in point (Johnson and Jesse 1979:370: Price 1983). The public has also subsidized agriculture through the government-financed development of irrigation systems in the Western U.S. (Hope and Sheehan 1983).

Another way of evaluating the equity and social sustainability of industrial U.S. food production is in the use of hired labor. Especially in the West, agriculture has been founded to a great extent on "noncompetitive labor either in the form of labor surplus, or highly mobile, unsophisticated immigrant populations" (Padfield and Martin 1965:253). When domestic surplus labor did not exist, the U.S. government supplied "other noncompetitive labor resources—e.g. prisoners of war, Puerto Ricans, Mexican immigrants, and . . . Mexican Nationals. This peculiar system has contributed immeasurably to a cost-efficient agriculture" (Padfield and Martin 1965:253).

Today, agribusiness in the Western U.S. strives to maintain its control over non-competive labor. Even though they can legally hire Mexican nationals under the H-2 or "green card" program, most growers have not because it is more expensive for them. Instead, most of the workers have been illegal. Agribusiness giants such as Tenneco and Sun Maid actively support immigration "reform" in the U.S. Congress which would preserve their special labor advantage. They favor an amendment to new immigration legislation authorizing as many as 350,000 foreign "guestworkers" which would allow them to continue control over a labor force unprotected by citizenship rights (Rural Coalition 1986). Social responsibility and equity, in this case in the form of fair wages, living and working conditions, appear not to be important considerations in U.S. agriculture. Indeed, the goal of short term production profits seems in many ways to be structurally opposed to these social goals.

Industrial agriculture has been based on an "abundant environment" approach. For example, crop selection assumes abundant supplies of water, fertilizer, pesticides and machinery (Boyer 1982). As it turns out, however, the environment may not be as abundant. Since the Great Depression of the 1930s, agricultural technology developed and adopted in the U.S. "has effectively separated fertility depletion from soil deterioration" (USDA 1981:87). The export push of the 1970s, encouraged by the government to finance the skyrocketing cost of imported oil, increased environmental and economic damage (Wessel 1983). Water shortages, groundwater overdraft and soil erosion, exacerbated by increasing energy costs, unstable and shrinking markets and increasing control by agribusiness multinationals are major problems in U.S. agriculture. In the West, heavily dependent on the use of water for irrigation, desertification[4] is a major problem. In southeast Arizona, for example, desertification is directly traceable to agricultural practices such as overgrazing and overdraft of groundwater (but also including climatic variation) (Dewhirst 1981; Sheridan 1981:60–64). As depth to water and the price for energy to pump it increase, cost of production increases (ACLRS 1981:128), and is a prime factor in abandonment of 191,000 to 237,000 acres of irrigated, harvested cropland in southeast Arizona (less Santa Cruz County) in the last 10–15 years (Meitl et al. 1983). Abandoned farmland is subject to increased wind and water erosion (Sheridan 1981; also Meitl et al. 1983). The environmental costs of industrial agriculture are usually not considered when assessing its economic sustainability.

The global dominance of industrial agriculture may affect African food systems in several ways. Food aid, which is supported by the industrial exporting countries as easing their domestic food surpluses while maintaining current world markets, may actually be a disincentive to increased production in Africa (OTA 1984:63–66). Over the longer term, food aid may be used to increase consumer preference for imported food. In Africa a major example is wheat used in bread (Dinham and Hines 1983: 141–143). While these indirect effects of the industrial agriculture model are important for an understanding of the African food system, I will focus in the following section on the direct effects of the promotion of this model for production in Africa itself.

---

[4]Desertification can be defined as occurring when one or more of the following symptoms are present: declining goundwater tables, salinization of topsoil and water, reduction of surface waters, unnaturally high soil erosion, and desolation of native vegetation (Sheridan 1981:1).

Another Green Revolution for Africa?

Agricultural development in Africa has been dominated by the idea that the technology of industrial agriculture could be transferred. The assumption has been that "any increase in productivity implies a heavier use of fertilizer, pesticides, and other purchased inputs" (Christensen et al. 1981:257).

The "Green Revolution", first developed in Mexico and Asia in the 1950s and 1960s, has at its center newly developed crop varieties with high response to and dependency on manufactured chemical fertilizers and pesticides, machinery and irrigation. Although introduced into Africa, the Green Revolution has not been widely adopted or "successful" there, partly because conditions are much different than in Mexico or Asia (Christensen et al. 1981:105–107). It may be that the very nature of the "biological" packages were inappropriate for the small-scale African farmer (see Richards 1985:39).

Many of the same problems created by industrial agriculture in the U.S. accompany its transfer to Africa. The structure of agriculture encouraged by the adoption of this industrial model may often work to the disadvantage of the limited resource, small-scale farmer, as well as the consumer (see Alverson 1984; Todaro 1985:312). For example, the industrial establishment has shown a pervasive neglect of traditional, locally-adapted crop varieties (FAO 1985; Okigbo 1977), referring to them disparagingly (and ignorantly) as "the horticultural equivalent of Indian corn" (Avery 1985:409). The Green Revolution in Africa is associated with land registration to establish ownership in the Western sense, which is "an invitation to create economic inequality", displacing traditional, egalitarian land tenure systems (Goody 1980:146; see also Reyna 1985). There is also evidence that some basic assumptions of this approach, such as large returns to inputs like manufactured chemical fertilizers, may not be valid (Diwan and Kallianpur 1985). Other basic components may have negative impacts, as with pesticides, which have caused great health and environmental problems (Bull 1982), and soil degradation caused by mechanization, chemical fertilizers and irrigation (Goody 1980; Berry, L. 1984:57,60).

Now USAID and others in the development establishment are calling for "another green revolution for Africa" (Brady 1985; McPherson 1985). The emphasis, at least publicly, now seems to be away from a resource abundance approach and on breeding for disease, pest and drought resistance, and a diversified environment. I have not, however, seen goals of the new Green Revolution for Africa concretely discussed in terms of social equity or environmental sustainability. Will the "new" Green Revolution reduce genetic variability and increase dependency and long term environmental and economic fragility? Genetic engineering is creating a "biorevolution" in the development of new crop varieties and is under the control of private multinational companies to a much greater extent than was the Green Revolution (Buttel et al. 1985). Many of these are chemical companies which have recently acquired seed companies, and a priority is to breed crops with increased herbicide resistance, making increased application, and thus sales, of herbicides possible (Sun 1986). To choose this route instead of increasing disease and pest resistance and weed competitiveness in food crops seems to be economically and not socially motivated. There is a need for a more detailed examination of the decision making processes, scientific theories, development goals, and probable long-term effects of any "Green Revolution" for Africa.

Traditional African Agriculture

Although the farmer is equipped with nothing more than a hoe, cutlass, fire and his own limited muscle power, there is probably little arable land in the [West African] . . . savannas that has not been cultivated at one time or another. . . . The process of degradation begins with the settlement of virgin land and ends. . . . [in] the final stage of degradation:. . . . trees succumb to lopping and felling, the soil to exhaustion and erosion. . . . [Rose Innes 1977:20]

As we have seen, the small-scale African farmer is now considered to be "economically rational". Examples of many types of behavior have become available which support this assertion: cultivation practices like mixed cropping (Legemann 1977), selection of adapted crop varieties (Kassan 1976), the allocation of production resources in terms of marginal returns (Levi and Havinden 1982), pregnancy rates and spacing of children (Cleveland 1986), the organization of the household (Netting 1969), and not participating in development schemes (Alverson 1984).

Production per unit of energy and capital is high in traditional compared to industrial agriculture, because little fossil fuel, manufactured inputs, or machinery are used. On the other hand, production per unit of labor and often per unit of land is frequently much lower. However, there is evidence that small-scale, labor-intensive production can be as productive of land as large-scale production (Bremen and deWit 1983; Cornia 1985). Household gardens, often neglected by agronomists, economists and anthropologists alike, can be as or more productive of land as traditional field production, and even large-scale industrial agriculture, and may even be more productive of labor than more extensive traditional field production (Cleveland and Soleri 1987; Lagemann 1977:55–56,94).

In addition, comparisons made with large-scale industrial agriculture in Africa are often unfair because they do not consider the greater government support, inputs, and often (as, for example, in southern Africa) the better soil and rain-fall resulting from the forced removal of small-scale subsistence farmers from the best land which was then developed into large-scale industrial farms (Weiner et al. 1985:277–282).

Traditional, small-scale agriculture can make use of labor and other productive local resources available in small increments, while minimizing risk and supporting social, religious and other important non-economic activities (Levi and Havinden 1982:54–71, 96–98). This characteristic is particularly important for the poor, for whom large investments of any resource may not be possible.

Traditional agriculture also appears to have incorporated a number of measures to conserve productive resources of soil, water and vegetation (Berry, L. 1984:106–107; Richards 1985:55ff.). For a livestock system in East Africa, for example, a low ratio of production to biomass ensures maintenance and stability without producing discernible environmental degradation (Coughenour et al. 1985). These researchers feel that to try to move a system evolved for maintenance and ecological stability toward one with a goal of production of surplus could mean ecological instability and environmental degradation, i.e. that industrial agriculture is basically incompatible with African ecology and traditional production systems.

However, it may not be valid to assume that because traditional systems, or parts of them, have survived through many generations, they are therefore adapted in the sense of being sustainable. It may also be invalid to assume that development is a matter of widespread support for traditional systems. Although it is difficult to measure change in potential productivity of traditional African production systems in the past, it may be that for most of Africa traditional agricultural systems were never "adapted". Rather, pressure on the environment was increasing so slowly, partially because of ample room for migration and a slowly growing population, prior to colonialism, that the imbalance never had a chance to manifest itself. In the East African example just cited, there is extensive human outmigration from the study area.

In spite of all the positive characteristics of traditional African agriculture, and its success in supporting the population for generations, it seems unable to cope with greatly increased population densities and changing social and economic conditions. Therefore, as practiced in much of Africa today, it has caused widespread environmental degradation and is associated with major social disruptions, such as male outmigration, and marginalization of women farmers (Cleveland 1986; Berry, L. 1984:50–65; NAS 1983:30–37; Rose Innes 1977). Certainly, traditional systems have been violently disrupted by the slave trade, colonial forced labor, economic exploitation, rapid population growth, expulsion from prime agricultural lands, and cultural imperialism (Berry, L. 1984:107–108). There is also no denying, however, that conditions have changed radically and irrevocably. It is likely, therefore, that even if traditional systems were formerly sustainable, they would not be appropriate without modification for the present, greatly changed and increasingly unstable conditions.

For example, decisions made by individuals in the context of viable social systems dependent on local ecosystems for survival may have balanced population and productive resources in the past. Yet in many cases these have been undermined by changes in the social and physical contexts of decision-making, due to increasing integration within a larger, money economy under colonial and post-independence governments. Seasonal wage labor migration by single young men was not formerly possible, thus they had to wait for their lineage to provide bride wealth, whereas now they can marry on their own. Under conditions of high mortality and severe social sanctions, fertility in Africa is controlled by postpartum abstinence. Decreasing mortality and changing social conditions lead to decisions by couples to shorten birth intervals to provide more household agricultural labor. In both of these situations decisions by individuals may be in their best interests, but work against their community by increasing fertility and thus population pressure of the land beyond the point of sustainability

(Cleveland 1986). Similarly, large herd size in the Sahel increases production for individual herders, but leads to an overall degradation of the range (Bremen and deWit 1983:1346).

However, a "tragedy of the commons" analysis of this phenomenon, leading to suggestions for either privatization of land tenure or government control (e.g. Frankenberger 1986), may be faulted for omitting both the possibility that past communal resource management systems could be adapted for the future, and the abundant evidence of private tenure system's capacity for resource destruction, not only in the U.S. and other industrial countries, but in Africa as well.

It may be, however, that many of the *elements* necessary for intensification and a sustainable increase in food production in Africa are already present and do not require the introduction of foreign models (see Alverson 1984; Nair 1983; Netting et al. 1980; Richards 1985). Indeed, the past introduction of such models and their attendant cultural and political baggage may have actually thwarted the development of traditional African agriculture (Alverson 1984), as in the neglect of the advantages of mixed cropping. One of the most important potential contributions to the future of the African food supply may be the investigation of past, present and changing systems of group resource use and population regulation.

Environmentally and Socially Sustainable Agriculture

It is hard to overestimate the importance of applying the correct standard to agricultural performance. I do not see how a stable, abundant, long-term agriculture can be built up and maintained by any standard less comprehensive than that of the perfect health of individual human bodies, of the community, and of the community's sources and supports in the natural world. [Berry, W. 1977:204]

The revolutionary changes of the last four decades in U.S. agriculture and their effect on society and the environment have led to fundamentally different approaches to food production, variously referred to as organic, alternative, ecological, biological or sustainable agriculture. While a growing number of LGUs and other establishment institutions are becoming more open to these alternatives, it appears to be primarily the economic, secondarily the environmental, and rarely the social aspects which are discussed.

As defined by the USDA, "organic" agriculture is "a production system which avoids or largely excludes the use of synthetically compounded fertilizers, pesticides, growth regulators, and livestock feed additives" USDA 1980:9). Most studies show that organic agriculture reduces both production costs and yields per unit land area (Lockeretz et al. 1981a; USDA 1980; CAST 1980), while the net profit is about the same as conventional farms in the U.S. (Lockeretz et al. 1981a). Organic farming can, "given suitable climatic conditions, markets and required inputs to be a productive and efficient farming option and reduce soil erosion" (OTA 1982:111). While successful on large farms as well, improvements in resource-conserving farm technologies could probably improve economic efficiency of small scale farms, and are consistent with the goals of small-scale farmers in the U.S. to achieve greater self-reliance and minimize risk (Young 1982:214). Anti-desertification methods demanding more intensive management for long-term productivity may be more readily put into practice by small-scale farmers (OTA 1982;128, 130). Organic agricultural practices dependent on natural fertility practices that reduce runoff and erosion are also important in maintaining fertility (USDA 1981:86).

While environmentally sustainable agriculture does not necessarily equal socially responsible agriculture, these two aspects are deemed by some to be inseparable. Efforts to improve the well-being of those adversely affected by the food system, such as limited resource, small-scale farmers, farm workers or consumers are usually met with opposition by the industrial agriculture establishment. This is especially true if they abjure incrementalist change in favor of structural change, without which there is "little hope of significantly improving the condition of the oppressed" (LaBelle and da Silva Goncalves 1984:357).

Ideology and values play a large role in the current and increasingly heated debate over alternatives to conventional agriculture in industrial countries (Lockeretz 1981b; Miller 1985). For example, the report on organic agriculture prepared by the USDA (1980) was immediately contested by an industrial agriculture establishment group, the Council for Agricultural Science and Technology (CAST 1980). Efforts for three years by congressional supporters of a farm bill meant to implement some of the recommendations in the USDA report have met with official opposition from the Reagan administration's USDA. Before finally being passed in 1985, the bill's sponsors changed its name from "organic" to "alternative" agriculture, and, finally, to the Agricultural Productivity Act, in order to appease the opposition. Sustainable agriculture in Africa as a synthesis of traditional and modern "scientific" methods is in its infancy. Efforts initiated from outside Africa may tend to slight traditional practices, as appears to be the case with a Dutch group promoting "ecological agriculture" at several sites in Ghana (van der Werf 1983, 1984). Some large-scale efforts have also been made, for example in Tanzania, where Nyerere (1983) has advocated organic agricultural practices, especially in composting and soil management. The strategy of starting with existing African production systems, and then adapting the most appropriate of alternative approaches being developed in the U.S. and other areas, offers the best hope for ecologically sustainable agriculture in Africa (see Harwood 1983).

Experiments with statist socialism such as Nyerere's in Tanzania or the State Farms in Ghana are quickly dismissed by the establishment as showing the inappropriateness of socialism for African agriculture (e.g. Eicher 1982). However, these may be more indicative of the inappropriateness of the type of socialist agricultural development in which the farmers have no say, and of the use of industrial agriculture models for Africa (Nyerere 1983; Miracle and Seidman 1968). As in the controversy over a resource management, this is an issue which is much influenced by value systems. An example is seeing as the obvious alternative to poorly managed government agricultural programs the support of "private sector suppliers of inputs" (Vengroff and Farah 1985:84), omitting communal systems.

Despite the record of the Green Revolution and the direction taken so far by the new biorevolution, there may be many possible applications of the advancing knowledge of crop improvement which could contribute positively to the African food supply. For example, guidelines have been proposed for crop breeding that reflect the situation of small-scale farmers and women in Africa for a USAID project. Since the project is meant to improve the health and nutrition of local people by increasing the availability of beans and cowpeas, a traditional focus on production is not enough. Important factors to consider are stability of yield, ability to yield without purchased inputs such as chemicals, multipurpose, e.g. leaf as well as seed consumption, ease of storage, processing and cooking, nutritional value, especially in weaning foods, and the effect on women's and men's workloads (Ferguson and Horn 1985:6–7). Anthropologists' advice to agronomists in a project in Malawi led to change in maize breeding programs, toward characteristics more suited to traditional farming systems (Spring 1985).

If "Africa's current economic crisis is structural, [and] rooted in unequal relations between nations and within divided societies", an effective international response must "foster genuine economic and social development based on principles of equality and democracy within African societies and between African states and the world's industrial nations" (Connell 1985).

Values And Development Alternatives In Africa: A Role For Social Scientists?

An important role for social scientists is to question assumptions about human nature, especially, perhaps, those of their own cultures. To allow the economists to define development "by what they do or study" simply because they are the dominant group among development practitioners (de Kadt 1985:551) is an abdication of responsibility. An awareness of anthropology's history in African colonial "development", may help prevent being drawn into the confining sphere of Western-style production agriculture, and becoming tied to its paradigms as the other agricultural disciplines including agricultural economics and rural sociology have (Friedland 1982). The debate on the future of African food system would be more productive if there were less hiding behind the safe walls of economic analyses and more focusing instead on the relation of *value systems* to power structures and development goals.

People, especially poor people, make decisions in contexts determined by forces beyond their immediate control. To simply help people adapt to these forces is not a solution to the current crisis in Africa or elsewhere, because it overlooks the real cause of the problems, and thereby increases the difficulty of changing the basic structure of a system that exploits them. Decision-making analysis (Barlett 1980; Gladwin 1982) is an example of a very important way in which anthropologists can contribute to African development. Yet unless it is set in the context of the power structure which determines parameters of farmers' decision-making it will be of little help in the long run, and it may be that "policies based on decision-making analysis have not succeeded because they do not address the source of power and patronage that shape resource allocation" (Berry 1980:333).

I believe that anthropologists must take a broader role in development than that advocated by currently popular "farming systems" approach. While farming systems proclaims that development must begin with an appreciation of the African farmer *in situ* and from her or his point of view, it may in essence still serve the economic goals of production agriculture. Most farming systems practitioners fail to take a larger view of the system (Altieri 1986; Garrett 1984). While some advocate research to "show how agricultural policies at the macro level affect and are affected by trends occurring at the micro level" (De Walt 1985:109), there is seldom an attempt to analyze the value system and political power structure of the micro-macro link, or environmental sustainability.

When anthropologists are told that their role in agricultural development should be to provide the information needed by biological agricultural scientists so that "their work can commence" and that they should stay out of the technical aspects of development (De Walt 1985:108), with no mention of the possibility of structural and cultural impediments to development in the *developed* world and the development establishment, this sells anthropology short on two scores.

First, it denies a proper role to the biological aspect of anthropology, with its emphasis on nutrition, demography, human biology, ecology, and evolution. For example, it has been suggested that "FSR projects should not be held accountable for nutritional consequences outside of their control" since "FSR projects which bring about improvements in food consumption may not always improve nutrition" because of "confounding influences" (Frankenberger 1985:2,3; see De Walt 1985 for contrary opinion). The same biological principles inform anthropology, nutrition and agriculture, and if development is truly viewed as a system, then the biological interface between different aspects of the system (and their attendant academic disciplines) is as important as the cultural interface. While most anthropologists are not agronomists, some at least are more qualified than agronomists to consider the interface between plant biology and human biology, and between both and culture.

Secondly, such a view limits the cultural aspect of anthropology to considering the poor, not the culture of the power structure that often creates their poverty. An almost complete lack of discussion in farming systems development literature of the possibility of the poor African farmer having control over her or his own development, leaves the development agent firmly in charge (see Gellar 1985). If development agency bureaucrats (Hoben 1980), biological agricultural scientists, and African bureaucrats (Berry 1984) are, like the poor African farmer, considered to be "rational", then their behavior can be fruitfully analyzed in terms of their decision-making environment. "Cultural paradigms" may be important predictors of their behavior, and their study may yield findings critical for promoting development.

My own experiences in Africa and as an administrator in an LGU international agriculture program have taught me that all of this is not easy. Most people in the U.S. agriculture establishment are not used to thinking in terms of value systems. They are, as Thomas Kuhn would put it, in the position of elaborating, and, to an increasing extent, defending the established paradigms of industrialized production agriculture (see George 1984:59–60). What is important is to increase the scope of discussion on development alternatives for Africa to include the tremendous resource of knowledge *within* Africa, the ferment of ideas and methods evolving from a challenging of conventional industrial agriculture in the U.S. and elsewhere, and an awareness of the cultural relativity of *all* approaches to the African food crisis.

Acknowledgements. I thank Daniela Soleri for her many valuable suggestions on several drafts of this paper; Anita Spring for comments delivered at the sessions on the African food crisis at the 1985 Annual Meeting of the American Anthropological Association, where an earlier version of this paper was presented; all of those who organized and participated in those sessions; and an anonymous reviewer.

References Cited

Achebe, Chinua 1959 Things Fall Apart. [First published 1958] New York: Fawcett.

ACLRS (Arizona Crop and Livestock Reporting Service) 1981 1980 Arizona Agricultural Statistics. Phoenix, Arizona: ACLRS.

Altieri, Miguel 1986 An Ecological Basis for the Development of Alternative Agricultural Systems for Small Farmers in the Third World. American Journal of Alternative Agriculture 1:30–38.

Alverson, Hoyt 1984 The Wisdom of Tradition in the Development of Dry-land Farming: Botswana. Human Organization 43:1–8.

Avery, Dennis 1985 U.S. Farm Dilemma: The Global Bad News is Wrong. Science 230:408–412.

Bartlett, Peggy 1980 Introduction: Development Issues and Economic Anthropology. In Agricultural Decision Making: Contributions to Rural Development. Peggy Bartlett, ed. Pp. 1–16. New York: Academic Press.

Berry, Leonard with the United Nations Sudano-Sahelian Office 1984 Assessment of Desertification in the Sudano-Sahelian Region 1978–1984. [Nairobi]: United Nations Environment Program.

Berry, Sara S. 1980 Decision Making and Policymaking in Rural Development. In Agricultural Decision Making: Contributions to Rural Development. Peggy Bartlett, ed. Pp. 321–335. New York: Academic Press.

———— 1984 The Food Crisis and Agrarian Change in Africa: A Review Essay, African Studies Review 27 (2):59–112.

Berry, Wendell 1977 The Unsettling of America: Culture and Agriculture. San Francisco: Sierra Club Books.

Boyer, J. S. 1982 Plant Productivity and Environment. Science 218:443–448.

Brady, N. C. 1985 Toward a Green Revolution for Africa. Science 227:1159.

Breman, H. and C. T. De Wit 1983 Rangeland Productivity and Exploitation in the Sahel. Science 221:1341–1347.

Bull, David 1982 A Growing Problem: Pesticides and the Third World Poor. Oxford: OXFAM.

Buttel, Frederick, Martin Kenney and Jack Kloppenburg, Jr. 1985 From Green Revolution to Biorevolution: Some Observations on the Changing Technological Bases of Economic Transformation in the Third World. Economic Development and Cultural Change 33:31–55.

CAST (Council for Agricultural Science and Technology) 1980 Organic and Conventional Farming Compared. Report No. 84. Ames, Iowa: CAST

Christensen, Cheryl, et al. 1981 Food Problems and Prospects in Sub-Saharan Africa: The Decade of the 1980's. Foreign Agricultural Economic Report No. 166. Washington, D.C.: U.S. Department of Agriculture.

Cleveland, David A. 1986 The Political Economy of Fertility Regulation: The Kusasi of Savanna West Africa (Ghana). In Culture and Reproduction: An Anthropological Critique of Demographic Transition Theory. Penn Handwerker, ed. Pp. 263–293. Boulder, CO: Westview.

Cleveland, David A., and Daniela Soleri 1987 Household Gardens as a Development Strategy. Human Organization 46 (3):259–270.

Cokorinos, Lee and James H. Mittelman 1985 Reagan and the *Pax Afrikaana*. Journal of Modern African Studies 23:551–573.

Connell, Dan 1985 Why are Africans Dying? The Mini-Monitor 2(3):5,7.

Cooper, Frederick 1981 Africa and the World Economy. African Studies Review 24 (2/3):1–86.

Cornia, Giovanni Andrea 1985 Farm Size, Land Yields and the Agricultural Production Function: An Analysis of Fifteen Developing Countries. World Development 13: 513–534.

Coughenour, M. B., J. E. Ellis, D. M. Swift, D. L. Coppock, K. Galvin, J. T. McCabe and T. C. Hart 1985 Energy Extraction and Use in a Nomadic Pastoral Ecosystem. Science 230:619–625.

Council on World Hunger, Development, and Trade 1984 World Hunger: Development and Trade. Washington, D.C.: Council on World Hunger, Development, and Trade.

Davenport, Charles, Michael D.Boehlje and David B. H. Martin 1982 The Effects of Tax Policy on American Agriculture. Agricultural Economic Report Number 480. Economic Research Service, U.S. Department of Agriculture, Washington, D.C.: U.S. Department of Agriculture.

de Kadt, Emanuel 1985 Of Markets, Might and Mullahs: A Case for Equity, Pluralism and Tolerance in Development. World Development 13:549–556.

Derman, William 1984 USAID in the Sahel: Development and Poverty. In The Politics of Agriculture in Tropical Africa. Jonathan Barker, ed. Pp. 77–97.

Dewalt, Billie 1985 Anthropology, Sociology, and Farming Systems Research. Human Organization 44:106–114.

Dewhirst, L. W. 1981 Introduction. Special Issue: The Future of Agriculture in Arizona. Progressive Agriculture in Arizona 31(4):2.

Dinham, Barbara and Colin Hines 1983 Agribusiness in Africa. London: Earth Resources Research Ltd.

Diwan, Romesh and Renu Kallianpur 1985 Biological Technology and Land Productivity: Fertilizers and Food production in India. World Development 13:627–638.

Eicher, Carl K. 1982 Facing up to Africa's Food Crisis. Foreign Affairs 61(1):151–174.

FAO (Food and Agriculture Organization of the United Nations) 1985 Broadening the Food Base with Traditional Food Plants. Report of the Expert Consultation held in Harare, Zimbabwe. Rome: Food Policy and Nutrition Division, FAO.

Ferguson, Anne E. and Nancy Horn 1985 Situating Agricultural Research in a Class and Gender Context: The Bean/Cowpea Collaborative Research Support Program. Culture and Agriculture No. 26:1–10.

Frankenberger, Timothy R. 1985 Inclusion of Food Consumption Concerns in Farming Systems Projects. mss. Prepared for the Nutrition Economic Group, Technical Assistance Division, Office of International Cooperation and Development, USDA.

———— 1986 Integrating Livestock into Farming Systems Research: An example from North Kordofan Sudan. Human Organization 45:228–238.

Friedland, William H. 1982 The End of Rural Society and the Future of Rural Sociology. Rural Sociology 47:589–608.

Garrett, Patricia 1984 The Relevance of Structural Variables for Farming Systems Research. Rural Sociology 49:580–589.

Geller, Sheldon 1985 The Ratched-McMurphy Model Revisited: A Critique of Participatory Development Models, Strategies, and Projects. Issue: A Journal of Africanist Opinion 14:25–28.

George, Susan 1984 Ill Fares the Land: Essays on Food, Hunger, and Power. Washington, D.C.: Institute for Policy Studies.

Gladwin, Christina H. 1982 The Role of a Cognitive Anthropologist in a Farming Systems Program That Has Everything. *In* The Role of Anthropologists and Other Social Scientists in Interdisciplinary Teams Developing Improved Food Production Technology. Pp. 73–92. Los Banos, Philippines: International Rice Research Institute.

Goody, Jack 1980 Rice-Burning and the Green Revolution in Northern Ghana. Journal of Development Studies 16:136–155.

Hart, Keith 1982 The Political Economy of West Africa Agriculture. Cambridge: Cambridge University Press.

Harwood, Richard R. 1983 International Overview of Regenerative Agriculture. *In* Proceedings of Workshop on Resource-Efficient Farming Methods for Tanzania. Pp. 24–35. Emmaus, Pennsylvania: Rodale Press.

Hightower, Jim 1978 Hard Tomatoes, Hard Times. Cambridge, MA: Schenkman Publishing Co.

Hoben Allan 1980 Agriculture Decision in Foreign Assistance: An Anthropological Perspective. *In* Agricultural Decision Making: Anthropological Contributions to Rural Development. Peggy F. Bartlett, ed. Pp. 337–369. New York: Academic Press.

Hope, Barney and Michael Sheehan 1983 The Political Economy of Centralized Water Supply in California. The Social Science Journal 20(2):29–39.

Howard, Rhoda 1983 The Full-Belly Thesis: Should Economic Right Take Priority Over Civil and Political Rights: Evidence from Sub-Saharan Africa. Human Rights Quarterly 4:467–490.

Johnson, Stanley S. and Edward V. Jesse 1979 The Southwest. *In* Another Revolution in U.S. Farming? Lyle P. Schertz and Others. Pp. 362–403. Washington, D.C.: USDA.

Kassam, A. H. 1976 Crops of the West African Semi-Arid Tropics. Hyderabad, India: International Crops Research Institute for the Semi-Arid Tropics.

LaBelle, Thomas and Jose da Silva Goncalves 1984 The Family Farm Program: Functionalist Designs and Conflicting Realities. Human Organization 43:352–357.

Lagemann, Johannes 1977 Traditional African Farming Systems in Eastern Nigeria: An Analysis of Reaction to Increasing Population Pressure. Munich: Weltform-Verlag.

Lappé, Frances Moore 1985 A Politics of Hope. Presented at the Conference Hunger: Looking beyond Famine, Tucson, Arizona.

Lappé, Frances Moore and Joseph Collins 1978 Food First: Beyond the Myth of Scarcity. Rev. ed. New York: Ballantine Books.

Latham, Michael C. 1984 Strategies for the Control of Malnutrition and the Influence of the Nutritional Sciences. Food and Nutrition 10 (1):5–31.

Levi, John and Michael Havinden 1982 Economics of African Agriculture. Essex, U.K.: Longman Group Ltd.

Lockeretz, William, Georgia Shearer and Daniel H. Kohl 1981a Organic Farming in the Corn Belt. Science 211:540–547.

———— 1981b [Letter to the Editor] Science 213:710,712.

McPherson, M. Peter 1985 Meeting the Challenge of Africa. Horizons 4(2):18–21.

Meitl, Joan M., Pamela L. Hathaway and Frank Gregg 1983 Alternative Uses of Arizona Lands Retired from Irrigated Agriculture. Tucson: Arizona: Cooperative Extension Service, College of Agriculture, University of Arizona.

Miller, Alan 1985 Psychosocial Origins of Conflict Over Pest Control Strategies. Agriculture, Ecosystems and Environment 12:235–251.

Miller, Thomas A., Gordon E. Rodewald and Robert G. McElroy 1981 Economics of Size in U.S. Field Crop Farming. Agricultural Economic Report Number 472. Washington, D.C.: Economics and Statistics Service, United States Department of Agriculture.

Miracle, Marvin P. and Ann Seidman 1968 State Farms in Ghana. LTC No. 43. Madison, Wisconsin: The Land Tenure Center, University of Wisconsin.

Morand, Catherine 1986 African NGOs Make Themselves Heard. United Nations Development Forum 14(2):15.

NAS (National Academy of Sciences) 1983 Environmental Change in the West African Sahel. Washington, D.C.: NAS.

Nair, Kusum 1983 Transforming Traditionally: Land and Labor Use in Agriculture in Asia and Africa. Riverdale, MD: Riverdale.

Ndumbu, Abel 1986 South Weighs Northern Views. United Nations Development Forum 14(3):1,10.

Netting, Robert M. 1969 Ecosystems in Process: A Comparative Study of Change in Two West African Societies. In Ecological Essays. National Museum of Canada Bulletin 230. D. Damas, ed. Pp. 102–112.

Netting, Robert M, David A. Cleveland and Frances Stier 1980 The Conditions of Agricultural Intensification in the West African Savannah. In Sahelian Social Development. Stephen P. Reyna, ed. Pp. 187–505. Abidjan, Ivory Coast: USAID.

Nyerere, Julius K. 1983 Opening Address. In Proceedings of Workshop on Resource-Efficient Farming Methods for Tanzania. Pp. 14–18. Emmaus, Pennsylvania: Rodale Press.

OTA (Office of Technology Assessment) 1982 Impacts of Technology on U.S. Cropland and Rangeland Productivity. Washington, D.C.: OTA.

———— 1984 Africa Tomorrow: Issues in Technology, Agriculture and U.S. Foreign AID. Washington, D.C.: OTA.

Okigbo, B. M. 1977 Neglected Plants of Horticultural and Nutritional Importance in Traditional Farming Systems of Tropical Africa. Acta Horticultura 53:131–150.

Padfield, Harland and William E. Martin 1965 Farmers, Workers and Machines: Technological and Social Change in Farm Industries of Arizona. Tucson: University of Arizona Press.

Perelman, Michael 1977 Farming for Profit in a Hungry World. Montclair, New Jersey: Allanheld, Osmun.

Pimentel, David and Marcia Pimentel 1979 Food, Energy and Society. London: Edward Arnold.

Please, Stanley and K. Y. Amoako 1984 The World Bank's Report on Accelerated Development in Sub-Saharan Africa: A Critique of Some of the Criticism. African studies Review 27:47–58.

Price, Barry 1983 The Political Economy of Mechanization in U.S. Agriculture. Boulder, CO: Westview.

Reyna, S. P. 1985 The Emergence of Land Concentration in the West African Savanna. Paper presented at the American Anthropological Association Annual Meeting, Washington, D.C.

Richards, Paul 1985 Indigenous Agricultural Revolution. London: Hutchinson

Rose Innes, R. 1977 A Manual of Ghana Grasses. Surrey, England: Land Resource Division, Ministry of Overseas Development.

Rural Coalition 1986 Immigration Bill: Reform its Not. Update June/July:4.

Schertz, Lyle P. 1979 A Dramatic Transformation. in Another Revolution In U.S. Farming? Lyle P. Schertz and Others. Pp. 13–41. Washington, D.C.: USDA.

Schultheis, Michael J. 1984 The World Bank and Accelerated Development: The Internationalization of Supply-Side Economics. African Studies Review 27:9–16.

Sheridan, David 1981 Desertification in the United States. Washington, D.C.: Council on Environmental Quality.

Spring, Anita (formerly with the Women and Agricultural Development Project, Malawi) 1985 (personal communication)

Steinhart, John S. and Carol E. Steinhart 1974 Energy Use in the U.S. Food System. Science 184:307–316.

Sun, Marjorie 1986 Engineering Crops to Resist Weed Killers. Science 231:1360–1361.

Todaro, Michael P. 1985 Economic Development in the Third World. 3rd ed. New York: Longman.

USDA (United States Department of Agriculture) 1980 Report and Recommendations on Organic Farming. Washington, D.C.: USDA.

――――― 1981 A Time to Choose: Summary Report on the Structure of Agriculture. Washington, D.C.: USDA.

――――― 1984 Sub-Saharan Africa. World Agriculture Regional Supplement. Review of 1983 and Outlook for 1984. Washington, D.C.: Economic Research Service, USDA.

――――― 1986 World Food Needs and Availabilities, 1986/87. Washington, D.C.: Economic Research Service, USDA.

206   David A. Cleveland

van der Werf, E. J. 1983 Ecologically Sustainable Agriculture as an Effective Means to Combat Desertification In Tropical Africa: The Case of Agriculture in Accra Plains (Ghana). Ecoscripts No. 22. Zandvoort, Netherlands: Stichting Mondiaal Alternatief.

——— 1984 Ecological Agriculture In Africa: The Agomeda Agricultural Project (Ghana). Ecoscripts No. 26. Zandvoort, Netherlands: Stichting Mondiaal Alternatief.

Vengroff, Richard and Ali Farah 1985 State Intervention and Agricultural Development in Africa: A Cross-National Study, Journal of Modern African Studies 23:75–85.

Vogeler, Ingolf 1981 The Myth of the Family Farm: Agribusiness Dominance of U.S. Agriculture. Boulder, Colorado: Westview Press.

Wangari, Esther and Mirjami Koivukari 1986 Women: The Plight and the Strength. In Africa Today: Learning From the Past. United Nations Development Forum 14 (5):8–9.

Weiner, Dan, Sam Moyo, Barry Munslow and Phil O'Keefe 1985 Land Use and Agricultural Productivity in Zimbabwe. Journal of Modern African Studies 23:251–285.

Wessel, James, with Mort Hantman 1983 Trading the Future: Farm Exports and the Concentration of Economic Power in Our Food Economy. San Francisco: Institute for Food and Development Policy.

Wisner, Robert N. and Tahereh Nourbakhsh 1985 World Food Trade and U.S. Agriculture, 1960–1984. Ames, Iowa: The World Food Institute, Iowa State University.

World Bank 1981 Accelerated Development in Sub-Saharan Africa: An Agenda for Action. Washington, D.C.: World Bank.

——— 1983 Sub-Saharan Africa: Progress Report on Development Prospects and Programs. Washington, D.C.: World Bank.

——— 1984 Toward Sustained Development in Sub-Saharan Africa: A Joint Program of Action. Washington, D.C.: World Bank.

Young, John A. 1982 Productive Efficiency and the Adaptations of Small-Scale Farmers. Human Organization 41:208–215.

The Role of Cassava in African Famine Prevention

Fatimah Linda C. Jackson, Ph.D.
and Robert T. Jackson, Ph.D.

University of Maryland
Departments of Anthropology and Human Nutrition
College Park, MD 20742

Introduction

Hunger, starvation, and famine are not new phenomena in human history. What is new and most troubling about them is that today we have the capacity, but perhaps not the will, to eliminate the most devastating of their physical consequences—severe wasting and death. Famine, as the most extreme expression of this continuum, can be defined as "a widespread lack of access to food that occurs when drought, flood, or war disrupts the availability of food in a society of chronically malnourished people." (The Hunger Project 1985). The societies which are most negatively affected by famines in this era are those which have the least ability to respond institutionally to the social and political deprivation that famines cause. Africa has faced no less than 23 famines since 1960 (Passmore and Eastwood 1986). Drought, destruction of crops by pests, and social dislocation caused by war are the main causes of these famines. With drought and insect attack on crops, the need for energy-dense staples that can be easily cultivated, stored, processed, and consumed has assumed increasing significance. In each of these areas, use of the tropical shrub cassava or manioc (*Manihot esculenta*) has emerged as the superior ecological choice.

The nutritional profile of famine

The misery and human suffering that famine causes is not just the result of an acute episode of deprivation following natural or man-made disasters, however. In Africa, famine is superimposed on a pre-existing foundation of chronic under-nutrition and nutrient deficiency (Payne 1985). Africa suffers from all of the major public health nutritional problems defined by the World Health Organization, including both ends of the spectrum of protein-energy malnutrition (kwashiorkor and nutritional marasmus), anemia due to iron deficiency, vitamin A deficiency, and endemic goiter and cretinism, as well as other nutritional problems.

With this in mind, it is not difficult to understand the serious medical and health problems that famines unleash. The reduction in food (and energy) intake associated with famines causes its victims first to lose their subcutaneous fat stores, followed by the loss of deeper fat stores. After these have nearly disappeared, the muscles start to waste away. Next the visceral organs (e.g., the liver and intestines) of the body begin to deteriorate. Wasting of the intestines decreases the supply of enzymes for digestion and absorption. The body tries to compensate for the consequent reduction in energy by reducing its metabolic rate. Edema often results from the low levels of serum albumin. Men often become impotent. Women often become amenorrheic. Pregnant women sometimes spontaneously abort their babies. Due to the decreased structural and functional integrity of the gastrointestinal tract and the fact that normal digestive surface and enzyme production is compromised, subsequent food may precipitate diarrhea. Diarrhea all too frequently leads to dehydration and cardiovascular collapse, frequently with fatal results (Latham 1979, Aykroyd 1971).

Famines and infections: the deadly synergism

Under-nutrition resulting from famines produces its deleterious consequences in a number of ways. People respond behaviorally to the decreased energy intakes by decreasing their energy expenditures. Deaths from famine are not only due to starvation, but are also frequently the result of infections. When the body's nutritional reserves are low, its capacity to fight off pathogenic organisms is reduced. Additionally, the presence of infection, irrespective of severity, may cause further deterioration in the nutritional status as invading organisms compete with the host for available nutrients. There is also metabolic loss of nitrogen, vitamins, and other nutrients that tend to cause a downward spiral in host nutritional status (Scrimshaw 1986). This situation has been described as the synergism of nutrition and infection, i.e., the result of both is more serious than the effects of either alone (Scrimshaw, et al. 1973). Furthermore, famine brings social disruption and confusion, increasing the likelihood that serious infectious diseases will occur (e.g., typhoid, cholera, tuberculosis, typhus). Most of the deaths in famines may actually be due to the these diseases rather than to starvation per se. Due to overcrowding in cities and near food distribution points, and the breakdown of normal sanitation and hygiene, infectious agents can pass with relative ease from one person to another. Decaying corpses present a very serious problem to health and hygiene and magnify the probability that infections will spread.

The ecological status and nutritional adequacy of cassava

The cassava plant is a tropical shrub native to the New World tropics. It is an extremely adaptable crop which grows best between 30°N and 30°S, at altitudes up to about 2000 meters, 500 to 600 mm rainfall per year, and ambient temperatures above 20°C. It is tolerant of periods of drought and of extremely poor or exhausted soils (Cock and Howeler 1978); under favorable conditions, it is one of the biologically most efficient producers of edible carbohydrate (Norman, et al. 1984, Cock 1982).

Cassava is one of the major food crops in the world. Its production exceeds 118 million metric tons per year (FAO 1980), 45 million metric tons of which is produced in Africa. Cassava is the staple crop for 500 million people around the world and is the most significant root and tuber crop in Third World countries. Data from the Food and Agriculture Organization indicate that in Africa an estimated 50 million people consume more than 500 kcal per day from cassava products. The worldwide production of cassava makes it the fourth most important source of food energy in the tropics. In Africa the cassava leaf as well as the root is eaten. Cassava leaf may be contrasted with spinach (Table I). Comparatively, cassava leaf is higher in calories, protein, fat, calcium, thiamine, riboflavin, niacin, and vitamin C.

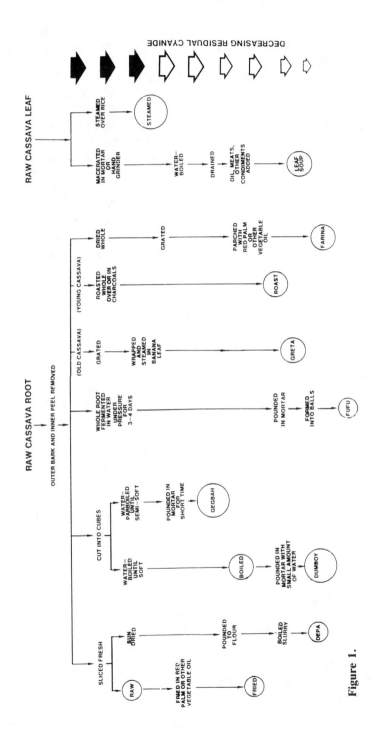

Figure 1.

Table I. Comparison of cassava leaf with spinach*

	Cassava leaf	Spinach leaf
Protein (%)	5.8	1.8
Calories	53	17
Fat (%)	1.1	0.2
Thiamine (mgs)	0.14	0.09
Riboflavin (mgs.)	0.26	0.16
Niacin (mgs.)	1.5	0.5
Vitamin C. (mgs.)	225	48
Calcium (mgs.)	175	66
Iron (mgs.)	1.7	2.4

Source: FAO, 1954;
*(Per 100 gram sample)

The nutrient composition of the root is contingent upon whether it is consumed fresh or dried as a flour or other product (Table II). As indicated in Tables III and IV, cassava flour compares favorably with grain flours and either white or sweet potato flours in calories and vitamin C but contains less protein than any of the above flours. The low protein contents of both the fresh root and cassava flour have been the major complaint against cassava as food by nutritionists (Passmore and Eastwood 1986, Byerlee and Eicher 1972).

Cassava is a poor food for children because of its low protein content. Growing children need substantially more and better quality protein per kilogram of their body weight than do adults. The biological value of cassava protein, like that of many other plant sources of pro-

Table II. Composition of fresh and dried cassava roots*

	Fresh	Dried
Protein (%)	0.9	1.5
Calories	109	338
Fat (%)	0.2	0.6
Thiamine (mgs.)	0.04	—
Riboflavin (mgs.)	0.2	—
Niacin (mgs.)	0.4	1.0
Vitamin C (mgs.)	27	—
Calcium (mgs.)	25	12
Iron (mgs.)	0.5	1.0

*(Per 100 gram sample)

Table III. Nutrient content of cassava compared with some cereals*

	Cassava	Rice	Wheat	Corn
Protein (%)	1.5	6.7	11.7	8.4
Calories	338	360	350	363
Fat (%)	0.6	0.7	1.5	1.2
Thiamine (mgs.)	—	0.8	0.32	0.18
Riboflavin (mgs.)	—	0.03	0.07	0.08
Niacin (mgs.)	1.0	1.6	1.7	0.6
Vitamin C. (mgs.)	—	—	—	—
Calcium (mgs.)	12	10	24	5
Iron (mgs.)	1.0	0.9	2.4	1.2

* (Per 100 gram sample)

teins, also decreases its value in meeting children's growth needs. Most adequate human diets provide between 10 and 15 percent of their energy in the form of protein. Cassava provides 3.3 percent of its energy in the form of protein. There is no place we know of in the world however, where adults or children consume cassava without also consuming other dietary sources of protein. Perhaps the main reason why cassava has been so maligned is because it became widely known to western nutritional scientists as the food the peasants ate, "belly-filler", during the hungry season (Lappe and Collins 1978). It was "discovered," as it were, during the 1970's when there was an explosion of interest in protein malnutrition (Byerlee and Eicher 1972).

In a famine situation however, the urgent need is for energy foods (Passmore and Eastwood 1986), and as such cassava could play a very useful role. Many people already rely upon cassava during the

Table IV. Cassava compared with potatoes*

	Cassava	White Potato	Sweet Potato
Protein (%)	1.5	1.7	1.1
Calories	338	70	97
Fat (%)	0.6	0.1	0.3
Thiamine (mgs.)	—	0.08	0.08
Riboflavin (mgs.)	—	0.03	0.04
Niacin (mgs.)	1.0	1.2	0.5
Vitamin C (mgs.)	—	8.0	19
Calcium (mgs.)	12	7.0	28
Iron (mgs.)	1.0	0.6	0.8

* (Per 100 gram sample)

hungry season. If infants and children are given adequate amounts of dried skim milk or other high-protein foods along with cassava, their protein needs can be satisfied. Cassava roots are not rich in vitamins and minerals. Correction of vitamin and mineral deficiencies may, therefore, have to wait until the worst of a famine situation is past, if leaves or other vitamin and mineral sources are not available.

Biocultural impediments to cassava use

Cicely Williams (1935), a British nutritionist, introduced the Western world to the word "kwashiorkor". Kwashiorkor is a Ghanaian word from the Ga language. It is loosely translated as the illness the older child gets when the new baby is born. After this word and the clinical symptoms that she described were introduced into the Western medical and scientific communities, there was a dramatic shift in research and applied nutrition emphasis. Rarely in science has there been such a mobilization of efforts, money, and talent as that which was begun by the recognition of the problem of kwashiorkor and protein deficiency.

Kwashiorkor is a disease characterized by edema (fluid retention) of the extremities, especially the legs. Children with this expression of calorie-protein malnutrition have a puffy, swollen-looking face, dull and pluckable hair, and a number of pathognomonic skin changes of the legs, forearms, knees, and elbows such as "flaky paint" dermatitis (Latham, 1979). The expression of this deficiency syndrome is quite dramatic. Nutritionists, pediatricians, biochemists, plant breeders, and agronomists are but a few of the many professionals who jumped on the protein bandwagon: the recognition of kwashiorkor as a clinical entity stimulated evaluations of the "worth" of various traditional foods on the basis of their protein content.

In response to the heightened concern with dietary protein, the International Maize and Wheat Improvement Centre in Mexico (CIMMYT), as well as many other international agricultural research centers, devoted much of their energies to the production of "quality protein" foods. This meant, for example, doubling the contents of lysine (to 4%) and tryptophan (0.5%) in maize (corn) at CIMMYT. The success of the efforts of many scientists ushered in a "green revolution." Many researchers believed that under-nutrition and hunger would be eliminated from the world (CIMMYT 1976). The excitement and enthusiasm, however, were short-lived. Applied nutritionists and anthropologists were among the first to realize that protein-energy malnutrition existed primarily because the poor in developing countries were not receiving enough food to eat, not simply because they were not receiving enough protein. Calculations were made which suggested that even given the usual cereal foods of the majority of children, an adequate caloric intake, in most instances, would insure an adequate protein intake (Gopalan 1975). In other words, the primacy of protein had begun to yield, under closer scrutiny, to the realization of energy deficiency as the major component of undernutrition in children.

By now, however, the notion of protein as panacea had already gained ascendancy. Thus cassava was already being viewed as irrelevant to the problem of protein-energy malnutrition because it had too little protein (Byerlee and Eicher 1972) and also because it was seen as a food eaten by the lower classes and therefore not likely to be accepted on a wider scale. Western ethnocentrism and bias against root crops assigned cassava an inferior role in the campaign to alleviate hunger, starvation, and famine in many Third World communities. Cereals, like rice, wheat, and maize, were given the major focus. Fortunately, the indigenous farmers tended to be more closely tied to traditional practices of demonstrated merit than to newly introduced Western agricultural and dietary prejudices. Thus, they continued to grow cassava even while they experimented with other crops. Throughout the world, many indigenous farmers remained receptive to the cultivation and consumption of cassava and the plant maintained its central role in their strategies for survival in the face of recurrent hunger, starvation, and periodic famine. What this experience should teach us is that we should improve the quality and quantity of the crops that we already have while trying to introduce populations to new crops. We should never dissuade people from consuming any food crop. Our aim should be to increase the diversity of the human diet rather than decrease dietary diversity.

Cassava's dietary history in Africa

Cassava appears to have been first introduced to Africa around 1600 A.D. (Jones 1959). The plant spread rapidly across West and Southwest Africa (especially Angola), into the interior regions (Zaire), and by 1700 A.D. it was established along the East African coast. Approximately 20 generations of West and Central Africans and perhaps 15 generations of East Africans have had some exposure to the crop. Cassava cultivars were first transported by the Portuguese to the West African coast where the plant was generally well accepted as a carbohydrate and dark green vegetable food source. Initially, Africans received the cassava but not the technology developed by the Amazonian Native Americans to detoxify, process, and store the plant for consumption. In this respect then, cassava's introduction into Africa was a classic case of the incomplete transfer of technology; the plant arrived minus the 6000 years of contact knowledge developed in South America to enhance its use. As a consequence, it became incumbent upon Africans to develop processing and storage strategies which would maximize the agricultural and nutritional potential of the plant while minimizing the persistence of toxic compounds in the final food products.

Traditional processing strategies

When cassava arrived in Africa, it frequently filled the dietary and cultural niche previously occupied by yams (*Discorea* spp.). Most indigenous groups initially processed the cassava as they had prepared the yams: removing the peel, cutting the root in segments, boiling to soften, and inevitably pounding the boiled root or leaf in a wooden mortar with a pestle to modify its texture and consistency and to improve the palatability of the final product. Other steps were subsequently added to lend variety to cassava's texture, consistency, and flavor and to enhance cassava's post-processing storage life.

During a recent investigation of traditional Liberian (West African) processing methods of cassava roots and leaves for dietary consumption, we observed over 15 distinct indigenous cassava food products. As depicted in Figure 1, these foods were the product of a variety of processing strategies. The roots may be fried, boiled, fermented under water as *fufu*, grated and steamed in a banana leaf, sun-dried and later pounded and boiled, roasted or eaten raw; young leaves may be macerated in a wooden mortar and pestle or in a hand-cranked meat grinder and boiled or simply steamed intact over rice. The type and duration of processing were aimed at increasing the diversity and palatability of the final product, increasing the storage potential of the highly perishable harvested fresh root, and decreasing the toxic component of the plant. Indigenous processing strategies were found to variably influence the amount of cyanide remaining in the final food product and that subsequently ingested.

Diffusion of the plant throughout the continent

The similarities between cassava and yams and the vastly superior storage potential of the intact cassava root greatly accelerated cassava's diffusion into the interior regions of tropical Africa. With most propagation by farmers done through the asexual planting of stalk cuttings from their most productive plants, there was selection over time for taller plants with the largest roots. In the tropical environment, stalk cuttings remain viable from 10 to 40 days, enough time to have been transported by foot to farms and kin groups in the more interior regions. The plant's ecological flexibility and high carbohydrate content has made cassava the most frequently cultivated and consumed reserve crop on the continent among traditional (subsistence) farmers and the primary year-round staple for very many groups. Indeed, throughout much of tropical Africa, cassava production and use has eventually supplanted extensive yam cultivation and use. In the savanna regions where grains remain the principal carbohydrate staple, cassava roots continue to be grown as a famine reserve and the leaves harvested periodically as a green vegetable. Of the various ecological advantages of cassava, the fact that cassava requires less moisture for its growth, makes it a prime candidate for famine situations, since many areas in Africa are drought-prone.

The factor of toxicity

In spite of cassava's excellent caloric content, its particular suitability for the humid tropical lowlands, its ability to grow well on nutrient-poor soils, particularly the oxisols and utisols of the humid rainforests (Ruthenberg 1971), its relative stability in annual yields, drought resistance, advantages for intercropping with short duration crops (Norman, et al. 1984) and its low labor requirement for cultivation, it has been the endogenous presence of cyanide compounds in the plant which has stymied the promotion of cassava as a major component of famine prevention in Africa. Cassava is one of the very few, but among the most important, of the food crops in which the content of cyanide can, under certain conditions of nutritional deprivation, create additional problems. Cassava's toxicity is the result of the endogenous presence of the cyanogenic glucosides linamarin and lotustralin, biological precursors of cyanide, in all parts of the plant. The presence of this toxin in the agricultural product and the critical lack of adequate data on the residual cyanide content of indigenous African foods derived from cassava have bolstered Western biases against root crops and contributed to cassava's depreciated role as a mitigant for chronic under-nutrition and famine.

Cassava's sublethal cyanide content is undeniable. Indeed, the plant's principal biomedical and bioevolutionary importance for humans emerges from the endogenous presence of bound and free cyanide in the plant and the potential for residual cyanide to persist in processed plant products (i.e., foodstuffs). Containing both the enzyme and the substrate needed for the production of hydrogen cyanide, the two come together when cells walls are damaged as the plant is initially prepared for consumption. In many cases, the presence of hydrogen cyanide can be detected aromatically, particularly when the young fresh raw leaves are macerated for later boiling.

No acyanogenic varieties of cassava have yet been found and the removal of the endogenous cyanogens from the agricultural product has been the focus of numerous plant breeding trials. Agricultural genetic engineers (Sadik, et al. 1974) have identified these substances as "undesirable" components of the plant and have targeted their elimination as a primary objective. Yet, the presence of these toxins serve to protect the plant from predation by viruses, bacteria, and larger organisms (including other mammals!) and to maintain a stability in plant yields. A significant reduction in plant cyanogen levels is directly correlated with a loss in agricultural yields in traditional subsistence environments (Hahn and Keyser 1985). In our shortsighted efforts to "improve" (that is, reduce) the toxic component of this major agricultural crop, we have completely discounted the potential for human cultural intervention and human biological adaptation to separately and synergistically modify the expression and consequences of the plant's toxicity.

African sociocultural responses to cassava

To understand how human behavior and biology might interface with cassava use and toxicity, it is essential that we identify the role that cassava plays in various subsistence communities. Data on African sociocultural responses to cassava are scant; however, we do know that since root products were already culturally acceptable as food, no stigma was associated with cassava consumption among most Africans. In the Republic of Liberia, among the ethnic groups electing to consume cassava as a staple, the plant and its products continue to assume a "super food" status. Among the Kru, Krahn, Grebo, Sappo, Mano, Gio, Bassa, and some Dei of Liberia, for example, it is given symbolically to the newborn and the newly delivered mother and is the principal weaning food. Among the Mano and Gio peoples of northcentral Liberia, a particular cassava root product called *gegbah* is seen as the food which has been crucial to their groups' survival during the days of tribal warfare. According to Mano and Gio legends, warriors would swallow large lumps of *gegbah* prior to going off to war. Because of this dietary practice and gegbah's density, these warriors could move quickly through the forests, wage war for a number of days, and return home without having had to stop and prepare meals or hunt for food while in the forests. This, of course, permitted them a strike advantage unavailable to other groups. In terms of cyanide toxicity, *gegbah* is particularly interesting because its cyanide concentration per unit area increases as the final product is produced. This is an unusual event in food science, where processing usually reduces endogenous toxicity. During famines, the production and ingestion of *gegbah* may have served a similar biocultural function, its slow gastrointestinal transit time forestalling the pangs of hunger and its unusually high residual sublethal cyanide content initiating a series of metabolic adaptations.

Major metabolic associations

It now appears that human biology may be profoundly affected by exposure to regular sublethal cyanide from dietary cassava (Oke 1973; Jackson, et al. 1985, 1986). Ingested sublethal cyanide is detoxified by several pathways with the production of thiocyanate being the most important. Thiocyanate production requires sulfur, usually derived from the sulfur-containing amino acids methionine and cysteine. Although thiocyanate is itself toxic, its toxicity is less than that of cyanide and most excess thiocyanate is usually excreted in the body fluids (urine, saliva, breastmilk, etc.). Some cyanide is detoxified into the cyano form of vitamin B12 and in the blood, cyanate may be formed from thiocyanate with hemoglobin acting as an enzyme (Oke 1973). Cyanide inhibits cellular respiration; at sublethal doses this toxin exhibits a wide range of effects on human metabolic systems. Twenty generations, perhaps even 15 generations of Africans regularly using cassava, could initiate a number of important physiological modifications which could impact on individual and group responses to food shortages and outright famine. One of the more obvious changes suggested by regular cassava use is alterations in glucose metabolism (Solomonson 1981). In a study of 82 adult Liberians consuming various levels of sublethal cyanide from cassava, higher levels of glycosylated hemoglobin were observed in those individuals regularly ingesting >0.9 mg CN/kg body weight/day (Jackson 1986). Glycosylated hemoglobin is an excellent index of long-term elevations in blood glucose levels. In a subsequent study using an animal model of West African dietary cyanide ingestion levels, direct evidence of blood glucose elevations were observed in response to higher dietary cyanide intakes (Jackson, et al. 1988) and further research in this area is clearly warranted.

Alterations in glucose metabolism coupled with a depression in thyroid activity (Delange, et al. 1982) may also induce major alterations in the rate of weight gain. Researchers in Zaire have suggested that chronic dietary cyanide may depress thyroid activity (Delange, et al. 1982) in iodine-limited groups. This effect may act synergistically with the elevated blood glucose levels to decelerate the rate of somatic weight gain. Sublethal cyanide's effect on thyroid function appears two-fold: iodine uptake by the thyroid gland is inhibited by cyanide (Delange, et al. 1982) and thiocyanate (the chief metabolite of cyanide detoxification) not only outcompetes iodide for uptake but also causes a rapid discharge of exchangeable iodide from the thyroid gland. It is possible that the lowered levels of T3 and T4 (thyroid hormones) and the higher blood glucose levels observed in individuals consuming high sublethal cyanide foodstuffs (1.2 mg CN/kg body weight/day) may depress protein synthesis, basal metabolic rate, and growth hormone production. In Africa where cassava consumption is so significant, under-nutrition chronic, and famine periodic, a pronounced slower growth among the very young may initially appear to be associated with considerably increased mortality and morbidity. At the individual level of analysis, such a scenario may appear maladaptive. However, at the population level of analysis, it may be ecologically more conservative; among older surviving children, the implications for slower growth are more difficult to assess. It is possible that in many parts of tropical Africa, a retarded rate of growth may act as a protective mechanism in nutritionally precarious times (e.g., during periods of seasonal agricultural inadequacy and famine). A smaller body size may provide an adaptive advantage during periods of caloric deprivation, particularly if coupled with other cultural and biological responses.

Interface of cassava and response to infectious disease

The synergism of under-nutrition and infection may also be influenced by cassava use. In the humid African tropics, the most favorable natural ecosystem on the continent for cassava cultivation and dietary use, an assortment of microbial pathogens are endemic and host immunological status represents a major determinant of overall health. Under environmental conditions of high pathogen prevalence, any compromise in immunoglobulin levels may result in an increased susceptibility to disease and a reduction in biological fitness. Sublethal cyanide ingestion requires sulfur for its *in vivo* detoxification to thiocyanate. Sulfane sulfur plays a critical role both in this detoxification (Westley 1981) and in the construction of immunoglobulins. So, any cultural practice which might reduce the availability of sulfur may affect immune status as well.

In a study of the impact of regular cassava diets on immune status (Jackson, et al. 1985) it was observed that cassava-derived sublethal cyanide at moderate to high levels of ingestion (0.6mg CN/kg body weight/day and above) appeared to raise levels of serum immunoglobulins in adult Liberians, particularly IgM levels. Several direct and indirect mechanisms may be responsible for these effects: dietary cyanide may stimulate immunoglobulin production by acting as an immunogen if it were bound to a macromolecular protein (e.g., carbamylated hemoglobin). In addition, bound forms of cyanide in the diet may also have antigenic potential. Certain sociocultural practices in Africa may also elevate immunoglobulin levels indirectly. In Liberia, as elsewhere in West Africa, traditional cassava processing methods may expose cassava eaters to higher levels of microbial contamination than they would otherwise encounter. Specifically these might include prolonged fermentation of peeled roots and subsequent fungal contamination, oral contact with intermediate products during *fufu* preparation, use of undisinfected, rough-surfaced wooden mortars and pestles for the protracted beating of intermediate and final cassava food products and the usual consumption patterns (i.e., food swallowed in lumps without prior mastication). Our observations of elevated IgM levels in these Africans are of possible clinical importance since this antibody has strong antibacterial capabilities, such as agglutination and activation of the complement system. In a region where such bacterial diseases as Hanson's disease (leprosy), louse-borne relapsing fever, yaws, and cholera are endemic, high levels of specific IgM may dramatically improve one's chances of survival, particularly if the condition of chronic under-nutrition is superimposed upon this exposure.

Cassava use may also have a less direct effect on susceptibility to infectious disease. Physiological levels of cyanates, secondary metabolic products of sublethal cyanide ingestion, have been shown *in vitro* to significantly modify the growth and development of *Plasmodium falciparum*, causative agent of falciparum malaria (Nagel, et al. 1980). Throughout Africa, falciparum malaria remains highly endemic, and is a consistent contributor to infant and child mortality, the most common cause of adult morbidity, and a well-known suppressor of immune function. The nutritional and immunological consequences on the host infected with falciparum malaria are well known; the parasite maintains its own growth and development at the expense of host iron and folate stores, and the presence of *Plasmodium* decreases the host's ability to respond to other endemic viruses, bacteria, and macroparasites. The presence of the parasite causes damage to the liver, spleen, and red blood cells. Host protein reserves are taxed in an effort to mount an immunological response. The parasite may even invade the brain. It is possible that dietary cassava ingestion could forestall the growth and development of *P. falciparum in vivo* in a manner similar to that observed *in vitro,* and place a ceiling on parasite proliferation and damage to the host.

Furthermore, one of the host enzymes which appear to be required by the parasite is red blood cell glucose 6-phosphate dehydrogenase. Studies using an animal model of West African patterns of sublethal cyanide ingestion suggests that moderate to high levels of ingested sublethal cyanide could reduce the availability of enzymatically active forms of this protein and perhaps indirectly impede parasite metabolism and survival (Jackson, et al. 1986). This could also have an important effect on immunological status and the subsequent host response to microparasitic (microbial) infection.

Summary

Cassava has great potential to alleviate the hunger and starvation that accompanies famines. In Africa, cassava is widely consumed and well-tolerated by millions of people. The conditions that precipitate hunger and famine in Africa (especially drought) make cassava especially relevant since the plant requires less moisture than most other crops such as maize, wheat, and rice for its growth and development. Cereals have a defined period when moisture is critical to plant growth and development; this is not the case with cassava. The hardiness of the plant allows it to survive circumstances and diseases that other staple crops could not. Furthermore, the storage potential of the intact root and its high carbohydrate content make it particularly appropriate when immediate survival depends upon adequate energy intake.

The presence of cyanide should not be a limit to cassava's utility in African famine prevention, since traditional processing methods very likely reduce residual cyanide to subtoxic levels. These sublethal cyanide levels may stimulate subsequent metabolic modifications in Africans and may prove to be of adaptive value under conditions of periodic hunger, starvation, and famine. The highly suggestive evidence that cassava positively influences the immune system by raising IgM levels is particularly exciting and reinforces the importance of assessing a major human food crop such as cassava from integrated multidisciplinary perspectives. Perhaps of greater importance than its role in famine prevention, however, is the regular use of cassava as a staple or co-staple food by Africans. Cassava plays a major role in increasing the energy intake in the African diet. It is a constituent of the diet of Africans in all areas of the continent. Many efforts have, and are being, made at international research centers to breed new varieties of cassava which have less cyanide and that contain higher protein contents. Although more could be done to increase the general productivity and cultivation of cassava, there have been numerous successes in cassava agriculture. CIAT and IITA located in Colombia, South America and Nigeria, West Africa, respectively, have active and relatively long-standing research programs devoted to all aspects of cassava husbandry. Moreover, we have already mentioned the fact that cassava is used quite frequently to sustain non-cassava eaters during times when droughts or pests reduce or destroy other, less hardy crops.

Given the increasing population pressures in some African countries and the decrease in arable land for cereal crops, cassava may play a significant role in future development thinking since it can be grown on less desirable land. Cereals are complemented with legume crops to augment their protein value and quality. This type of complementarity could also make cassava much more nutritionally balanced as well.

The fact that cassava requires less labor-intensive cultivation practices is also important. People decrease their energy expenditure when their energy intake is chronically low. Although there are seasonal variations in energy expenditure associated with crop production, the need for less energy to cultivate cassava makes it especially important in periods of decreased food and energy availability (Payne 1985).

Most of the recent studies examining the nutritional status of Africans indicates that overall food production has not kept pace with the growth in population. The shortfalls in the amount of food available has been made up by imports and food aid (United Nations 1986). Cassava, therefore, has several advantages, not the least among which are that it has already been accepted by the African people and has a niche or place in their diet and cultural patterns.

Literature Cited

Aykroyd, W. R. 1974. *The conquest of famine.* Chatto and Windus, London pp. 7–23.

Aykroyd, W. R. 1971. Definition of different degrees of starvation. In *Famine: Nutrition and Relief Operations in Times of Disaster,* ed. by Blix. Uppsala: Almquist and Wiksells.

Byerlee, D. and C. K. Eicher. 1972. Rural Employment, Migration, and Economic Development: Theoretical Issues and Empirical Evidence from Africa. Africa Rural Employment Study, Paper No. 1, Department of Agricultural Economics. East Lansing: Michigan State University.

Centro Internacinal de Mejoramiento de Maiz Y Trigo. 1976. 1976 CIMMYT Review. El Batan, Mexico.

Cock, J. H. 1982. Cassava: a basic energy source in the tropics. *Science* 218:775.

Cock, J. H. and R. H. Howeler. 1978. The ability of cassava to grow on poor soils. In *Crop Tolerance to Suboptimal Land Conditions,* ed. by G. A. Jung. Madison, WI: American Society of Agronomy. pp. 145–154.

Delange, F., F. B. Iteke, and A. M. Ermans. 1982. *Nutritional Factors Involved in the Goitrogenic Action of Cassava.* Ottawa, Canada: International Development Research Centre.

FAO. 1954. *Food Composition Tables—Minerals and Vitamins—for International Use.* No. 11. Rome: FAO.

FAO. 1980. *Production Yearbook.* Volume 34. Rome: FAO.

Gopalan, C. 1975 Protein versus calories in the treatment of Protein-Calorie Malnutrition: Metabolic and population studies in India. In *Protein-Calorie Malnutrition,* R. E. Olson, ed. New York: Academic Press. pp. 329–351.

Hahn, N. and Kaiser. 1985. Ibadan, Nigeria: International Institute for Tropical Agriculture.

The Hunger Project. 1985. *Ending Hunger: An Idea Whose Time Has Come.* New York: Praeger.

Jackson, L. C. 1986. Hyperglycemia and chronic exposure to sublethal dietary cyanide: Does regular cassava eating predispose to diabetes? *American Journal of Physical Anthropology* 69(2):218.

Jackson, L. C., E. F. Bloch, R. T. Jackson, J. P. Chandler, Y. L. Kim, and F. J. Malveaux. 1985. Influence of dietary cyanide on immunoglobin and thiocyanate levels in the serum of Liberian adults. *Journal of the National Medical Association* 77(10):777–82.

Jackson, L. C., J. P. Chandler, and R. T. Jackson. 1986. Inhibition and adaptation of red cell glucose-6-phosphate dehydrogenase (G-6-PD) in vivo to chronic sublethal dietary cyanide in an animal model. *Human Biology* 58(1):67–77.

Jackson, L. C., M. Osegura, S. Medrano, and Y. L. Kim. 1988. Carbamylation of hemoglobin in vivo with chronic sublethal dietary cyanide: Implications for hemoglobin S. *Biochemical Medicine and Metabolic Biology* 39:64–8.

Jones, W. O. 1959. *Manioc in Africa.* Stanford, CA: Stanford University Press.

Lappe, F. M. and J. Collins. 1978 *Food First: Beyond the Myth of Scarcity.* New York: Ballantine Books.

Latham. M. C. 1979. *Human Nutrition in Tropical Africa: A Textbook for Health Workers.* Rome: FAO.

Nagel, R. L., C. Razento, H. B. Tanowitz, and M. Wittner. 1980. Effect of Na Cyanate on *Plasmodium falciparum* in vitro. *Journal of Parisitology* 66(3):483–87.

Norman, M. J. T., C. J. Pearson, and P. G. E. Searle. 1984. *The Ecology of Tropical Food Crops.* Cambridge: Cambridge University Press.

Oke, O. L. 1973. The mode of cyanide detoxification in chronic cassava toxicity. Proceedings of an Interdisciplinary Workshop, ed. by B. Nestel and R. MacIntyre. Ottawa, Canada: International Development Research Centre.

Passmore, R. and M. A. Eastwood. 1986. *Human Nutrition and Dietetics.* Eighth Edition. Edinburgh: Churchill Livingston.

Payne, P. R. 1985. The nature of malnutrition. In *Nutrition and Development,* ed. by M. Biswas and P. Pinstrup-Andersen. Oxford: Oxford University Press. pp. 1–19.

Ruthenberg, H. 1971. *Farming Systems in the Tropics.* Oxford: Clarendon Press.

Sadik, S., O. U. Okereke, and S. K. Hahn. 1974. Screening for Acyanogenesis in Cassava. Technical Bulletin No. 4. Ibadan, Nigeria: International Institute for Tropical Agriculture.

Scrimshaw, N. S. 1986. Consequences of hunger for individuals and societies. *Federation Proceedings* 45:2421–26.

Scrimshaw, N. S., C. E. Taylor, and J. E. Gordon. 1973. Interactions of nutrition and infection. *American Journal of Medical Sciences* 237:367–403.

Solomonson, L. P. 1981 Cyanide as a metabolic inhibitor. In *Cyanide in Biology,* ed. by B. Wennesland, E. Conn, C. Knowles, J. Westley, and F. Wissing. London: Academic Press. pp. 11–28.

Spalding, E., J. McCrae, I. H. E. Rutishauer, and J. M. Parkin. 1977. A study of severely malnourished children in the Gambia. *Journal of Tropical Pediatrics and Environmental Child Health* 23:215–19.

United Nations. 1986. First Report on the World Nutrition Situation. Subcommittee on Nutrition of the United Nations Administrative Committee on Coordination. New York.

Westley, J. 1981. Cyanide and sulfane sulfur. In *Cyanide in Biology,* ed. by B. Vennesland, E. Conn, C. Knowles, J. Westley, and F. Wissing, London: Academic Press. pp. 61–76.

Williams, C. D. 1935. Kwashiorkor: a nutritional disease of children associated with a maize diet. *Lancet* 2:1151–2.

Seasonality of Vegetable Use and Production On Swazi Nation Land: Problems and Interventions

John J. Curry

601 Blick Drive
Silver Spring, MD 20904

Rebecca Huss-Ashmore

Department of Anthropology
University Museum
University of Pennsylvania
Philadelphia, PA 19104-6398

Doyle Grenoble

Department of Horticulture
The Pennsylvania State University
University Park, PA 16802

Douglas Gama

Malkerns Research Station Horticultural Programme
PO Box 4
Malkerns, Swaziland

While increased agricultural production is central to solving Africa's food problems, it is increasingly plain that production must be linked to consumption concerns (Gittinger, et al. 1987). This includes both the consumption preferences of African households as economic units and the consumption needs of family members as biological units. The linkages between African agricultural production and both of these types of consumption issues have only begun to be explored (Huss-Ashmore, these volumes). However, as Frankenberger (1985) notes, the inherent seasonality of agricultural systems is one of the most important links. In this chapter, we describe research by the Swaziland Cropping Systems Project into the seasonality of vegetable use and production on Swazi Nation Land (communal tenure land). We first present an overview of nutritional concerns relevant to the project, and then outline a program of research and intervention aimed at changing the seasonality of vegetable production.

The Importance of Seasonality

Seasonality is a characteristic feature of the tropical landscape. Indeed, in their discussion of the relationship between seasonality and rural poverty, Chambers, Longhurst, and Pacey have observed that:

> seasonal variations occur in most of the human activities and natural processes which directly concern rural life . . . It is difficult to find any aspect of rural life in the tropical third world which is not touched by seasonality.
>
> (Chambers, et al. 1981:6,xvi)

Consequently, patterns of seasonal fluctuation have been studied by a number of researchers and policy makers in areas such as climate, energy availability and utilization, labor allocation, food availability, morbidity, malnutrition, indebtedness, and poverty.[1] Much of the emphasis in seasonality studies has been placed on the consequences of seasonal constraints or stresses in the local production system—a system most often dominated by rainfed production of staple food crops. The literature is replete with such studies, a review of which is beyond the scope of this paper. Irrigation, when incorporated into most models of seasonality, seems to be regarded more as an external element of change rather than an integral feature of seasonal processes. For example, Chambers, et al., assert that:

> agricultural seasonality does not always reflect the seasonality of climate because of irrigation. By using stored or non-seasonal water (whether from dams, rivers,

---

[1]For a review of this literature, see Chambers, et al. 1981, Huss-Ashmore, et al. 1988, and Longhurst 1986.

or the ground) cultivation may artificially (emphasis ours) spread more around the calendar, bringing new and different flows of food and income, labour demands and threats to health. As irrigation spreads . . . annual patterns of variation along many dimensions can be expected to change.

(Chambers, et al. 1981:6)

Irrigation is certainly an important method for extending the cropping calendar for the staple grain in many systems (e.g., Asian rice systems). However, in other circumstances, crops under irrigation may themselves have a pattern of seasonality imposed upon them by conditions of climate, diseases and other pests, and labor shortages which occur during the rainy season. These cultivars, then, can only be accomodated into the cropping pattern under irrigation in the dry season, i.e., at a time of year when such constraints are minimized.

Patterns of seasonal availability and scarcity, although different from rainfed crops, are no less pronounced in many irrigated crops. Similarly, there is a seasonality to patterns of price fluctuation that reflect conditions of supply and demand. Such patterns can have profound consequences in terms of consumption, and therefore in terms of the health and well-being of the population.

Vegetable growing by small farmers in Swaziland is just such a case where seasonal constraints severely limit cultivation during the rainy season. Most of the production of the main vegetables grown (cabbages, tomatoes, onions, Swiss chard, beets) is restricted to winter (dry season) production under irrigation. Such conditions of production create a seasonal pattern in terms of availability of vegetables, prices paid and received for them, and their consumption by people in both rural and urban areas. Efforts to assist these farmers to overcome the seasonality of vegetable production should have implications for the profitability of vegetable growing for producers, the availability of vegetables for consumers, and consequently, the health and nutritional well-being of both.

This paper describes the efforts of the Malkerns Research Station (MRS) Horticultural Programme, assisted by the Swaziland Cropping Systems Project, to address the issue of seasonality of vegetable production through its summer vegetable program. The program employed a modified Farming Systems Research methodology (Low 1986) to identify problems associated with summer vegetable production on Swazi Nation Land (SNL), and to test—both on the research station and on individual farms—technological solutions to these problems. This method emphasizes rigorous screening of new technologies on-station in the early stages of research, prior to testing on farmers' fields, and is described in detail elsewhere (Grenoble and Gama 1988).

In addition, this paper illustrates the use of food consumption and nutrition information by an agricultural development project to identify areas for research and potential intervention. This is a strategy which has been increasingly recommended (FAO 1982, 1984; Frankenberger 1985, Mokbel and Pellett 1987, USAID 1983) but rarely employed. In this case, dietary data collected by the Cropping Systems Project showed a strong seasonality to both nutritional content of the diet and to vegetable use (Huss-Ashmore 1987, 1988). Expanded vegetable production was seen as one way to even out some of the fluctuation in dietary variety.

Nutritional Concerns in Swaziland

While Swaziland's nutritional problems are modest by African standards, there are nonetheless indications that the nutritional environment could be improved. For example, the recent National Nutrition Survey indicated that 30% of preschool children in rural areas were stunted (National Nutrition Council 1986). Stunting was most prevalent among children 18–24 months of age, and among rural families on Swazi Nation Land (i.e., as opposed to title deed or plantation land). Lack of a cash income also appeared to be associated with nutritional problems. While much of this stunting was thought to be related to diarrheal disease, consumption patterns were also implicated. Young children were less likely than the rest of the family to receive starches other than maize, and were also less likely to receive oil, margarine, or other calorically dense foods. Dietary variety was low, with some children receiving little more than dilute maize gruels. Dietary variety for the rest of the family was also low, with legumes and groundnuts eaten by less than 10% of the households surveyed (National Nutrition Council 1986:16).

Cappetta (1983) confirms the impression of suboptimal food consumption patterns for many Swazi households. In her survey, 60% of households showed inadequate caloric intake, and 20% were deficient in protein. Intake of fats was very low overall, comprising less than half the recommended proportion of calories. Calcium, riboflavin, niacin, and vitamin A were deficient for at least 50% of households. All of these deficiencies were exacerbated seasonally.

These studies show a rural Swazi diet which is either regularly or seasonally lacking in calories and variety, particularly for low-income households. Interested in possible production solutions for these problems, the Cropping Systems Project added a diet and nutrition study to its program of socioeconomic research. The project was particularly concerned with the dietary impact of introduced production technology (hybrid maize, legumes, irrigated vegetables) and with the effect of herbicides on edible wild greens, an important traditional component of the Swazi diet.

From February, 1986, through March, 1987, the project conducted field interviews on dietary intake with a sample of approximately 100 women and 50 preschool children (less than five years of age) drawn from homesteads cooperating with the project. Each woman was asked once a month to recall for the previous 24 hours all food prepared by her household, the number of persons eating in the homestead, and all food eaten by the woman herself and by her preschool child (if she had one). In addition, anthropometric measurements were taken at two points during the study to determine nutritional status of the sample.

The initial anthropometric survey showed signs of suboptimal nutrition in a significant proportion of sample households. Forty-seven percent of sample children were below 90% of standard (less than 90% of the median) height for age, compared to international standards (Huss-Ashmore 1987). Twenty percent were below 80% of standard weight for age. These are the recognized cutoff points for stunting and wasting, respectively. Acute malnutrition, as measured by weight for height, arm circumference, and triceps skinfold was less common; however 13% of children in the sample were below the 25th percentile in weight for height. Nutritional problems were also seen among the women sampled. While 20% were obese, 28% were underweight and up to 24% were low in either fat or muscle (Huss-Ashmore 1987).

While poor nutritional status often reflects factors other than diet (e.g., workload, infection, sanitation), results of our dietary survey indicated that food consumption is a major constraint, even for these supposedly "progressive" households. For women in these households, average caloric intake was well below the 2235 kcal per day recommended by the FAO/WHO/UNU (1985). Intakes of fat, vitamin B6, folic acid, and calcium averaged less than 50% of recommended daily allowances. In addition, for many of the areas studied, summer is a time of particular stress, with caloric intake for adult women averaging as much as 18% percent below winter intake. This is a pattern recorded (although not quantified) as long ago as 1947 (Kuper 1980), and which four decades of economic change have not completely eradicated.

The seasonality of African diets is a widely recognized phenomenon, related to both economic and ecological factors (Huss-Ashmore and Goodman 1988). Scarcity of food reserves, labor time, and cash during the pre-harvest period all limit dietary intake. Many African populations, including rural Swazis, rely heavily on wild foods during this time. While our survey shows that consumption of maize varies little over the course of the year, vegetable and legume use is highly seasonal. Improving the seasonal distribution of these products is therefore both an important channel for dietary improvement and a feasible goal for agricultural development in Swaziland.

Seasonality of Vegetable Use

At the start of the Cropping Systems Project in 1982, horticulturalists from MRS and the project consulted printed sources, farmers, extension workers, and other horticulturalists to determine general production practices and constraints to vegetable production for SNL farmers. During this initial phase, the seasonality of vegetable production and marketing became apparent. Grenoble (1984) noted that most of the vegetables grown in Swaziland were produced during the winter and marketed between August and November. He suggested that emphasis should be placed on shifting some of the production to summer:

> It has long been recognized that fresh vegetables are in short supply during summer and fall and that this period provides the best markets and prices. However, farmers continue to have great reluctance to grow vegetable crops for this time.
> (Grenoble 1984:4)

This reluctance to devote much time to summer vegetables was also noted in 1983 by Hunting Technical Services in their evaluation of

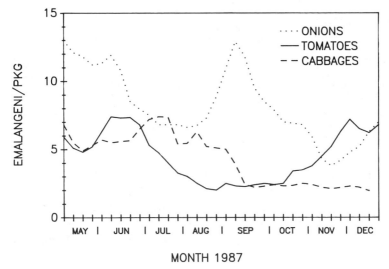

Figure 1. National Agricultural Marketing Board prices for vegetables, 1987. Emalangeni per pocket (onions), box (tomatoes), or bag (cabbage).

Swaziland's Rural Development Area programs. They attributed this reluctance to a conflict with maize production that would result if vegetable growing were attempted at that time of year (Hunting Technical Services 1983:C35). This production seasonality is reflected in the market share to which vegetable producers in Swaziland have access in the local markets. In their study of vegetable marketing in the central area of Swaziland (Mbabane, Matsapha, Manzini), Sterkenberg, et al. noted that "The vegetables produced in Swaziland take their share of the Central Areas sales during the winter months" (Sterkenberg, et al. 1982:46). This implies that those vegetables marketed in Swaziland during the summer are imported from outside the country.

The seasonal fluctuation in market prices is illustrated in Figure 1 by National Agricultural Marketing Board data on average prices for onions, tomatoes, and cabbages for May through December, 1987. Peak prices for onions occur in early May, when last season's onions have long since been sold, and in early September just before the winter season's crop is harvested. Tomatoes command their highest prices in early June before winter tomatoes are available, and in late November to early December, after the summer season (with its higher

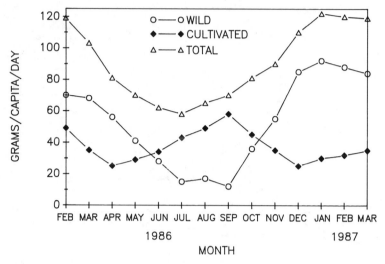

Figure 2. Green vegetable use by weight for women in sample households (three-month running average).

humidity and disease load) has begun. Cabbages reach their price peak slightly later, in June and July, and continue to drop steadily during the winter, reaching a low in the early spring.

The seasonality of vegetable market availability is mirrored in records of dietary consumption. Using cabbage as an example, maximum consumption is recorded in September and October, the months when prices are lowest. Peak prices correspond to the period in early winter when very few green vegetables of any kind are consumed. Figure 2 shows the seasonal consumption of both wild and cultivated green vegetables. Only 29% of women in our sample reported eating vegetables of any kind[2] on their interview day in June, contrasted with 79% in January. This seasonality is especially striking for green vegetables. This category is particularly important, because it constitutes the most frequently consumed relish or side-dish eaten with the staple maize porridge.

As Figure 2 shows, the high consumption of green vegetables dur-

---

[2]The "vegetable" food group included both starchy and non-starchy vegetables, but excluded dried legumes.

ing summer is due almost entirely to wild greens. This includes a number of different plants, principally *ligusha (Corchorus spp.)*, various species of *Amaranthus, Bidens pilosa,* and pumpkin leaves. While pumpkin leaves are not precisely wild, they are not cultivated for their own sake, but are treated as a "windfall" vegetable, in the same manner as wild greens. All plants in this group grow as weeds or intercrops in cultivated fields, and are harvested during the course of other agricultural tasks. By contrast, domesticated vegetables (mostly cabbage, with some Swiss chard and beet greens) are grown in gardens or special plots, often under irrigation.

The heavy nutritional reliance on wild greens during the summer places a constraint on the use of herbicides for small farmers. Many of these farmers report that labor for weeding is in short supply during the summer (particularly as more children attend school) and that timely weeding limits maize production. Use of herbicides could eliminate this bottleneck, but would also remove a critical dietary resource. The Cropping Systems Project currently recommends the use of post-emergence herbicides after the period of peak palatability for wild greens. However, development of a cultivated source of summer greens which could be grown in garden plots would give farmers greater flexibility.

With this in mind, the horticultural section installed a trial at the Malkerns Research Station during the 1987–88 growing season to evaluate several varieties of *Amaranthus*—seed for which is commercially available in Swaziland. Both farmers and extension workers have expressed interest in obtaining seed for traditional vegetables to include in summer and winter gardens. Such greens should also have a modest commercial potential during the winter by supplying urban markets at a time when this item is difficult to obtain.

While the seasonality of green vegetables is probably the most important in nutritional terms, starchy vegetables such as potatoes, pumpkins, gourds, vegetable melons, and onions are also seasonally available. Figure 3 shows the intra-annual distribution of starchy vegetable consumption. Spring and early summer stand out as periods when few such items are reported. Pumpkins and sweet potatoes are particularly important during the period of peak availability, substituting to some extent for maize. Because onions are usually used in cooking, rather than as a separate food item, it is likely that their use is underestimated by our dietary records.

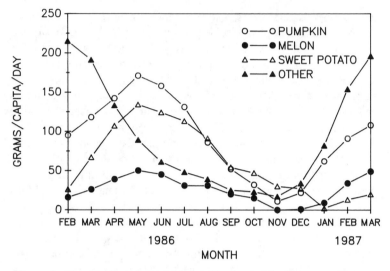

Figure 3. Use of selected starchy vegetables by weight for women in sample households (three-month running average).

The Summer Vegetable Program

Responding to the marked seasonality of vegetable production in Swaziland, horticulturalists from Malkerns Research Station and the Cropping Systems Project undertook a program of research and extension for summer vegetables. This program followed a modified version of a standard Farming Systems Research methodology. This type of methodology usually involves five stages: a diagnostic stage in which problems are identified, a design stage in which alternative solutions are suggested, a testing stage (on-station and on-farm) for proposed solutions, a dissemination stage in which successful technologies are communicated to other farmers, and an evaluation stage, in which the rate of adoption is assessed (Norman and Baker 1986). In Swaziland, the lack of known technological solutions to horticultural problems has led researchers to emphasize multiple diagnostic and testing stages, with a particularly heavy emphasis on exploratory testing at the research station. The remainder of this paper describes the stages of research used by the summer vegetable program, using cabbages, tomatoes, and onions, potentially successful summer cultivars, as examples.

Table I Production outcomes of summer vegetable crops by 14 Phophonyane irrigation scheme homesteads.

Production outcome	Number of homesteads
No crops attempted	4
Crops destroyed in seedbed	3
Crops planted to field	(7)
Tomatoes	7
Cabbages	6
Beans	3
Onions	1
Spinach (Chard)	1
Crops sold	(6)
Tomatoes	5
Cabbages	4
Beans	1

Source: Watson and Malaza 1984: Table 4.

Diagnostic Stage: Identification of Problems and Solutions

Early impressions concerning the seasonality of vegetable production were confirmed by a series of diagnostic surveys conducted by the Cropping Systems Project. These included informal surveys conducted in three of the Rural Development Areas and the Phophonyane irrigation project. These surveys provided clues as to why farmers were reluctant to grow vegetables in the summer. The surveys revealed that, in addition to an increase in disease and pest problems, summer vegetable production faced the problem of labor shortages due to competition with homestead maize production. Even at the Phophonyane irrigation scheme, there was a low level of vegetable production and sale during the summer. Table I summarizes the summer vegetable production activities of 14 farmers monitored at the scheme. It is apparent that even those farmers who attempted summer crops did not all have sufficient production to sell.

Watson and Malaza (1984) identified five factors which were principally responsible for low summer production of auxiliary crops. The most important of these was the simultaneous production of dryland maize, which limited land, labor, and capital resources available for other enterprises. Other problems included high temperatures and crop pests, torrential rains, shortage of tractors for land preparation, and insufficient extension services.

Based on these and other surveys, the Horticultural Section identified the following constraints to vegetable production in general:

1. Lack of reliable information on market demands and prices;
2. lack of transport to reach markets;
3. inability to store fresh produce at the homestead;
4. a limited variety of fresh produce available at one time to attract buyers;
5. lack of reliable product information (including pest control);
6. water shortage for irrigation in the dry season;
7. lack of suitable varieties for summer production; and
8. shortage of cash to purchase inputs.

(Grenoble and Gama 1988:4–5)

Solutions to a number of these problems lie outside the scope of a Cropping Systems Project. However, where technological responses seemed appropriate, the Horticultural Section was able to test possible solutions.

Testing Stage: On-Station and On-Farm

Given the importance of pests and high temperatures as obstacles to summer production, the section first began screening vegetable varieties suitable for summer cultivation by testing them at the Malkerns Research Station. This program of variety screening involved searching for cabbages with heat tolerance and tomatoes with disease resistance. For cabbages, the number of varieties having heat tolerance which are recommended to SNL farmers has increased from one in 1982 to five in 1988 (Grenoble and Gama 1988). For tomatoes, on-station screening included varieties, lines, and cultivars which were reported to be resistant to bacterial wilt, the most serious limitation to summer tomato production.

Following the on-station variety screening, on-farm tomato trials were conducted in 10 Rural Development Areas. In these trials, a wilt-resistant variety, Rodade, was compared to a farmer's variety, Karino. The resistant variety was acceptable to farmers who had bacterial-infested soils; however, it was considered inferior to the farmers' variety in terms of fruit size and tolerance to early blight. Additional varietal screening is now being done at the Research Station in an attempt to find a resistant variety that also has other characteristics desirable to farmers. In addition, the horticultural section is investigating pre-planting soil treatments and other cultural practices that may help to control disease.

The work with vegetables exemplifies the problems faced by horticulturalists in Swaziland when trying to apply a standard Farming Systems methodology to their research. Within the standard research framework, pre-existing technologies would be surveyed, and the most promising choices tested extensively on farmers' fields. Indeed, the on-farm testing program is a critical component of standard Farming Systems practice, since it familiarizes farmers with the potential for innovation under their own agricultural conditions. However, for Swaziland, most of the technology available for solving horticultural problems (e.g., varietal resistance, chemical control of pests) is untried by researchers and unfamiliar to farmers. Horticulturalists argue that technological payoffs are obtained more efficiently by devoting a greater proportion of time to on-station screening, particularly during the earlier phases of the research. Credibility of the program is also increased by not exposing farmers repeatedly to unsuccessful experimental technology. On-farm work is therefore reserved for verification and demonstration of on-station results.

This modified Farming Systems approach was applied by the Horticultural Section to its research on long-day onions. As Grenoble and Gama (n.d.) have noted, various factors influence bulb formation in onions, the most important being photoperiod or daylength. Onions can be classified as short-day types with a required photoperiod between 12 and 14 hours, and long-day types requiring photoperiods in excess of 14 hours. In Swaziland, short-day varieties are commonly grown in winter, and are harvested from June to September. Consequently, onions must be imported during other times of the year.

The section felt that if a variety of long-day onion could be found that would bulb within the rather narrow tolerance limits of summer day-length in Swaziland, summer production would be possible. This would benefit not only the producer, who could take advantage of favorable prices in summer, but also consumers, who would have greater access to this nitrogen-rich vegetable.

The long-day onion research program began with on-station screening of long-day varieties. With this program, the researchers hoped not only to identify varieties that form bulbs under summer conditions in Swaziland, but also to try out cultural practices which would enhance bulb formation in selected cultivars. The most important goal was to demonstrate to Swazi farmers that summer production of onions was possible.

During the initial research season, the section tested seven long-day onion varieties imported from the United States, plus two short-day varieties as a control, using two seeding dates and two levels of fertilizer. The two highest-yielding varieties (Pronto S and Rocket) produced up to 24 tonnes per hectare of dry-bulb yield, with a low percentage of undesirable growth characteristics. These two varieties, as well as six additional long-day varieties, were tested at the research station during the following two growing seasons. Three of the new varieties tested, although currently grown in South Africa, were judged not to be adapted to Swazi conditions.

Along with the expanded screening trial, the section conducted an on-farm assessment of the six most promising long-day varieties. Trials were conducted at 15 sites, although shortage of moisture or hail damage prevented data collection at seven of these. At the eight remaining sites, three varieties (Pronto S, Garnet, and Rocket) showed at least 85% of the plants producing usable bulbs. Interviews with farmers at the conclusion of the trials showed that all farmers were satisfied with all three of the successful varieties. Although summer onions were a new crop, farmers were generally pleased with the possibilities for summer onion production. On the basis of the four years of varietal evaluations and the on-farm trials, the Horticultural Section decided to recommend all three varieties to SNL farmers for future cultivation.

Dissemination Stage: Publications and On-Farm Demonstrations

As a result of the vegetable testing program, five varieties of cabbage, one variety of bacterial wilt-resistant tomato, and three varieties of long-day onions have been recommended to farmers for summer production. These recommendations are being disseminated through the extension service in two ways. First, extension publications such as field support guides, production guides, and fact sheets are currently being revised to include the results of the trials and production information for long-day onions.

Second, the Horticultural Section is conducting a verification and demonstration "trial" of these onion varieties on farmers fields during the current cropping season. Research assistants for the Cropping Systems Project are cooperating with the National Subject Matter Specialist for horticulture to set up the trials and to explain their results to farmers and extension agents. Although the on-farm demonstrations under the supervision of the research assistants have experienced some difficulties in installation of the plots and propogation of the vegetables, many of the plots under the direction of the Subject Matter Specialist have thrived. Research station and project horticulturalists predict that these trials will provide useful data on varietal performance under an expanded set of agroclimatic conditions.

Conclusions

The success of a development effort such as the summer vegetable program can be judged in several ways. The ability to identify or develop potentially successful technology is certainly one criterion for evaluation. However, as Gilbert, et al. (1984) point out, the ultimate indicator of success for technological innovation is its adoption by farmers. In the past, Farming Systems projects have tended to put relatively more energy and time into the diagnostic and testing stages of their research and less into evaluation and dissemination. As a result, more is usually known about the productive potential of new agricultural technology than about its actual impact on local farming systems.

In the case of the summer vegetable program in Swaziland, success will depend not only on the ability of new cultivars to survive during the rainy season, but also on the willingness of farmers to plant them. Since that decision would involve the reallocation of labor at a time when labor is traditionally scarce, vegetables would have to carry their own incentives. One such incentive would certainly be their cash value, if they could be successfully marketed. Another incentive might be their value as a dietary supplement for the producer's household.

Evaluating the long-term success of such a project should involve not only farmer's opinions of the suitability of individual crops, but also the degree to which production of these crops is increased. This would involve monitoring the market and household availability of vegetable items at different points in the year, and tracing the channels through which they are acquired. Where nutritional issues are involved, as in the case of Swazi vegetables, rural diets should also be monitored for the increased inclusion of target crops. Simplified qualitative food recalls or food frequency interviews at different seasons could provide valuable information on the dietary impact of new agricultural technology.

Linking agricultural research to consumption concerns seems an obvious direction to take for improving agricultural production in Africa. Nutritional and dietary problems can provide both a framework for identifying research problems and criteria for the evaluation of technological innovations. Farming Systems Research, which takes its point of departure from the circumstances and constraints of the farmer, is a logical framework for the inclusion of these concerns. The Horticultural Programme of the Malkerns Research Station and the Swaziland Cropping Systems Project provides an example of research linking production and consumption through its emphasis on summer vegetables. By including critical but unorthodox issues such as seasonality and nutrition, this research increases its potential to improve the quality of life for farmers on Swazi Nation Land.

Acknowledgments

This research was supported by USAID and the Swaziland Cropping Systems Research and Extension Training Project. The authors would like to thank Janis Goodman, David Lewis, Phindile Malaza, and Thokozile Sibiya for their help.

Literature Cited

Cappetta, M. 1983. Population, food, and nutrition: Swaziland 1940–1982. in *The Swaziland Rural Homestead Survey*, ed. by F. DeVletter. Social Science Research Unit, University of Swaziland: Kwaluseni.

Chambers, R., R. Longhurst, and A. Pacey, eds. 1981. *Seasonal Dimensions to Rural Poverty.* Frances Pinter: London.

FAO. 1982. *Integrating Nutrition into Agricultural and Rural Development Projects. A Manual.* FAO: Rome.

———— 1984. *Integrating Nutrition into Agricultural and Rural Development Projects. Six Case Studies.* FAO: Rome.

FAO/WHO/UNU. 1985. Energy and protein requirements. *Report of a Joint FAO/WHO/ UNU Expert Consultation.* Technical Report Series No. 724 WHO: Geneva.

Frankenberger, T. 1985. *Adding a Food Consumption Perspective to Farming Systems Research.* USAID/USDA: Washington, DC.

Gilbert, E. J., D. W. Norman, and F. E. Winch. 1980. *Farming Systems Research: A Critical Appraisal.* MSU Rural Development Papers No. 6. Michigan State University: East Lansing.

Gittinger, J. P., J. Leslie, and C. Hoisington. 1987. *Food Policy. Integrating Supply, Distribution, and Consumption.* Johns Hopkins University Press: Baltimore.

Grenoble. D. W. 1984. Horticultural production and research in Swaziland: An end-of-tour report. Swaziland Cropping Systems Research and Extension Training Project: Malkerns Research Station, MalKerns, Swaziland.

Grenoble, D. W. and D. M. Gama. n.d. Long-day onion production studies. Malkerns Research Station: Malkerns. (Mimeo)

———— 1988. An overview of horticulture in Swaziland. Paper presented to the Workshop on Farming Systems Research, sponsored by the Swaziland Cropping Systems Project and CIMMYT. Nhlangano, Swaziland.

Hunting Technical Services. 1983. Review of the Rural Development Areas Programme. 2 Vols. Ministry of Agriculture and Cooperatives: Mbabane, Swaziland.

Huss-Ashmore, R. 1987. Report of the food consumption survey. Part I: Anthropometrics, food group use, and food consumption by weight. Swaziland Cropping Systems Project and Ministry of Agriculture and Cooperatives: Mbabane, Swaziland.

———— 1988. Report of the food consumption survey. Part II: Nutritional content of women's diets. Swaziland Cropping Systems Project, MalKerns Research Station: MalKerns, Swaziland.

Huss-Ashmore, R. and J. L. Goodman. 1988. Seasonal changes in work, weight, and body composition for women in highland Lesotho. In *Coping with Seasonal Constraints,* ed. by R. Huss-Ashmore, J. J. Curry, and R. K. Hitchcock. *MASCA Research Papers in Science and Archeology,* Vol. 5, pp. 29–44.

Huss-Ashmore, R., J. J. Curry, and R. K. Hitchcock, eds. 1988. *Coping with Seasonal Constraints. MASCA Research Papers in Science and Archeology,* Vol. 5. MASCA, University of Pennsylvania: Philadelphia.

Kuper, H. 1980. *An African Aristocracy.* New York: Africana Publishing Co.

Longhurst, R., ed. 1986. *Seasonality and Poverty. IDS Bulletin* 17(3).

Low, A. R. C. 1986. On-farm research and household economics. In *Understanding Africa's Rural Households and Farming Systems.* ed. by J. L. Moock. Westview Press: Boulder. pp. 71–91.

Mokbel, M. and P. L. Pellett. 1987. Nutrition in agricultural development in Aleppo Province, Syria. 1. Farm Resources, Rainfall and Nutritional Status. *Ecology of Food and Nutrition 20:1–14.*

National Nutrition Council. 1986. Key Results of the Swaziland National Nutrition Status Survey. Government of Swaziland: Mbabane.

Norman, D. W. and D. C. Baker. 1986. Components of Farming Systems Research, FSR credibility, and experiences in Botswana. In *Understanding Africa's Rural Households and Farming Systems,* ed by J. L. Moock. Westview Press: Boulder. pp. 36–57.

Sterkenberg, J. J., A. J. Diphoorn, and K. P. Spaarman. 1978. The production and marketing of vegetables in Swaziland. Unpublished manuscript.

USAID. 1983. Editorial Experts for USAID. *Food Consumption and Nutrition Effects of International Development Projects and Programs: An Annotated Bibliography.* USAID Bureau for Science and Technology, Office of Nutrition: Washington, DC.

Watson, V. and P. Z. Malaza. 1984. Phophonyane irrigation scheme. A case study of emergent cash cropping on Swazi Nation Land. The Swaziland Cropping Systems Project: Malkerns, Swaziland.

The Lesson of Rwanda's Agricultural Crisis: Increase Productivity, Not Food Aid

Edward Robins

Anthropology Department
University of Wisconsin
River Falls, WI 54022

Introduction

Nineteen-eighty-four was an interesting year for Rwandan agriculture. The long rains, ordinarily tapering off at the end of May, stopped abruptly in mid-April. The early termination of the rainy season caused a serious production shortfall in beans, Rwanda's most important food crop, prompting the Government of Rwanda (GOR) to request 69,000 metric tons (MT) of emergency food aid from international donors. It was not until the end of 1986 that the last of the 40,000 MT which the donors agreed to provide were delivered. While most of the imported food arrived well after the "crisis" had passed, and may have had a slight depressing effect upon domestic food markets, the crisis itself was noteworthy mostly for the attention it drew to the state of agricultural, and more broadly, economic development in Rwanda: its chronic weaknesses, the failure of development programs to have much impact on economic growth, the Government's agricultural strategy of *auto-suffisance alimentaire* (food self-sufficiency), and the tactics employed by households to meet their food and cash needs under ordinary and extreme circumstances.

While relief efforts in the Horn of Africa captured the world's attention at the time, Rwanda looked inward at the precariousness of its own food production system and posed a fundamental question: How can domestic agricultural production be increased? Increased production is often viewed strictly as a supply-side issue and presupposes that it is a lack of modern technology which handicaps the producer.

A closer look at the Rwandan situation, however, reveals that effective demand for food is low; most Rwandans—more than 90% of the households—are also producers of food. Raising demand is thus problematic and a principal reason why farmer interest in increasing production is also low. The problem in Rwanda is one of too many producers producing too many of the same products, too little profit being realized as a result, and low overall productivity. Inadequate technology is one component of the production problem; the farmer's apparent disinclination to produce more is another. The question of how to increase production is then really three questions: how to increase the number of individuals involved in and reliant on food markets; how to increase their capability to purchase food in those markets; and, how to increase the capability of producers to meet increased demand. The first two questions are about increasing the number of new, productive employment opportunities and income; the third question is about agricultural technology and infrastructure.

The 1984 crisis called to the forefront the approach to agricultural development taken by the GOR: self-sufficiency in domestic food crop production and minimal food imports. Yet 1984 witnessed a Government request to donors for emergency food aid in a situation whose crisis proportions were never fully defined. While the total amount of aid requested was relatively small, the food emergency demonstrated that a more careful look at food imports, domestic food production, and overall food security was called for. The decision to import food was questionable from the start, and more so 6–12 months later when the food that did arrive, and well past when it was needed, began to compete with locally produced foodstuffs in domestic markets. More significantly, the measures required to receive and distribute the emergency food diluted scarce Rwandan human and material resources and directed attention away from real problems in production and marketing. This was most dramatically illustrated by the effort the GOR's Agricultural Survey and Policy Analysis Unit (SESA) was asked to undertake in designing and implementing an Early Warning System (EWS) to forecast future shortfalls. By 1987 the EWS still was not debugged and still of questionable utility in Rwanda.

That emergency food aid can be an appropriate, temporary response to an outbreak of actual or impending food scarcity is not in doubt. However, food aid can disguise more pervasive and serious problems in agriculture such as technology inappropriate for the needs of a growing population, weak infrastructure, and policy poorly suited for agricultural growth. More insidiously, food aid can promote a dependency mentality in recipient nations in which needed reforms are not taken, investment in agriculture is assigned a low priority, the incentive structure for agriculture is not strengthened, and self-reliance is discouraged. The resources it requires in donor and host country monies, transport, and administration, time and energy—in the Rwanda case at least—could otherwise be better spent on creating new or modified agricultural and economic structures than on repairing cracks in existing structures. Emergency food aid is the wrong response to insufficient and low agricultural productivity.

This paper argues that to overcome chronic weaknesses in rural food production and enterprise systems, Rwanda will need solutions which provide technologies for increasing yields and productivity while sustaining resource bases. In addition, it will need stable food markets to encourage some producers to allocate more labor to off-farm and revenue-generating activities while reducing the risks of merchants and lowering their costs; sufficient demand to encourage yet other producers to increase production; enterprise growth and increased employment opportunities for income generation; greater reliance upon private sector entities, especially indigenous non-governmental organizations (NGOs), for defining and implementing economic and social development programs and relieving Government of this drain on its human and material resources; and overall, greater diversification and specialization of households to promote interdependence among producers and reduce their economic autonomy.

The principal goal of Rwanda's agricultural system as currently defined by the GOR is self-sufficiency in food production. It is appropriate to the extent that is focuses resources on increasing domestic food production. However, it must be part of a more sweeping reform program for increasing productivity, increasing the size of the population dependent upon food markets, and increasing domestic and regional trade. It is argued that the formidible task of economic development in Rwanda will not be advanced by autarky, not be advanced by replicating the autonomous farm model throughout the country, and not be advanced by focusing resources and energies on food aid.

Section I below summarizes key features of Rwandan agriculture and leads to a description in part II of the 1984 drought and its consequences. There follows a discussion of measures needed in sub-Saharan Africa for economic and agricultural growth through the development of sustainable technologies and increased income-earning opportunities. Section IV concludes with another look at Rwanda and a strategy which it can adopt to increase food and economic security for households and the nation at large.

Rwandan Agriculture

Rwandan agriculture is at an abyss. Yields are stagnating, eroded and over-exploited hillside soils threaten the future of production, and additional land to put under cultivation is minimal. With population density on arable land estimated at 390/km^2 and the population growing at an annual rate of 3.7%, it is more than the agricultural future of the nation which is at stake. Yet Rwanda's record of agricultural production and economic growth since Independence has been impressive. The GDP has grown annually by almost 6%, nearly double the average for sub-Saharan Africa, and average annual increases in food production have exceeded the rate of population growth. The problem in Rwanda's future is that the methods which have been employed in the past will not suffice for the coming years. Fundamental economic adjustments and development investments are needed to support the growth curve (Robins, et. al. 1987).

Agriculture in Rwanda is practiced by more than one million households, over 90% of the total population of 6.5 million, on holdings averaging less than 1.2 hectares of land. While the distribution of parcels is unequal—57% of the households farm land averaging just over .5 hectares in size, while, on the other end, 16% of the households own 43% of the land on farms averaging 3.26 hectares— the unevenness of the distribution is low by comparison to many countries in Latin America and Asia. Larger parcels are positively associated with increased sales of food but do not appear to be clearly linked to increased per capita caloric consumption and better nutritional status (Loveridge, et. al. 1988). Since 1978, density on arable land has increased by 28% while average farm size has decreased by 30% (Delepierre 1985).

**Table I. Total production of eight major food crops, 1985
(in metric tons)**

Crop	2nd Season 1985 (Feb.–May 1985)	1st Season 1986 (Sept.–Dec. 1985)	Total
Bananas	1,089,309	973,491	2,062,800
Sweet potatoes	424,392	402,152	826,544
Manioc	186,453	169,529	355,982
Beans	98,340	200,119	298,459
Potatoes	113,326	137,231	250,557
Sorghum	156,447	19,578	176,025
Maize	13,349	123,416	136,765
Peas	7,531	13,136	20,667

(source: SESA 1986)

The Rwandan household cultivates an average of 14 fields divided into five blocks distributed across one or more hillsides. This dispersal pattern is a key feature of the farmer's strategy to minimize the risk to the household's agricultural livelihood. With much microvariation in soils, gradient, and even weather—localized hailstorms can destroy a crop in minutes—the Rwandan producer trades off the additional labor required in farming parcels a kilometer or more from the house for the additional security of having spread his/her risk.

Eight food crops dominate the Rwandan agricultural system (Table I): bananas, sweet potatoes, manioc, beans, potatoes, sorghum, maize, and peas. Production has shifted to tubers and away from grains, especially sorghum, as population has grown and the need has increased for greater per hectare yields. While average annual food production increases since Independence in 1962, roughly 4.3%, have been greater than the rate of population growth, this has not come about through increases in yields but rather through double and triple cropping, putting marginal land into production, year-round cultivation of wet bottom lands (*marais*), and shifting production from grains to tubers at an average annual rate of 5.9% between 1974 and 1983 (Delepierre 1985).

Beans, Rwanda's most important source of protein and 2nd greatest source of calories, are not produced in quantities sufficient to meet domestic demand. In the first six months of 1986, 15,000 to 20,000 MT of beans were unofficially imported from neighboring countries (SESA 1987). The precariousness of Rwanda's production system is further indicated by its reliance on pulses and cereals: more than 30% of the diet comes from 2% of production. Some 40% of the population has sub-standard diets, calculated either on the basis of total calories consumed (ENBC 1986; Loveridge et. al. 1988) or the proportion of low weight and malnourished children seen at nutrition centers (UNICEF 1985). By the year 2010 Rwanda could have more than 15 million people, or more than 1100 persons per square kilometer of arable land. With yields stagnating and nearly all available land under production, it is staggering to contemplate Rwanda's future in the absence of fundamental investments in agricultural technology, infrastructure, and enterprise development.

Rwanda's agricultural exports are dominated by two crops: coffee and tea. Together they account for 85% of Rwanda's foreign exchange earnings. Coffee is grown by 50% of all households on parcels of about 0.1 hectare. While the farmgate price for coffee has been held relatively constant since 1980 at 125 FRw/kg, or about 70 cents per pound, despite international market fluctuations, in real terms prices have fallen by over 25% during the period. Tea, by contrast, has not suffered as great a real price decline. Tea is grown mostly on industrial estates or in village tea schemes on the acid soils of Rwanda's highlands. Tea and coffee together account for some 12% of the total income of Rwandan households.

Differences in production by region are notable. There is considerable agroecological variation throughout the country, from the savanna-like east, where rainfall averages 700-1000 mm/year, to the central plateau, where rainfall increases to 1200 mm/year, to the Zaire-Nile divide, where 2000 mm or more may fall each year. Population density follows the pattern for rainfall, being lowest in the east at 107/km^2 and over 470/km^2 in the northwest. The production pattern corresponds to regional differences in rainfall and altitude, although some crops are grown virtually throughout the country. These latter include the banana, the Rwanda's most important crop, in a variety for cooking, another used for the production of beer, and a third, sweet table-type. The banana occupies fully one-third of all agricultural land. Other widely grown crops include beans, maize, sorghum, sweet potato, and manioc. Peas, peanuts, soy, wheat, potatoes, and coffee show clear regional variation. Generally, the eastern and south central regions produce more than one-half the nation's bananas (55%), peanuts (87%), sorghum (66%), manioc (56%), and beans

(50%). The mountain highlands, by contrast, produce most of the peas (58%), maize (70%), wheat (99%), and potatoes (85%). Nearly one-fifth of all coffee is produced in the southwestern corner of the country; the central and eastern plateaus account for much of the rest (Robins, et. al. 1986).

Rwandan households produce mostly for home consumption, although 25% of all food is purchased. Cash income is earned through the sale of coffee, tea, food crops and livestock; home brewed banana beer; and remuneration for labor in roughly equal proportions. Average annual household income is about $550/year. The low purchasing power of most rural households is reflected in the proportion— 59%—of total private consumption attributable to the rural population. The urban population, 5% of the total in Rwanda, accounts for more than 40% of all private consumption expenditures (ENBC 1986).

Low overall household income belies the relatively high involvement of Rwandan households in the market. Rural households spend 21% of total cash income on food and beverages, 22% on non-food items, 26% on goods needed for production, and 22% on financial transactions. Yet overall income and demand remain low. Where income is greater, a relatively lower proportion is devoted to food purchases while the demand for clothing, education, and household utensils increases. Currently little investment is made in agriculture. Only 14% of the gross value of agricultural sales is represented by expenditures for agricultural production (ENBC 1986).

Rwandan agriculture, in sum, is focused on food crops, with notable regional variation in production, and two export crops. Agricultural performance has been excellent since Independence, largely the result of more extensive agronomic practices, but not likely to continue to perform as well in the future without fundamental investments in new technology and infrastructure. Most households depend upon food markets to supplement their own production, using cash obtained from the sale of banana beer, crops, and labor. Overall household income, however, is undiversified and low. In the future, food markets will be even more important as the population grows to include more consumers and relatively fewer producers. Currently, there is limited incentive for producers to increase production for market on a sustained basis; producers thus invest little of their cash income in agriculture.

The Agricultural Crisis of 1984

A production shortfall for the drought-shortened season of 1984 (February-May) is indicated when compared to the same season of 1985 (considered to be average). Table II reveals that for 1984, key crops experiencing shortfalls were:

1) peas, 61% of normal;
2) beans, 65% of normal;
3) manioc, 81% of normal
4) sweet potatoes, 82% of normal; and
5) sorghum, 91% of normal.

Overall, tonnage for the eight basic food crops was 1,923,923 MT for the second season of 1984 and 2,089,147 MT for the same season in 1985, or a shortfall of 165,224 MT (SESA 1986). Per capita caloric production for 1984, at 825,000/year or 2260/day, was the lowest in more than 10 years (Loveridge, et. al. 1988).

Donors pledged to help make up the shortfall in the absence of knowing its magnitude at the time. Of the 40,000 MT pledged, 2,541 MT or 6.4% of the total arrived before the end of 1984. Another 25,218 MT or 63.8% arrived throughout 1985. Some, but not all, of the remainder arrived in 1986, two years after the period of food scarcity (Neel 1986). Of this total, 25,100 MT of emergency food aid was distributed to needy families identified by local (communal) councils in the areas hardest hit by the drought—91 of 143 communes. If each

Table II. Food crop production,
1984 short season vs. 1985 normal season (MT)

Crop	1984	1985
Peas	1,158	7,531
Beans	64,376	98,340
Manioc	151,594	186,453
Sweet potatoes	348,033	424,392
Sorghum	142,802	156,447
Bananas	1,075,924	1,089,309
Maize	15,175	13,349
Potatoes	121,400	113,326
TOTAL	1,923,923	2,089,147

(source: SESA 1986)

family in those communes shared equally in the food rations, they would have received approximately 40 kgs/household, or less than 8 kgs/person of supplementary food over a 2 year period. The remainder of the food arrived as commercial food imports. Nearly all the wheat (92% in 1983) and more than one-half the rice marketed in Rwanda is imported. TRAFIPRO, a cooperative, in collaboration with the grain storage and marketing parastatal, OPROVIA, markets imported grains. They have encountered difficulty in selling them at a price higher than the market price for domestic grains. A lower price, however, creates problems for commercializing local production. The President of Rwanda has been firm in insisting that imported foodstuffs be sold at a price "clearly higher than domestic products" in order to stimulate, not discourage, domestic production (Habyarimana 1986). Nonetheless, food imports, distributed either free to needy families, as salaries for local development projects, or arriving unofficially from Zaire and Uganda, find their way into local markets, depressing prices for locally produced foodstuffs. The impact this is having upon income-earning opportunities for rural households is considerable, as discussed below.

While the magnitude of the shortfall and its impact upon households was not truly of crisis proportions, the emergency aid temporarily distracted officials and donors from the reforms needed in agricultural policy, research, private sector initiatives, and the policy formulation process. In each instance the prevailing trend was hostile to agricultural growth and economic development. Agricultural policy included floor prices for crops marketed in Rwanda but grown elsewhere; research, already weakened by a shortage of trained scientists, was not focused on priority crops and regions; the growth of small enterprises was constrained by tax and tariff regulations and credit schemes; and agricultural policy was formulated on some basis other than the results of scientific data collection and analysis. The rural cultivator, who recognized the need for reform, did not share the Government's perception of the "crisis." Several field trips undertaken by the author between May and August 1984 revealed that households were anticipating a return to normal the following season, employing tactics to bring in the next harvest a few weeks early (by planting beans in the *marais* during the dry season rather than on hillsides after the first rains of September), and increasing their consumption of manioc, the leaves of both manioc and sweet potato, and beer bananas. Notably absent from the statements of farmers was the perception of crisis in agriculture resulting from the seasonal shortage of rain.

The allocation by the GOR and the donor community together of scarce resources and energies to the 1984 crisis should not be lightly dismissed. The U.S. Government alone furnished an additional $1 million for transport costs. The squandering of Rwandan resources was unaffordable. The Ministry of Agriculture's Policy and Survey Unit (SESA) was asked by the Government in October of 1984 to devise and implement an early warning system (EWS) to forecast future production shortfalls. The soundness of this decision was questionable at the time given that periodic shortfalls rarely endure more than a single season and, as the record demonstrates, imported emergency food does not arrive when it is most needed. SESA has spent more than three years trying to de-bug the EWS, noteworthy otherwise mostly for its attempt to use farmer opinions during the growing season to assess the character of the particular agricultural season and anticipated crop yield. SESA has, in a relatively short time, established one of the best agricultural data bases in Africa, and performs timely data collection and analysis with important policy implications. It is a SESA study which revealed that most Rwandan households are net purchasers of beans and that floor prices benefit mostly foreign producers and a few large Rwandan ones (SESA 1987). This finding has prompted the GOR to reassess its price policy for beans. SESA's impact as a policy and survey unit is watered-down, however, when it is asked to devote its limited resources to early warning projections.

Africa, Food, and Economic Development

According to World Bank estimates, more than 40% of the almost 500 million people of sub-Saharan Africa have sub-standard diets. This figure corresponds roughly to the proportion of *households* in Rwanda in which caloric intake is under 2100 per person per day (ENBC 1986), the estimated cut-off for adequate nutrition. African agriculture, and to a lesser degree, high rates of population growth, have been held accountable for the declining state of well-being on the continent since Independence. Because new agricultural and family planning technologies have the potential to boost welfare levels in these highly visible domains, the bulk of attention and donor dollars have been funneled into projects and programs designed to increase the supply of appropriate technologies. In Rwanda, a proliferation of donor-funded agricultural projects (there were more than 100 of them in 1986) was nonetheless failing to have much of an impact upon the agricultural sector. In December, 1986, the Ministry of Agriculture convened to perform a "self-assessment" for rectifying the wastefulness of past programs.

The demand side of the agricultural production equation, which expresses household interest in technology adoption, is less visible for its locus in out-country settings among relatively voiceless populations. Yet it is the true indicator of rural readiness for productivity increases. For these producers, it is not only the availability of new technology but an improved incentive climate which is needed to promote technology adoption, increase productivity, and improve the ratio of people to resources. Local empowerment to articulate the areas in which reforms must be taken is currently promoted at the grassroots level by indigenous NGOs. Increased know-how and improved technologies are part of this process, but these latter alone cannot bring about the changes needed to increase overall productivity and rural welfare. While policy reform, natural resource management, and support to the private sector are on today's development agendas, still it is technology development which captures most of the interests of planners and the dollars of donors. A new development agenda is called for which will increase the demands of producers for new ideas and technologies at the same time that those technologies are being developed and touted. Food aid may be fit into this agenda as an interim supply measure, until nutritional levels are improved, but does not address the basic demand problem and may even exacerbate it.

For sub-Saharan Africa as a whole, between 1960 and 1980, per capita food production fell by 1% annually; three-fourths of the growth in output during the period was the result of an expansion in area cultivated (Staatz 1988). The reasons for the failures of African agriculture are summarized by Hyden (1986). In what he calls, "features peculiar to Africa's political economy," Hyden cites the absence of intermediate technology (such as the wheel and plow), the lack of institutional mechanisms for the exploitation of land, and systems and modes of production which are precapitalistic in nature and yield low levels of productivity per unit of land. Specialization of production is minimal; agriculture, in most instances, is extensive; and productivity gains, when they occur, are translated into a reallocation of household labor to off-farm activities. The African farmer is largely independent of other groups and institutions in society. Being essentially an autonomous unit of production, the household—only to a limited degree—exchanges goods. Structural interdependence is relatively low. Because production is so extensively controlled by the peasant, argues Hyden, African governments are less well placed (when compared to Asian or Latin American) to influence agricultural development. Improving the organizational instruments of government, such as extension, is ineffective because the African farmer is not structurally well-integrated into the wider economic system. There is an opportunity here, we would add, which NGOs are currently exploiting, for non-State entities to gain the confidence of farmers.

Africa's independent rural producer, though not tied to Government, is integrated into personal support networks in which economic, social, and political functions are intertwined. Household decisions are based on how to best use resources for economic, social, and political ends, and not strictly to maximize profit or productivity. Of particular importance is the strategy to spread risk, which pre-adapts the rural producer to opportunities for maximizing gains and reduces the impact of development efforts narrowly tied to improving producer efficiency. The African will invest in patronage as well as productivity; efficiency of production may be traded-off for socio-political support. (This tendency may change in the future, however, as a true business class and greater economic interdependence evolve.)

Hyden's African portrait presents an interesting dilemma for applied social science. How much of the African's "nature" should be changed and how much exploited by new models for development? The practice of maximizing opportunity for gain, for example, will be a key component in a strategy calling for increased diversification, increased specialization, and increased interdependence. On the other hand, the African's alleged disdain for efficiency poses a serious threat to growth processes dependent upon greater productivity. Should the former predisposition be retained and the latter "deleted" from the African's character? It is instructive to recognize in this instance that the lack of efficiency which Africans exhibit is largely a function of their structural autonomy. Greater specialization and interdependence will result in greater efficiency of production.

Greater diversity of production also can help to mollify the current dependence of African nations upon narrow export markets, a circumstance generated by the illusion of African comparative advantage in marketable tropical crop production. Lofchie and Commins (1982) argue that when key exports—coffee, tea, peanuts, cocoa, cotton, and palm oil—are sold for foreign exchange, the revenues they generate are variable because international markets for these commodities are so elastic. African governments thus are forced to budget expenditures in the absence of knowing how much foreign exchange they will have from year to year. Their problem is compounded by the nature of the commodities they import: rice, wheat, and corn—all staples. By purchasing them in relatively small quantities in what are essentially "spot" markets, scarce foreign reserves are siphoned from debt financing and purchases of petroleum and other primary goods. Rather than adhering strictly to this mistaken notion of comparative advantage in crops for which substitutes are readily available, changed relationships among producers, consumers, and investors are what these authors argue for, so that multi-sectoral development takes place.

Key domains, exclusive of export agriculture to developed nations, include domestic food crop production, regional trade, and growth in small scale manufacturing and service industries. Increasing food crop production entails, inter alia, better management of the natural resource base. Soils in much of Africa are endangered by erosion and leaching. Traditional fallows are no longer practiced as population densities increase. Fragile soils will weaken further in the future if soil-enhancing technologies are not applied. Failure to address the deterioration of natural resources threatens African agriculture fundamentally. With no more than 20% of the arable land on the continent currently under production, it is not too late to institute improved land use management practices. While increased crop production will not occur without improved seeds and incentives as well, a failure to improve soils and better manage lands will renew interest in applications of imported fertilizers. African nations can ill afford to use limited cash reserves for fertilizer purchases as an alternative to better resource management.

Growth in small scale manufacturing and service enterprises for employment and income generation is equally needed in Africa. Most households are unable to meet their needs through food crop production alone. While some producers can continue to focus on export crops if reliable food markets are operating, others need to supplement on-farm production with non-farm employment. Small manufacturing enterprise development may require policy reform, as argued by Mead (1988) in the case of Rwanda. Overall, much central decision-making and investment must be shifted to local and private entities in order to both create new employment opportunities and reduce government budget deficits.

Staatz (1988) offers a reminder that the restructuring of African economies must be accompanied by measures for slowing domestic inflation. A reduced role for Government in buying and selling agricultural outputs and inputs can help to accomplish this by transferring these activities to private entities. At-risk households, as net buyers of food, are particularly vulnerable to inflation, need income, and benefit from new employment opportunities. Other producers will require improved access to land, labor, credit, fertilizer, seeds, and transport in order to respond to new market opportunities. The role for Government is to develop those domains where private interests are minimal, i.e., infrastructure and research.

For high-risk households, food aid can be helpful as a measure to alleviate the short-term burdens of economic restructuring by depressing food market prices. Yet the tradeoffs involved make the food aid option a questionable one at best. Supplemental food for food-insecure households can free government resources for other social services, encourage price stabilization, and, in Food For Work programs, promote infrastructure development. On the other hand, imported foods which drive market prices lower are detrimental to net sellers and their employees. Stable food prices can reduce incentives to traders for buying and storing grain and weaken this key component in the evolution of the agricultural economy. Overall, food aid can discourage self-reliance, postpone agricultural reform, increase dependency upon donors, and permit investment in agriculture to dwindle. By competing directly with local production, food assistance undermines the domestic food price structure and acts as a disincentive to local agriculture. Host country abuses of food aid have a more insidious impact. Food used to support patronage, withheld from the needy for political gain, distributed only when bribes are paid, and transported at inflated prices are a tool used against the interests of at-risk households. Lofchie and Commins (1982) argue that food relief programs generally widen the gap between the rich and poor. It is also an argument *against* sound natural resource management, they conclude, and a "dead-end" approach (1982: 22).

If food aid is more likely to induce crisis in agriculture than forestall it, then reducing the *need* for this type of assistance, reducing the insecurity of households, must be a fundamental objective of agricultural and economic development strategies. Although this can be accomplished in part by increasing agricultural output through the introduction of high yielding technologies, in fact the cash needs of families are such that in the absence of reliable food markets and sufficient demand for food, increased agricultural production alone will not provide families with the revenue for such household necessities as building materials, school uniforms and fees, and health care. Realistically, it is not even likely that families on small parcels cultivating weak soils will be capable of meeting all of their own food needs. In a more diversified economy, households could also grow wood for sale, make brick, process food for resale, or enter the service sector. Crawford (1988) notes that focusing only on food production is not the best way to increase food security at the household level since most households depend also upon cash crops and nonfarm employment for income. Mead's (1988) argument for diversification includes the observation that rural manufacturing enterprises which are pure family undertakings have the least favorable prospects for productivity, sustainability, and growth. He underscores the need for greater specialization and socio-economic interdependence. A program of food security thus is constructed on overall economic development, where Africa's mass of rural and urban poor are integrated through their participation in production, food, and labor markets.

The increased participation of private entities in implementing and managing the new economy can relieve overburdened and inefficient African bureaucracies and help reduce Government budget deficits. This transfer of responsibility presumes greater investments in Africa's human resources. The dearth of African researchers at Independence is well known. A more vital private sector requires a literate populace, competent vocational training programs, and an infusion of information on events and technologies across borders regionally and beyond. While Rwanda devotes nearly one-fourth of its budget to education, and similar attempts elsewhere have reduced illiteracy throughout the continent, human resource weaknesses limit the beneficiary spread of development. Donors have helped with long term training overseas and technical assistance and materials for public schools, and private, often church-operated, school programs have played key roles. In the future there will need to be a greater reliance upon accredited private schools. An educated populace generates its own momentum for development; educated farmers more readily try out new technologies, for example.

Much of the potential for the private management of development lies with indigenous African non-governmental organizations (NGOs). Fundamentally grass-roots in orientation, NGOs do not confuse the rural population as government extension programs have done with hidden agendas and conflicting interests. Local NGOs are more in touch with local needs, are staffed by private citizens, work for the objectives set by the people themselves, and help individuals and communities to develop both by defining, designing, and implementing development assistance programs, and by educating the uninformed rural dweller of what is possible and how it can be accomplished. In order to profit most from the services NGOs offer, the rural citizenry must be literate and have confidence in their own abilities to track plans, activities, and financial accounts. Otherwise they are prone to suspect the intentions of individuals whose methods they do not comprehend. Government suspicion of these organizations, based on their independence of the State, as noted by Derman (1988), may not diminish for some time, but ultimately a greater need for the private sector to share the costs and burdens of development will generate greater true democracy in these nations and help to improve the standard of living for the majority of people on the continent.

Agriculture, Income, and Food Security in Rwanda

La production vivriere nationale est serieusement menacee par la concurrence de vivres exterieurs introduits dans le pays par les organismes d'aide alimentaire.

Domestic food crop production is seriously threatened by competing imported foodstuffs brought into the country under food aid programs. (Dialogue 1986: 67)

The goal of food self-sufficiency in Rwanda has received considerable attention within the country over the past five years. While there is no general agreement on whether it can be achieved, how so, or, in fact, if it is appropriate, the debate nonetheless highlights Rwanda's interest in increasing food crop production and providing sufficient basic foods for its exploding population. Commercial food imports and food aid are viewed by many in Rwanda as hostile to this objective, depriving Rwandans of production and income-earning opportunities and, worse yet, acting as disincentives to local initiatives. The President of the Republic has voiced his opposition to the importation of foods which can be otherwise produced in Rwanda, while interviews with receipients in food-for-work programs reveal their distaste for food in lieu of cash.

The agricultural crisis of 1984 prompted a closer look at food imports and domestic food production as donors and Government attempted to back up "conventional wisdom"—that Rwanda was self-sufficient in bean production, for example—with hard data. Neel (1986) has demonstrated that food imports are depriving Rwandans of income-earning opportunities, especially if food processing and distribution can be improved to lower per unit production costs and make domestic production more competitive with imports. The case of rice is instructive. In 1986, more than 3,500 MT of rice were imported (2,880 MT as food aid distributed to projects), while as much as 2,000 MT of Rwandan rice were stocked in-country. Locally produced rice sold for 80 FRw/kg. Imported rice, by comparison, was selling for 67 FRw/kg—taxes and transport included. Of the 80 FRw/kg market price, local Rwandan producers were receiving 25 FRw/kg. Competitively priced rice, according to Neel, would provide an important source of income for over 17,000 families, each cultivating a 5 *are* (50 m x 50 m) parcel yielding 4,000 kg/ha/year. Similarly, based on substitutions for imported wheat, milk, and malt, Neel concludes that additional revenues could be provided for 72,640 families cultivating 10 *ares* of wheat yielding 1,500 kg/ha; 10,698 families selling 1,800 liters of milk annually; and 54,000 families raising malt on 10 *ares* with yields of 1,500 kg/ha/year. In total, this represents additional sources of income for 165,000 families, or 16% of the households in Rwanda. Producing vegetable oil domestically and increased production of tobacco constitute other income-earning opportunities for Rwandan families.

Neel's demonstration is not an argument for ceasing all food imports, but for considering domestic production, commercial food imports, and food aid in the global context of agricultural and overall economic development. Economies of scale militate against Rwanda competing with Thailand in rice production, for example; yet

Rwandan smallholders with access to parcels in the wet valley bottoms (the *marais*) may find rice an interesting seasonal alternative in an improved *marais* cropping pattern. Having this and other options, the Rwandan smallholder would introduce new possibilities into farm management decision-making, setting in motion an evolution of the agricultural economy toward greater diversity, specialization, and interdependence.

Diversification of production is critical. Households are already purchasing food and obtaining cash income. Net purchasers of food have the most diversified sources of income of all rural households (Loveridge, et. al. 1988). Yet when this income is derived exclusively from sales of agricultural products, these households have the lowest value of consumption per capita. The proportion of tubers to pulses and grains they grow on-farm is also greater than is the case for other households. The Rwandan household which must purchase food, and this includes most of them, is most secure when it derives income from a variety of sources, but is at risk nutritionally when selling only the crops it produces to satisfy cash needs.

Regional specialization of crop production is already occuring in Rwanda, as previously noted, although most families are still interested in producing staples for household consumption. Most families too rely upon food markets for nearly one-fourth of their food needs. Nineteen-eighty-four was a demonstration of the importance of food markets to rural households. Over 70% of the households in Rwanda made-up shortfalls with food purchases (Loveridge, et. al. 1988). In the case of beans, the most important crop affected by the drought, unofficial imports from Zaire and Uganda brought beans to Rwandan markets. A key role was played by private traders. An active merchant class is a stimulus to rural economic development: it can help to integrate markets and keep prices at affordable levels. To do this successfully merchants need to keep transport costs low and be assured of agricultural surpluses. They do *not* benefit from food aid or food subsidies, which can make the transport and storage of food unprofitable. Improved rural roads are important for getting crops from farms to pick-up stations; improved technologies are key for increasing yields. The incentives to farmers to participate in this system should come more from an increase in the availability of consumer goods than from floor pricing; the latter not only discourages private traders but in Rwanda has been demonstrated to reward essentially foreign and a few large domestic producers (SESA 1987).

Private traders who have agricultural surpluses to distribute can help to promote reliable rural food markets, where affordable prices are the norm and in which rural households can have confidence. Under such circumstances, the "risk-spreading" strategy of African producers can be profitably employed to search for non-food production employment opportunities. These will provide the income for making food purchases, create incentives for food producers, and support private trader activity. As rural, non-farm enterprises grow and expand, the increased availability of consumer goods in the market will serve as an additional incentive to producers of all kinds, and the economy will grow.

For this to happen in Rwanda there needs to be productive applied agricultural research for improved seeds, improved cropping patterns, sustainable resource management, and improved and accessible infrastructure. In addition, economic policy reforms are needed to eliminate floor prices for food crops, permit regional food crop exports (especially for the potato), and promote small enterprise development. Each of these elements is key in the evolution of the rural economy.

1. *Agricultural Research.* Technologies applicable to Rwanda's numerous agro-ecological zones are needed for increasing yields and sustaining the resource base. While experiments are ongoing for improved seeds which are moisture tolerant for the highlands, and drought tolerant in the eastern savannas, everywhere there is a need for technologies for improving soil fertility and quality. Low-cost technologies such as agroforestry and the application of green manures are the most promising at this time. More than 100 "failed" attempts have prompted Rwanda's Agricultural Research Institute (ISAR) to focus more specifically on farmer perceptions of production constraints and the development of a critical mass of agronomic scientists in a few key crop areas.

2. *Infrastructure.* In Ruhengeri Prefecture farmers have left potatoes in fields because they cannot get them to market. An improved system of rural roads is essential in a country in which there are no village aggregates of people. The dispersed homestead settlement

pattern which prevails in Rwanda requires improvement of the rudimentary system of tracks which penetrate the hillsides. Credit, too, is needed by farm households as new opportunities arise; the cooperative *Banques Populaires* are the best candidates to provide this.

3. *Training.* As discussed earlier, training is needed to upgrade skills and improve management, especially of rural cooperatives and other NGOs. In the area of enterprise development, more know-how is required for product application/adaptation in the Rwandan context.

4. *Private Sector.* Traders, small entrepreneurs, and local NGOs are the key actors in privatising rural economic development. NGOs in particular, for their grass roots composition and orientation, must assume more of the role in organizing, instructing, and representing the interests of rural dwellers. Rwanda already has a good base upon which to build. While cooperative efforts are well known to farmers, there being thousands of informal cooperatives (*groupements*) throughout the country, organizations such as IWACU have an excellent track record in reaching cooperatives with training for improved management and financial accountability. Numerous small NGOs such as ARDI (*Association Rwandaise pour le Developpement Integre*) are being aided by the Canadian Government under a program of support for *micro-realisation,* or small-scale local development. The many church-affiliated NGOs have a long and successful record in promoting improved health and education. Recently one of these, ADRA (the development arm of the Adventist Church), began a program of "Rodale" or regenerative gardening based on improved composting, terracing, and mulching for the production of nutritious vegetables for home consumption and the improvement of soils. More active NGOs are fundamental to economic growth in Rwanda. Their *raison d'etre* are well summarized by Musengimana (1986) in his discussion of Duhamic-Adri.

5. *Business Climate.* Reforms are needed, as summarized by Mead (1988), to encourage small and medium enterprise development. These pertain to taxes, which currently are biased against small firms in a way that penalizes them when they try to grow and expand, credit, which is not accessible to small entrepreneurs and, tied to credit, bankable proposals (which requires technical assistance and training). Rwanda also needs a "size-neutral" policy for do-

mestic industries to enable small as well as large-scale producers to profit from protection from foreign competition, and better dissemination of information on available technologies, equipment, and products to expand the conceptual universe of Rwandan entrepreneurs. It will be especially important to promote research on products and markets which will help to demonstrate how to link high and low potential markets to diffuse employment, how to make seasonal enterprises more profitable year 'round, and how to promote construction, commerce, and services, as well as manufacturing, as enterprise options for their relatively high labor content, expenditure elasticities, and impact on opening up new markets.

The consequences of these actions will be increased specialization and the diversification of household activities. The basic elements are already in place. Agricultural production varies by region and awaits improved technologies and stronger markets. The interest in maximizing opportunity is a feature of the rural household's strategy. Private traders are active, moving surpluses from eastern Rwanda to other regions and integrating markets (Bylenga and Loveridge 1987). Greater incentive to produce surpluses will render markets everywhere more reliable and the food in them affordable. Policy reforms are being studied. Research results do reach decision-makers and are discussed in Government. A more thorough reform program can evolve from the process already established.

The next steps are critical. Currently only 11% of the Rwandan labor force is outside agriculture (Khiem 1987). With the economically active population increasing at the rate of 90,000/year, agriculture will not be able to absorb them all in the future. New labor-intensive technologies, such as agroforestry, offer some relief, as does the distribution of labor to eastern Rwanda, where the largest surplus producers are located and most constrained, by their own estimation, by a shortage of labor. But employment must be found mostly outside traditional agriculture to provide the income needed to generate economic growth. This will require market research and policy reform for enterprise development, reliable food markets to give net purchaser households the confidence to try non-food production employment options, production-enhancing agricultural technologies, and free private trader activity to regularize the integration of food markets (disrupted minimally by food aid). The poorest and most food-insecure households are also those most dependent on food markets and off-farm income. The most successful measures for improving their overall health and well-being promote affordable food in local markets and the income with which to purchase it.

Bibliography

Bylenga, Sharon and Scott Loveridge 1987 Integration Regionale des Prix Alimentaires au Rwanda, 1970–1986. Department of Agricultural Economics. Michigan State University. East Lansing.

Crawford, Eric 1988 Factors Affecting Household Food Security. National Committee for World Food Day. Washington, D.C.

Delepierre, Georges 1985 Evolution de la Production Vivriere et les Besoins d'Intensification. Premier Seminaire sur la Fertilisation des Sols au Rwanda. Ministry of Agriculture. Kigali.

Derman, William 1988 Democracy, Self Determination and Processes of Empowerment. National Committee for World Food Day. Washington, D.C.

Dialogue 1986 Intensification Agricole. ASBL Dialogue. Kigali.

ENBC (Enquete Nationale sur le Budget et la Consommation des Menages) 1986 Milieu Rural. Ministry of Plan. Kigali.

Habyarimana, Juvenal 1986 Discours du President de la Republique Rwandaise. Agence Rwandaise de Presse. Kigali.

Hyden, Goran 1986 African Social Structure and Economic Development in R. Berg and J. S. Whitaker, eds., Strategies for African Development, pp. 52–79.

Khiem, Nguyen 1988 A Study of the Construction Sub-Sector. Investment Incentives Studies Working Paper No. 8. Ministry of Finance and Economy. Kigali.

Lofchie, Michael and Stephen Commins 1982 Food Deficits and Agricultural Policies in Tropical Africa in The Journal of Modern African Studies, 20:1, pp. 1–25.

Loveridge, Scott, Serge Rwamasirabo, and Michael Weber 1988 Selected Research Findings from Rwanda that Inform Food Security Policy Themes in Southern Africa. Michigan State University Agricultural Economics Staff Paper 88–89. East Lansing.

Mead, Donald 1988 Non-Farm Income and Food Security: Lessons from Rwanda. Department of Agricultural Economics. Michigan State University. East Lansing.

Musengimana, Simeon 1986 Connaissez-vous Duhamic-Adri? in Dialogue 117, pp. 129–133. ASBL-Dialogue. Kigali.

Neel, Henri 1986 Aide Alimentaire Ambigue in Dialogue 117, pp. 67–78. ASBL-Dialogue. Kigali.

Robins, Edward, Alex Dickie, David Gow, Susan Hoben, Yolande Jemai, Valens Ndoreyaho, and David Wilcock 1986 The Rwandan Social and Institutional Profile. Agency for International Development. Africa Bureau. Washington. D.C.

Robins, Edward, Stuart Callison, Rose Marie Depp, Patrick Fleuret, and Michael Fuchs-Carsch 1987 The Rwanda Country Development Strategy Statement. Agency for International Development. Kigali.

SESA (Services des Enquetes et des Statistiques Agricoles) 1987 Quelques Observations sur les Programmes de Fixation des Prix Plancher et Recherche sur le Haricot au Rwanda. Ministry of Agriculture. Kigali.

1986 Rapport sur les Enquetes de Production. Ministry of Agriculture. Kigali.

Staatz, John 1988 Food Supply and Demand in sub-Saharan Africa. Committee on World Food Day. Washington, D.C.

UNICEF 1985 Analyse de la Situation de l'Enfant Rwandais. United Nations Children's Fund. Kigali.

Food, Farmers, and Organizations in Africa: Anthropological Perspectives, with Implications for Development Assistance

Patrick Fleuret

Bureau for Africa
U.S.A.I.D.
Washington, DC

Introduction

Food in Africa is probably one of the most serious and intractable human issues in the post-WWII era. In the short term we saw 7–12 million people severely affected by food shortages during the 1983/85 famine period; over the long term, we must contend with the fact that Africa is the only major region of the world where food production per capita is declining—at a time when population growth rates are increasing and Africa's capacity to finance food imports is weakening (World Bank 1984, USAID 1986). Large-scale humanitarian assistance is the obvious short term response, but African nations and donor organizations must also find effective answers to the long-term problem—and here our direction is not so clear, because there are many competing visions about what needs to be done. Moreover, observers both within and without the donor community question the efficacy of existing patterns of development assistance, which, two decades or more after their independence, seem to have contributed little to helping African nations deal with growing crises in food production and consumption. Obviously this paper will not resolve the debate on food and agriculture strategies in Africa. The purpose is

The views expressed in this paper are those of the author alone and should not be attributed to the U. S. Agency for International Development or any unit thereof.

more limited: to clarify the range of objectives that need to be considered; to ensure we are fully aware of the variety of alternative—or complementary—strategies that are feasible or promising; and to identify a few key questions we need to keep before us as we seek to assist Africa in achieving long-term food self-reliance. This paper explores these questions by presenting some propositions about food, farmers, and organizations that are based upon intensive study of African agricultural development at the level of the household and village.

Some Thoughts about Objectives and Strategies

Most often we approach the problem of food in Africa by identifying production shortfalls—a way of thinking about food issues that focuses our efforts immediately on technology development, input supply, marketing, commodity prices, and other familiar elements of the debate on agricultural development. Plainly there is a need for production increases, and plainly it is important to think about improving the effectiveness and efficiency of basic agricultural institutions in Africa. These are important and legitimate development objectives. But there are at least two other ways of thinking about food in Africa, which for the sake of convenience might be labelled the consumption perspective and the trade and commerce perspective. Moreover, no assessment of development alternatives in Africa can be complete without tackling explicitly the difficult question of organizational and institutional performance—what we want to do must be grounded in a realistic appraisal of what we can do. Each of these topics— consumption, production, trade, and institutional capacity—is considered in turn below. A final section offers conclusions.

The Food Consumption Perspective

If every family in Africa grew all the food they ate, and ate all the food they grew, then solving Africa's production problem would solve the food problem too. But in Africa today it is usually a mistake to think of rural families as "subsistence farmers", because there is considerable, though variable, participation in markets for food crops, commercial commodities, and labor. This is attended by substantial variation in the capacity to grow or purchase food, which in turn is reflected in important variations in consumption levels and nutritional status at the level of the community and household. Very often, those who need food most are those with the least access to productive resources and the least access to productive employment. In other words, solving the food production problem is not the same thing as solving the food problem—because those who need food are very often those who have little capacity to produce it and little capacity to buy it. This line of thinking suggests that improved education and expanded employment opportunities are also legitimate overall development objectives in Africa, in the sense that progress on these fronts will address critical components of the food problem. It will be helpful to examine these propositions in more detail.

The procedures used to define the "African food problem" also very largely define the solutions sought. Thus, for instance, since per capita food production has apparently declined in Africa over the past 20 years, it seems obvious to conclude, as have most donor organizations, that the focus of development assistance must be on programs to improve food production. Moreover, since the production decline is conceived in aggregate terms, it seems sensible to mount mass agricultural development programs to tackle the problem on a broad front. But the concept of "aggregate food supply" should be handled with care. Aggregate declines in per capita production shed little light on the essential questions of *who* lacks food, *where,* or *why.* Thus the fact that there is an overall lack of food tells us almost nothing about what should be done to improve matters.

By contrast, household- and village-level studies of food consumption and production in Africa show quite plainly that the "African food problem" is concentrated within several very specific segments of the population (Bantje 1982, Fleuret and Fleuret 1980, 1983, Jakobsen 1978, Little 1982, Republic of Kenya 1981). In general, these are (a) households that are landless or nearly so; (b) households without access to multiple sources of income, including food crops, commercial crops, and non-farm employment; (c) households where the principal child care-givers have not completed their primary education; and (d) households headed by single women. We must take account of this significant variation within the rural population with regard to both consumption patterns and production potentials. The implications for African development will emerge as we consider each of these issues in turn: access to land, access to multiple income streams, access to education, and the special question of women-headed households.

The Land-Poor

In Africa those who are landless or effectively so constitute surprisingly large and growing proportions of the population in many countries. This is because high- and moderate-potential land is usually limited; population is often growing rapidly; and political-economic institutions are generally working toward an increasing concentration of land ownership (Bruce 1985, Haugerud 1983, Noronha 1984, Riddell 1985). The land-poor may pursue one of several strategies to stay alive and raise their families: migration to cities in search of informal and formal sector employment; movement to large-scale plantations (sisal, sugar, tea) to join residential labor forces; migration to marginal or semi-arid zones where land is available but not well-suited to agriculture; squatting or tenancy on under-utilized large-scale holdings in more productive zones. In all these settings families usually find it difficult to obtain enough food—but it would be a mistake to diagnose their problems in strictly agricultural terms. Those who have been squeezed out of the bottom of the rural economy by demographic, economic, and political processes need productive employment, not agricultural technology. Smallholder agriculture in Africa can continue to absorb a sizable proportion of the growing rural labor force, particularly if supported by the spread of labor-using technologies; but there is no country where all of the projected labor force growth can be absorbed in smallholder agriculture. We must also question whether a process of agricultural intensification (involution?) is really a viable vision for the future of Africa, where most production now and in the future will continue to be carried out by already over-burdened women cultivators on infertile soils under extremely variable rainfed conditions characterized by very sharp and somewhat unpredictable fluctuations in seasonal and annual labor requirements.

Most African Cultivators Cannot be Called "Subsistence Farmers"

In Africa today it is usually a mistake to think that rural households are engaged only, or even primarily, in subsistence farming. In nearly every country for which studies are available we see that (a) a substantial proportion of the adult male population and an increasing number of women engage in casual, formal, or seasonal wage employment; (b) very few farmers anywhere do not produce something for sale, be it food, export crops, livestock, or handicrafts; and (c) anywhere from 15–80% of total household income is generated by non-farm activities (Brown 1983, Burnham 1980, Due 1986, Hill 1972, Pollet and Winter 1976, Reboussin 1986, Sperling 1985). Moreover, some studies have shown that members of households that maintain consistent access to multiple income streams are usually wealthier, healthier, and better nourished than households without such options (A. Fleuret 1984, Fleuret and Fleuret 1983, Gans 1963, Graedon 1980, Kwofie et al. 1983, Tripp 1981). This is because wage employment, commercial agriculture, and livestock production serve as hedges against food crop failure; and continued staple food production is a hedge against the failure of commercial crops, the failure of the specialized marketing channels associated with them, the loss of a job, or catastrophic herd loss. Diversified households are well-protected against—and are well-placed to adapt to—changes in the availability of or markets for food, cash crops, and labor.

Once it is recognized that "farmer" decision-making is influenced both by the desirability of maintaining multiple income streams and by markets (however imperfect) for labor and other non-food commodities, it becomes possible to begin considering the possibilities inherent in non-food agricultural programs and non-agricultural programs generally, and to capitalize upon some powerful linkages between food production and other elements of the rural economy. For instance, many studies have shown clearly that improved food production technologies are adopted almost solely by households with substantial monetary reserves achieved through commercial agriculture, wage employment, or some combination of these. For the most part, only households such as these are able to gain access to improved technologies (Collier and Lal 1979, Hart 1982, Haugerud 1981, Raikes 1978, Thoden van Velzen 1974); equally important, wealthier households can afford both the cost of innovative technologies and the risk of innovation failure. The implication is that more food crop research and extension can accomplish little unless the population of potential adopters is expanded; and historically, this has happened primarily through expansion of the production of commercial crops and through non-farm employment growth. Instead of building on this demonstrated relationship, official development assistance has tended to fund public-sector extension and credit programs, which accomplish almost nothing by comparison, aiding primarily wealthier farmers who could finance innovations themselves (Donald 1976, Donaldson and Von Pischke 1973, Lele 1975, Leonard 1986).

Basic Education Will Help the Food Problem.

Households headed by those without primary education suffer food problems for two main reasons: most importantly, parents are less able to obtain non-farm jobs that generate additional income streams; also, lack of education is part of a complex bundle of factors involving attitudes and food beliefs that sometimes results in people not making the best use of food available to them. Literacy and numeracy also help farmers decide for themselves how best to use innovative agricultural technologies. The clear implication is that support for basic education—especially among women—should be a priority. This does not mean unthinking support for massively expensive public education bureaucracies; it means improving the effectiveness, efficiency, and financial soundness of existing schooling systems.

Woman-Headed Households are at the Heart of the "African Food Problem"

Woman-headed households constitute a significant proportion (at least 15–30%) of smallholder populations nearly everywhere in Sub-Saharan Africa (Brown 1983, Fortmann 1984, Gordon 1981, MacCormack 1979, Nyhus and Massey 1986, Obbo 1986, Oboler 1985). Women become heads of household for a variety of reasons: (a) they may never have entered a marital union; (b) they may have been widowed, divorced, or abandoned; or (c) they may be married but the husband lives and works so far away and returns so seldom that he has little impact on household affairs. Households headed by women experience food problems because (a) they have reduced access to land and other agricultural inputs; (b) they have meager labor resources within the household and usually cannot afford to hire outside labor; and (c) they have reduced access to indigenous social support systems founded on ties generated through marriage and descent. Such households are also relatively unlikely to adopt and benefit from food production technology. To be blunt, there is little that can be done about this in any direct fashion. This is not because woman-headed households have no potential, but because direct interventions to assist this (or any other) specific category of households run into serious organizational difficulties, a point to which we will return.

Employment Generation is a Policy Issue of Growing Importance.

The foregoing discussion of issues revolving around access to land, non-farm income, education, and woman-headed households suggests, from many different starting points, that there is a great need in Africa for growth in non-agricultural employment. Donor organizations and African governments have a limited stock of ideas in this area: policy reform, to change relative factor prices in favor of labor-using technologies; financial or technical assistance programs to make capital and specialized expertise available to small-scale private enterprise; and provision of foreign exchange, to ease constraints on imports of steel, cement, equipment, and other commodities needed for industry and commerce. At the moment, however, it is difficult to be optimistic about the efficacy of any of these. Policy reform discussions tend to revolve around commodity, not factor prices, because the former are relatively more amenable to adjustment while the latter are deeply embedded in fundamental political-economic institutions. The benefits of commodity import programs are captured disproportionately by the state and by major industrial enterprises. And financial or technical assistance programs, which are intended to target financial and commodity resources more narrowly, add complex organizational components that have been of doubtful utility in Africa. These pessimistic remarks suggest that much more research is needed to better understand the sources and conditions of employment growth in Africa; this set of issues will become dramatically evident to policy-makers in the next two or three decades, and the time to invest in knowledge generation is now.

The Food Production Perspective

All of the foregoing argues that mass research and production interventions for "the rural poor" are largely irrelevant to the needs of those who really lack food in Africa. What the food-deficit groups need is not agricultural technology, but education and employment. Nevertheless, Africa does need more food production—where is it to come from? And what sort of development assistance programs are likely to stimulate further food production? These questions are explored below.

Surplus Food Production is Concentrated in a Small Proportion of the Rural Population.

In Africa, production of *surplus* food is concentrated among a minority of farming households. Although data on these points are spotty, it is probable that only about 30–40% of rural households in most countries are capable of producing a marketable surplus with the land, capital, and labor resources available to them (Hart 1982, Marter and Honeybone 1976). What is the implication for development assistance? The most obvious point to question is how much effort should be devoted to research and extension programs aimed at developing and spreading technologies suited to "the majority of smallholders". It is not unfair to suggest that the mass programs supported in the past have been most effective at generating employment within the mass bureaucracies created to administer them. Perhaps technology development and transfer programs should concentrate on the minority of rural farming households that are committed to farming as an occupation, and that have the basic resources that are required to undertake investment and innovation.

A two-pronged rural development strategy of the sort suggested here would simultaneously focus scarce agricultural development resources on a producer population that can effectively respond, while recognizing Africa's overwhelming and increasingly urgent need for expansion in education and employment to benefit the majority of the rural population who are truly poor by increasing their effective demand for food and other necessities. A responsible overall development policy must recognize that the "problem populations" who lack food are not now and will not become an independent category of self-sufficient small farmers. It is much more likely that they will become a landless rural proletariat, and unless steps are taken now to provide them with substantial and growing employment opportunities, they will in future become a source of grave domestic difficulties, social and economic.

Our Understanding of Farmer Behavior is Too Simplistic, but Our Agriculture Research and Production Interventions are Too Complicated.

In an earlier era it was thought that African cultivators were lazy, unmoved by profit factors, or tradition-bound. Those perceptions have been replaced by a current view—just as distorted—that the African farmer is the primordial "economic man", shrewdly calculating the costs and returns associated with alternative investment options. Agricultural economists and anthropologists have added to this the concept of "risk", recognizing that the likelihood of a pay-off is as important as the magnitude—but despite much agreement that risk is an important consideration, it is not really factored into "our" plans for "them". Moreover, there are other dimensions to agricultural decision-making in Africa that we do not generally appreciate at all.

It is best to view resource allocation and decision-making at the household level as based upon at least four simultaneous strategies: (a) maximization of monetary returns on investment (Bauer and Yamey 1959, Helleiner 1975, Jones 1960, Miracle 1976); (b) management of risk and uncertainty caused by ecological, economic, and institutional unpredictability (Belshaw and Hall 1972, Johnny et al. 1981, Linares 1981, Netting 1968); (c) preservation of access to productive resources over the long term through investment in social relationships (Berry 1983); and (d) maintenance of a negotiated, everchanging network of reciprocal exchange relationships among decision-makers within and among households (Guyer 1980, Jones 1983). One or the other of these strategies may dominate in some places at some times, but none is ever entirely outside the decision calculus, and all influence the allocation of household resources and therefore the response to agricultural programs.

At this point it would be conventional to suggest that donor organizations and African agricultural organizations need to support more research and give more attention to devising "technical packages" that fit neatly into this complex decision-making environment. In fact, that is the direction that official agriculture and rural development programs have taken—ever more complicated design efforts, ever larger and more diverse technical assistance teams, more funds devoted to complex farming systems research that often emphasizes improved farm management practices, bigger and better extension organizations—all predicated upon the unexamined assumption that assistance programs and national agricultural institutions must somehow capture, understand, and improve upon local farmer decision-making and resource allocation, presenting the results back to the farmer in the form of "optimal technical packages". The problem is that there is not time and money enough in the world to create institutions capable of doing this consistently—and if, occasionally, an "optimum technical package" does work, it will suit only a small minority of farmers and likely be out of date when conditions change next season.

It is easy to forget that rural society and economy in Africa are changing continuously in response to many stimuli. Donors and government officials generally cannot design projects or organizations capable of responding to the complexity of changes taking place, which suggests we should not try to create organizations expected to replicate and improve upon all the allocative decisions that African producers must make. Our programs are predicated upon the assumption that donor and host country officials—yes, and academics—can make better decisions than farmers—a proposition for which there is little evidence in Africa. But rather than supplanting farmer decision-making, what about improving the environment within which farmer decisions are made? The principle involved is to try to respond to the underlying logic of farmer resource allocation, rather than to influence the specific shape of particular allocative decisions. Thus, future interventions should focus on:

- improving the reliability of input supply and marketing systems. This must be done not primarily by strengthening existing public or private monopolies/monopsonies but by (a) supporting viable alternatives so that the failure of one agency or firm has minimal impact on the system as a whole, and (b) by encouraging the elimination of policies and programs that inhibit the movement of farm supplies and marketed commodities;
- rehabilitating, maintaining, and extending basic agricultural infrastructure (transport, storage, and communications systems) so that people, commodities, and information can travel freely and reliably;
- increasing the range of inputs and production options available to farmers. Donors and host countries have little capacity to improve

upon allocative decisions made by farmers, but *can* provide farmers the varied resources and sound information they need to find better solutions to their diverse, changing circumstances; and

• concentrating agriculture research on plant genetic problems (resistance to disease, insects, and water stress, improved utilization of soil nutrients) that are of importance to any farmer, rather than on finely-tuned technological packages (dependent upon complex adjustments in farm management practices) that are frequently relevant to none.

Finally, it is important to note that genetic improvements embodied in planting materials will work whether or not there is an extension agent around. And if basic planting and application instructions are provided with packaged inputs, the need for extension agents is further reduced. Thus the benefits of applied research and improved inputs can often be delivered to farmers independently of the extension service; this is an important advantage in Africa, where extension services are monumentally ineffective and equally expensive. It must be recognized that the very large bureaucratic and even autocratic extension services commonly found throughout Africa are built on the assumption that farmers cannot figure out very much for themselves— a proposition that is manifestly untrue. Africa's farmers need better education and better access to information through modern communication media much more than they need improved public extension services.

The Trade and Commerce Perspective

This is not an area about which anthropologists have very much to say. But it is an area that we ought to consider. It is by no means clear that, over the long-term, each African country should seek to produce all or even a major proportion of its own food. It is, however, very clear that commercial agricultural exports, domestic wage labor, and international migration for wage employment provide substantial earnings that support indigenous agricultural and economic development at all levels from the nation on down to the household (Berg Associates 1985, Pearson and Cownie 1974, Stein 1979). The potential role of trade and commerce becomes even more important when we consider that population growth and a declining resource base will make it difficult to fulfill even very conservative targets for per capita food production increases over the next 15–20 years. The economist's favored "comparative advantage" framework is probably too simplistic to provide a valid assessment of the production options open to African nations, because the international market is dynamic (and fundamentally distorted in favor of developed nations), and because domestic African political considerations will dictate a certain allocation of resources to food production regardless of efficiency considerations. Farmers will also think first about their need for household food security. But we still need to consider to what extent Africa's long-term food needs can be met through growth in international trade and commerce, including migration. This line of thinking takes us into the unfamiliar areas of export development, multi-national investment, trade agreements, and the like—but our unfamiliarity with these approaches should not blind us to their potential power, which ought to be made to work for Africa in the future as it has worked against Africa in the past.

A Realistic Perspective on Organizations in Africa

No development resources—money, commodities, ideas—can have an effect in Africa except through the actions of organizations. Decisions about which organization or set of organizations to employ for the implementation of a particular development initiative are critical because the institutional mechanism can be either a link or a barrier between development resources and the people intended to benefit from them. In Africa, the "barrier" problem is particularly serious. There are at least seven overlapping reasons for this.

* First, institutional mechanisms usually emerge as a by-product of technical discussions among donor organizations, intermediaries (universities, firms, PVOs), and government officials; such mechanisms are often aimed more at expediting the commitment of funds and preserving programs than at solving real implementation problems or meeting farmer needs.
* Second, institutional performance is difficult to predict in any case,

especially when the tasks involved are new (which is characteristic of development interventions).

- Third, our understanding of particular organizational types is sometimes based more on what they have accomplished in the U.S. than on how they perform in Africa. Our misguided enthusiasm for "farmer's" cooperatives is a case in point. They are usually run by governments, not farmers, and even those that are in some sense farmer-run must struggle within tightly constrained regulatory environments. The principle is more general: we don't adequately appreciate that African institutions must have their own sources of political, social, and economic legitimacy, and that these influence institutional performance in ways that might not track with Western expectations.

- Fourth, most African organizations are weak, we are unsure how to strengthen them, and when we *do* succeed in building institutions the result may be perverse. The livestock ministries and regional development authorities we helped strengthen in the Sahel, for instance, are arguably impeding rather than facilitating rural development; similarly with the parastatal sector in Tanzania.

- Fifth, most interventions, whether explicitly "integrated" in nature or not, depend on stable performance from a system of institutions, the failure of any one of which will endanger the objectives of the intervention. It is not unusual, for instance, to find projects that will not work unless a donor organization, a U.S. university, firm, or PVO, a government ministry (or two or three), and district level officials all agree on objectives and procedures. Needless to say, the result is quite often implementation failure (which may or may not be perceived by program administrators and evaluation teams). Planners usually recognize only a small part of these organizational systems, and have little influence over them anyway.

- Sixth, we are generally insensitive to the inherent weaknesses of African institutional systems. Development programs tend to assume optimal performances when we should know from experience that minimal performances are the rule. Moreover, the complex program objectives favored particularly by social scientists (for instance, narrow targeting of benefits to special categories of disadvantaged farmers or to women) tend to place major and generally unworkable demands on organizations that are struggling in the first place.

• Finally, international development organizations have many problems of their own: ponderous and unpredictable systems of project and program development, rigid approaches to financial accountability, a confusing and constraining tangle of restrictions on procurement of goods and services, and (in the case of A.I.D. and other bilateral agencies) a need to work within shifting legislative and executive guidelines in response to special constituencies. These factors in combination make it difficult for African organizations to develop coherent programs, sound objectives, realistic budgeting procedures, or effective financial management practices. Moreover, too much time of African staff and managers is taken up with meeting donor requirements; too little time is left for implementing their own programs.

With this as background, it should be easy to understand why so much of what the international community has attempted in agriculture and rural development has been difficult and costly to implement, and often ineffective as well. There are two possible responses to this institutional complexity: (a) maintain current program objectives, but attempt to improve the planning and implementation of the programs by seeking better understanding of the organizational dimensions of development; or (b) recognize the very real organizational constraints present, admit that our capacity to change them is marginal and very often ill-informed in any case, and abandon current objectives in favor of ones that are more feasible and more effective within existing organizational parameters. Recent A.I.D. policy papers on "Institutional Development" and "Local Organizations in Development" represent attempts to do the former; this paper suggests we might also give some attention to the latter. A development strategy grounded in realistic appreciation of the constraints imposed by organizational systems in Africa would include the following elements: (a) more non-project assistance; (b) simpler projects; (c) minimization of procurement problems by concentrating on large quantities of strategic commodities (steel, fertilizer) rather than complicated assortments of equipment and supplies; and (d) program concentration in countries with adequate administrative capacity.

Such a withdrawal from complex direct interventions need not mean abandoning our interest in assisting the rural poor; recent A.I.D. programs to provide steel for hoes in Uganda, commodity and financial support to basic education in Zimbabwe, and rural roads in Western Kenya show that the needs of the rural poor can be met very well through simplified programs and projects of the sort suggested above.

Conclusion

This review of issues arising in official approaches to food, farmers, and organizations in Africa reveals a single, fundamental paradox: although our strategies and programs are founded upon a demonstrably weak understanding of African development dynamics, our project interventions are extremely deterministic, attempting to specify optimal solutions to production and organizational problems when we do not even know what is possible, let alone what is best. The only reasonable conclusion is that we need better understanding, coupled with programs that are less vulnerable to mistaken assumptions about what Africa's people need.

Better understanding does not necessarily mean funding more research, although there is certainly room for that. Rather, "better understanding" means making better use of the information already available to those who seek it.

Our understanding of African development can be improved, but it will never be complete, because of the complexity and speed of changes taking place in Africa and in the world generally. This means there will always be a significant element of uncertainty in our strategies, programs, and projects. We can best adapt to this uncertainty (a) by avoiding over-designed and over-determined interventions that make too many assumptions about what needs to be done and how, and (b) by directing our resources toward programs and projects that address basic, obvious constraints within simple administrative frameworks.

Finally, we need to re-examine very seriously our present conviction that Africa's most pressing needs are exclusively in the realm of rural development and smallholder food production. We have not given sufficient consideration to the potential of a strategy oriented around employment generation and education as well as food production; we may have abandoned too readily the unromantic but nevertheless essential objective of infrastructural development; and by choosing to emphasize production-related agriculture and rural development interventions we have gotten entangled in major institutional problems for which there are probably no solutions but the passage of time. The point is, our strategy must be based not only on what we would *like* to do, but on a realistic assessment of what we *can* do; and the last ten years of experience in Africa point toward a return to basics.

References Cited

Bantje, H. 1982 Food flows and dietary patterns in Ikwiriri village. University of Dar es Salaam Bureau for Resource Assessment and Land Use Planning Research Paper No. 74.

Bauer, P. T., and B. S. Yamey 1959 A case study of response to price in an underdeveloped country. Economic J 69:800–805.

Belshaw, D. G. R., and M. Hall 1972 The analysis and use of agricultural experimental data in tropical Africa. E Afr J of Rural Development 5(1):39–71.

Berg Associates 1985 Intra-African trade and economic integration. Vol. I and II. Mimeo.

Berry, S. 1983 Agrarian crisis in Africa? A review and interpretation. Paper presented to the Joint African Studies Committee. New York: Social Science Research Council and the American Council of Learned Societies.

Brown, B. 1983 The impact of male labour migration on women in Botswana. African Affairs 82:367–388.

Bruce, J. W. 1985 Land tenure issues in project design and strategies for agricultural development in Sub-Saharan Africa. Madison, Wisconsin: the Land Tenure Center.

Buch-Hansen, M., and H. Marcussen 1981 Contract farming and the peasantry. Roskilde University Center Research Report No. 18.

Burnham, O. 1980 Opportunity and constraint in a savanna society. New York: Academic Press.

Collier, P., and D. Lal 1979 Poverty and growth in Kenya. IBRD mimeo.

Donald, G. 1976 Credit for small farmers in developing countries. Boulder, Colorado: Westview Press.

Donaldson, G. F., and J. D. von Pischke 1973 A survey of small farmer credit in Kenya. A.I.D. Spring Review of Small Farmer Credit, Vol. III, Kenya. Washington, DC: USAID.

Due, J. 1986 Intra-household gender issues in farming systems in Tanzania, Zambia, and Malawi. Paper presented at a conference on Gender Issues and Farming Systems Research and Extension. University of Florida, Gainesville.

Fleuret, A. 1984 Household organization, labor, and diet in Taita. ms.

Fleuret, P., and A. Fleuret 1980 Nutrition, consumption, and agricultural change. Human Organization 39:250–260.

Fleuret, P., and A. Fleuret 1983 Socio-economic determinants of child nutrition in Taita, Kenya: a call for discussion. Culture and Agriculture 19(8):4, 16–20.

Fortmann, L. 1984 Economic status and women's participation in agriculture: a Botswana case study. Rural Sociology 49(3): 452–464.

Gans, B. 1963 Some socio-economic and cultural factors in West African paedriatrics. Arch Dis Childhood 38:1–12.

Gordon, E. 1981 An analysis of the impact of labour migration on the lives of women in Lesotho. J of Dev Studies 17(3):59–76.

Graedon, T. 1980 Nutritional consequences of rural-urban migration. Paper prepared for USAID.

Guyer, J. 1980 Household budgets and women's incomes. Boston University African Studies Center Working Paper No. 28.

Hart, K. 1982 The political economy of West African agriculture. Cambridge: Cambridge University Press.

Haugerud, A. 1981 Economic differentiation among peasant households: a comparison of Embu coffee and cotton zones. University of Nairobi Institute for Development Studies Working Paper No. 383

Haugerud, A. 1983 The consequences of land tenure reform among smallholders in the Kenya highlands. ms.

Helleiner, G. K. 1975 Smallholder decision-making: tropical African evidence. In: Agriculture in Development Theory, L. G. Reynolds (ed.), pp.27–52, New Haven: Yale University Press.

Hill, P. 1972 Rural Hausa: a village and a setting. London: Cambridge University Press.

Jakobsen, O. 1978 Economic and geographical factors influencing child malnutrition. A study from the southern highlands, Tanzania. University of Dar es Salaam Bureau of Resource Assessment and Land Use Planning Research Paper No. 52.

Johnny, M., J. Karimu, and P. Richards 1981 Upland and swamp rice farming systems in Sierra Leone: the social context of technological change. Africa 51:596–620.

Jones, C. 1983 The impact of the Semry I irrigated rice project on the organization of production and consumption at the intra-household level. Paper prepared for USAID.

Jones, W. O. 1960 Economic man in Africa. Stanford Food Research Institute Studies 1:107–134.

Kenya, Republic of 1981 Child nutrition in rural Kenya. Nairobi: Central Bureau of Statistics, Ministry of Economic Planning and Community Affairs.

Kwofie, K., E. Brew-Graves, and G. Adika 1983 Malnutrition and pregnancy wastage in Zambia. Soc Sci Med 17:539–43.

Lele, U. 1975 The design of rural development: lessons from Africa. Baltimore: Johns Hopkins University Press.

Leonard, David 1986 Developing Africa's Agricultural Institutions: putting the farmer in control. In: Strategies for African Development, R. Berg and J. Whitaker (eds.), Berkeley: University of California Press (forthcoming).

Linares, O. 1981 From tidal swamp to inland valley: on the social organization of wet rice cultivation among the Dida of Senegal. Africa 51:557–595.

Little, P. 1982 Food production, marketing, and consumption in the semi-arid area of Baringo District. Rome: FAO.

MacCormack, C. 1979 Control of land, labour, and capital in rural southern Sierra Leone. ms.

Marter, A. and D. Honeybone 1976 The economic resources of rural households and the distribution of agricultural development. University of Zambia Rural Development Studies Bureau. Mimeo.

Miracle, M. P. 1976 Interpretation of backward-sloping labor supply curves in Africa. Econ Dev and Cultural Change 24:399–406.

Netting, R. 1968 Hill farmers of Nigeria. Seattle: University of Washington Press.

Noronha, R. 1984 A review of the literature on land tenure systems in Sub-Saharan Africa. IBRD mimeo.

Nyhus, S., and G. Massey 1986 Female-headed households in an agro-pastoral society. Paper presented at a conference on Gender Issues in Farming Systems Research and Extension. University of Florida, Gainesville.

Obbo, C. 1986 Some East African widows. In: Widows in African Societies: Choices and Constraints, B. Potash (ed.), pp. 84–106, Stanford: Stanford University Press.

Oboler, R. 1985 Women, power, and economic change: the Nandi of Kenya. Stanford: Stanford University Press.

Pearson, S. R., and J. Cownie 1974 Commodity exports and African economic development. Lexington, Massachusetts: Heath.

Pollet, E., and G. Winter 1978 The social organization of agricultural labor among the Soninke (Dyahunu, Mali). In: Relations of Production, D. Seddon (ed.), pp. 331–356, London: Frank Cass.

Raikes, P. 1978 Rural differentiation and class formation in Tanzania. J of Peasant Studies 5(3):285–325.

Riddell, J. C., et al. 1985 Country profiles of land tenure: African. Madison, Wisconsin: the Land Tenure Center.

Sperling, L. 1986 Wage employment among Samburu herders. ms.

Stein, L. 1979 The growth of East African exports and their effect on economic development. London: Croon Helm.

Tripp, R. 1981 Farmers and traders: some economic determinants of nutritional status in northern Ghana. J of Trop Ped 27:15–22.

U.S. Agency for International Development 1986 Report to congress on U.S. development assistance to Africa. Washington, DC: USAID.

Van Velzen, H. T. 1972 Staff, kulaks, and peasants. In: Socialism in Tanzania, Vol. 2, L. Cliffe and J. Saul (eds.), Nairobi: East African Publishing House. World Bank 1984 Toward sustained development in Sub-Saharan Africa: a joint program of action. Washington, DC: the World Bank.

INDEX

Abortion, 90
Adaptation (adaptive strategies), 4, 218, 220
Agribusiness, 190
Agro-pastoralism (mixed farming), 4, 24, 113
Alcoholism, 90, 99
Authorite des Amenagements des Vallees des Volta (AVV), 47–51, 59

Basal metabolic rate (BMR), 220
Beer, 82–84, 90, 91, 129, 130, 250, 251, 254
Boreholes, 170
Bride-service, 96
Bridewealth, 66

Carrying capacity, 8, 9, 13, 14, 17
Cash crops (*see also* export crops), 40, 49–51, 66, 68, 78, 87–90, 96, 111, 114, 121, 123, 259
  Cocoa, 56, 257
  Coffee, 56, 78, 80, 86, 87, 94, 114, 250, 251, 257
  Cotton, 48–51, 54, 59, 114, 170, 257
  Papaya (papaine), 87
  Peanuts (groundnuts), 37, 38, 63, 65, 84, 114, 118, 122, 123, 129, 130, 230, 250, 257
  Pyrethrum, 78
  Quinquina (quinine), 78, 80, 86–88
  Sisal, 272
  Sugar, 20, 272
  Tea, 78, 80, 81, 86, 87, 114, 250, 257, 272
  Tobacco, 114, 118, 122, 123, 129–131, 261
Child labor, 52
Church, 92, 94, 260, 264
Cloth, 88, 89

Club de Amis du Sahel (Club), 60
Comite Permanent Interetats de Lutte contre la Secheresse dans le Sahel (CILSS), 60, 61
Cooperatives, 264, 281
Corvee labor, 51, 77
Crafts (handicrafts), 116, 273
Cyanide (in cassava), 216–223

Dairying, 4, 110
Dams, 5–7, 18–23, 32, 33, 35, 36, 38, 40, 55, 61, 184
Desertification, 8, 10, 14, 190, 196
Disease (*see also* malnutrition, morbidity), 12, 192, 220
  Acquired Immune Deficiency Syndrome (AIDS), 100
  Cholera, 209, 221
  Diarrhea, 83, 208, 230
  Goiter, 88, 208
  Leprosy, 221
  Louse-borne, 221
  Malaria, 221
  Onchocerciasis, 47, 49
  Tick-borne, 12
  Tuberculosis, 79, 209
  Typhoid, 209
  Typhus, 209
  Yaws, 221
Divorce, 119, 130, 274
Drinking water, 18, 19
Drought, 34, 44, 60, 112, 143, 185, 188, 192, 207, 222, 252, 263

Early warning system (EWS), 254
"Economy of affection," 107, 108, 255, 256
Eggs, 129
Electricity (*see also* hydropower), 20, 21, 31, 33, 35

289

"Entitlement," 132
Ethnic conflict (*see also* war), 95
Export crops (*see also* cash crops), 18,
    21, 80, 87, 88, 184, 251, 273
Extension (agricultural), 30, 125, 126,
    130–132, 143, 153, 232, 238, 241,
    279
European Economic Community (EEC),
    47, 49, 50

Fallowing, 52, 82, 122
Famine, 185, 188, 207, 208, 216, 217,
    219, 220, 222, 269
Farmers' organizations, 127
Farming systems, 76, 80, 92, 97, 108,
    133
    Farming Systems Approach (Farming
    Systems Research), 107, 108, 118,
    131, 141–143, 149, 150, 199, 200,
    236–242
    Male and female systems, 110–112, 115
Female-headed households, 81, 109, 115,
    117–132, 271, 274, 275
Fertility (as a factor in population
    growth), 52, 53, 194
Fertilizers, 187, 189, 191, 196, 257,
    258, 282
Fire (as land management), 192
    Range fires, 11
Fish, 4, 19, 22, 24, 88, 96
Flood, 19, 20, 22, 38, 207
Flood recession agriculture, 22, 24, 38
Food aid, 190, 245–247, 252–265
    Food for Work, 258
Food and Agriculture Organization
    (FAO), 5, 10, 116, 139, 191, 209,
    230, 232
Food Crops (*see also* vegetable produc-
    tion)
    Bananas, 82, 83, 87, 90, 91, 129,
    249, 250, 252, 254
    Beans, 78, 81–85, 118, 122, 170,
    197, 245, 249–254, 261, 262
    Cow peas, 19, 197
    Maize, 19, 82, 83, 87, 96, 114, 118,
    121–131, 170, 198, 214, 222, 230–
    235, 249–252, 257

Manioc (cassava), 78, 82–86, 89, 99,
    114, 207–223, 249, 250, 252, 253
Millet, 19
Rice, 20, 33, 35, 36, 38, 39, 55, 62,
    88, 114, 116, 214, 222, 229, 253,
    257, 261
Peas, 249–252
Potatoes, 235, 249–252, 263
Sorghum, 19, 66, 78, 83, 84, 87,
    249, 250, 252
Sweet potato, 82, 118, 122, 211, 249,
    250, 252, 253
Taro, 82
Wheat, 214, 222, 250, 251, 253, 257,
    261
Yams, 82, 215, 216
Food energy (calories), 13, 82, 208,
    209, 212, 216, 222, 223, 230, 250,
    254
Food policy, 139, 140, 142, 145, 154
Food processing, 97, 111, 197, 218, 261
Food security, 34, 68, 78, 112, 117,
    132, 246, 259, 280
Food self-sufficiency, 34, 107, 109, 132,
    133, 245–247, 260
Forests (forestry), 6, 7, 12, 33, 56, 58,
    59, 76, 88, 154, 263, 265
    Tropical woodlands, 6
Fuel, 39, 192

Gambia River Development Organization
    (OMVG), 31–33, 35–38, 40
Game (meat), 88
Gardening, 96, 116, 193, 264
Gender, 75, 90–92, 96, 97, 99, 109,
    113, 116, 131, 132, 142
Glossinae (tsetse fly), 16
Gorillas, 80
"Green Revolution," 191, 192, 197, 213

Hailstorms, 249
Health programs (health care), 79, 86,
    88, 186, 259
    Mother-child health, 79
Housing, 131, 170, 259
Hunger, 29, 75–78, 87, 139, 182, 207,
    213, 218, 222

Seasonal hunger, 82, 220
Hydropower (*see also* electricity), 5, 20–22, 31

Immune function, 220–222
Industrialization, 109
Infanticide, 90
Integrated rural development, 118
International Institute for Tropical Agriculture (IITA), 223
International Livestock Center for Africa (ILCA), 9
International Maize and Wheat Improvement Center in Mexico (CIMMYT), 213
International Monetary Fund (IMF), 9, 37, 98
Involuntary relocation, 23
Irrigation, 5, 18–22, 29, 31–33, 38, 39, 55, 60–64, 130, 184, 189–191, 229, 237

Lactation, 87
Land concentration, 43–46, 54, 60, 67, 68, 272
Land grant universities (LCU's), 140, 153, 188, 189, 195, 200
Latrines, 123
Livestock, 4, 8, 10–13, 15, 16, 18, 19, 21, 24, 33, 84, 94, 108, 110, 118, 145, 154, 193, 251, 273, 281

Male-headed households, 108, 117–132
Malnutrition, 78, 79, 82, 87, 90, 207, 208, 212, 220, 250
  Anemia, 208
  Goiter, 88, 208
  Kwashiorkor (*bwaki*), 79, 86, 87, 208, 213
  Marasmus, 79, 208
  Protein energy malnutrition (PEM), 79, 208, 213, 214
  Stunting, 79, 230, 231
  Vitamin A deficiency, 208
  Wasting, 231
Manufacturing, 257
Market vendors, 110

Marxist development, 184
Migration, 6, 14, 17, 45, 51–53, 56, 60, 66, 90, 109, 112, 115, 119, 120, 194, 272, 279, 280
Milk, 113, 213, 261
Mines (minerals), 33, 37, 98, 183
  Cobalt, 98
  Copper, 98
  Gold, 94, 95
Monopsonies, 48, 92, 278
Morbidity (*see also* disease), 220, 221
Mortality, 52, 186, 194, 220, 221
Mountains, 76, 80, 251
Muslim, 63

Non-governmental organizations (NGO's), 247, 255, 256, 260, 264
Nutrition, 34, 75, 77, 83, 84, 92, 96, 139, 181, 186, 197, 199, 209, 213, 217, 223, 228–232, 242, 248, 255, 273
  Sex differences, 96–97

Off-farm employment, 21, 52, 81, 115, 130, 259–260, 271, 274, 275
Orchards, 55, 56
Organization of African Unity (OAU), 29
Overgrazing, 7–9, 14–16, 190
Overpopulation, 77, 97
Oxfam America, 159

Palm oil, 78, 85, 257
Parastatals, 5, 20, 46–49, 51, 53, 58–62, 64, 67, 68, 98, 107
Pastoralism, 4, 5, 7, 8, 10–15, 17–21, 23, 24, 113
Pest control, 11, 142, 238, 239, 279
  Herbicides, 187, 231, 235
  Insect control (insecticides), 11, 47, 49, 187, 279
  Pesticides, 189, 191, 196
Petroleum, 64, 86, 190, 257
Plantations, 6, 56, 78, 79, 84, 85, 86, 93, 95, 230, 272
Plow cultivation, 113, 116, 255
Pollution, 18

Water, 7
Population growth, 33, 51–53, 65, 90,
    186, 194, 248, 254, 257, 261, 269,
    272, 280
Pregnancy, 87, 120, 192, 208
Private voluntary organizations (PVO),
    24, 161, 163, 170, 176, 280, 281
Proletariat, 53, 56, 57, 59, 68
Protein, 13, 16, 17, 96, 209, 211–214,
    220, 230

Rainfall, 15, 29, 33, 80, 83, 118, 193,
    209, 238, 245, 250
Ranching, 4, 6, 12, 13, 16, 18, 23, 93,
    94
Rangelands, 4, 5, 7, 10, 11, 13–15, 17,
    23
Reciprocity (exchange relationships), 277
    Generalized, 57
    Negative, 57
Remittances, 112, 115
River basin development, 5, 8, 18, 24,
    29–31, 34, 37, 60, 62

Sahel, 3, 7, 8, 14, 15, 18, 29, 34, 36,
    43, 64, 67, 68, 195, 281
Sanitation, 59, 209
Savanna, 18, 43–46, 60, 61, 64, 67, 68,
    192, 250, 263
Seasonality, 227–230, 232–236
Senegal Valley Development Authority
    (OMVS), 19–22, 62
Slave trade, 186, 194
Smuggling, 94, 95
Soils, 36, 49, 52, 80, 99, 190, 192,
    193, 209, 216, 239, 248, 249, 257,
    259, 272
Soy flour, 84, 87
Starvation, 78, 208, 209, 222
Steppe, 18
Structural adjustment, 98

Subsistence agriculture, 18, 85, 95, 270,
    272
Sustainable agriculture, 182, 193, 195,
    196, 197
Swamplands, 81

Thyroid activity, 219
Tractors, 116, 238
Traders, 54, 94, 95, 100, 112, 264, 265
"Tragedy of the commons," 8, 9, 12,
    14, 23, 195

Undergrazing, 15, 16
United Nations Development Programme
    (UNDP), 33, 36, 40, 60, 64
United States Agency for International
    Development (USAID), 12, 14, 16,
    22, 34, 37, 47, 53, 76, 85, 119,
    142–144, 148, 153, 184–186, 188,
    191, 197, 242, 269, 282
United States Department of Agriculture
    (USDA), 196
United States Peace Corps, 76
Urbanization, 29, 33, 109

Vegetable production, 227–229, 232–
    240, 264
Veterinary programs, 11, 12, 84, 94,
    145, 147, 149

War (see also ethnic conflict), 112, 207
    Civil war, 62
West Africa, 7, 29, 30, 31, 32, 34, 35,
    40, 43–47, 60, 61, 64, 68
Wild foods, 231, 232, 234, 235
Wildlife, 154
Women in Development, 142, 148, 150
World Bank (International Bank for Re-
    construction and Development), 4–
    7, 12, 18, 21–24, 37, 44, 63, 67,
    98, 139, 170, 184, 185, 269
World Health Organization (WHO), 208,
    232
World Resources Institute, 6